Colin Murphy's Political Plays

Colin Murphy's Political Plays

100 YEARS OF IRISH HISTORY

Inside the GPO
The Treaty
Haughey|Gregory
Guaranteed!
Bailed Out!

COLIN MURPHY

methuen | drama
LONDON • NEW YORK • OXFORD • NEW DELHI • SYDNEY

METHUEN DRAMA
Bloomsbury Publishing Plc, 50 Bedford Square, London, WC1B 3DP, UK
Bloomsbury Publishing Inc, 1385 Broadway, New York, NY 10018, USA
Bloomsbury Publishing Ireland, 29 Earlsfort Terrace, Dublin 2, D02 AY28, Ireland

BLOOMSBURY, METHUEN DRAMA and the Methuen Drama logo are trademarks of
Bloomsbury Publishing Plc

First published in Great Britain 2026

Copyright © Colin Murphy and Contributors, 2026
Inside the GPO copyright © Colin Murphy, 2026
The Treaty copyright © Colin Murphy, 2021, 2026
Haughey|Gregory copyright © Colin Murphy, 2019, 2026
Guaranteed! copyright © Colin Murphy, 2020, 2026
Bailed Out! copyright © Colin Murphy, 2026

Colin Murphy has asserted his right under the Copyright, Designs and Patents Act, 1988, to be identified as author of this work.

Cover design by Lara Himpelmann
Cover images: European Flag © jaanalisette / Getty Images,
Irish Republic Flag © National Museum of Ireland

All rights reserved. No part of this publication may be: i) reproduced or transmitted in any form, electronic or mechanical, including photocopying, recording or by means of any information storage or retrieval system without prior permission in writing from the publishers; or ii) used or reproduced in any way for the training, development or operation of artificial intelligence (AI) technologies, including generative AI technologies. The rights holders expressly reserve this publication from the text and data mining exception as per Article 4(3) of the Digital Single Market Directive (EU) 2019/790.

Bloomsbury Publishing Plc does not have any control over, or responsibility for, any third-party websites referred to or in this book. All internet addresses given in this book were correct at the time of going to press. The author and publisher regret any inconvenience caused if addresses have changed or sites have ceased to exist, but can accept no responsibility for any such changes.

No rights in incidental music or songs contained in the work are hereby granted and performance rights for any performance/presentation whatsoever must be obtained from the respective copyright owners.

All rights whatsoever for plays in this collection are strictly reserved and application for performance etc. should be made before rehearsals begin to Lisa Richards Agency, United House, North Road, London N7 9DP. No performance may be given unless a licence has been obtained.

A catalogue record for this book is available from the British Library.

A catalog record for this book is available from the Library of Congress.

ISBN: HB: 978-1-3505-6401-5
PB: 978-1-3505-6402-2
ePDF: 978-1-3505-6403-9
eBook: 978-1-3505-6404-6

Series: Methuen Drama Play Collections

Typeset by RefineCatch Limited, Bungay, Suffolk
Printed and bound in Great Britain

For product safety related questions contact productsafety@bloomsbury.com.

To find out more about our authors and books visit www.bloomsbury.com and sign up for our newsletters.

For my parents, my first producers
For Martin Kelly, my first director
For Ruth, my first reader
For Zack, Iseult and Elena, my first audience

Contents

List of Illustrations viii

A note by Michael D. Higgins 1

Introduction 3

Inside the GPO 11

The Treaty 67

Haughey/Gregory 133

Guaranteed! 195

Bailed Out! 255

Illustrations

1. Michael Glenn Murphy as Tom Clarke, clutching a copy of the Proclamation, in *Inside the GPO*. ©Photo by Pat Redmond   65

2. Jonathan White as Prime Minister David Lloyd George delivering an ultimatum to the Irish delegation in *The Treaty*, in the Kevin Barry Rooms at the National Concert Hall, Dublin.
   (R to L, Karen Ardiff, Ian Toner, Patrick Moy, Shadaan Felfeli, Simon O'Gorman, Jonathan White, Ali White and Camille Lucy Ross.)
   ©Photo by Ste Murray   132

3. Peter Coonan as Barry, Ruairí Heading as Tony Gregory and Janet Moran as Eileen in *Haughey|Gregory*. ©Photo by Anthony Woods.   194

4. (L to R) Darragh Kelly as the Taoiseach, Peter Hanly as the Minister for Finance and Peter Daly as the Governor in *Guaranteed!*.
   ©Photo by Pat Redmond   253

5. Ali White as the Narrator and Peter Daly as Michael Noonan in *Bailed Out!*.
   ©Photo by Pat Redmond   313

A note by Michael D. Higgins

Colin Murphy's work is among those whose work in a special way seeks to make an affirmation of the power of theatre to inform, to provoke, and, perhaps most importantly, to cultivate the empathy that is essential to any functioning democracy, continuing the long tradition of Irish theatre as a space for political reflection and social change.

In *Political Plays: 100 Years of Irish History*, Colin continues this project and indeed tradition. History of great political and social struggle is brought to life with clarity and depth, reminding us that history not envisaged as something distant or static is a living force that continues to shape our society.

Colin Murphy offers us a timely contribution to all who seek to understand the complexity of our past and to engage with the ongoing work of building a more just and inclusive Ireland.

Michael D. Higgins was president of Ireland from 2011 to 2025.

Introduction

In September 2008, I had a one-year old child, a precarious foothold in Irish journalism and an unfinished play in a drawer. And then the Irish government guaranteed the banks.

If that period is hazy in memory, the reason is not just sleep deprivation. The news came in blizzards; it was bewildering. Even though I was a journalist — or perhaps all the more so because I was a journalist — I felt myself steadily more alienated from the national conversation, as politics (about which I believed I knew something) was stealthily taken over by economics (about which I knew nothing).

Still, I did immediately realise *something* about the bank guarantee. A group of men locked in a room overnight trying to solve a life-or-death problem. . . It sounded like a play. I assumed somebody would soon write it. But nobody did.

Then an email came in from Fishamble theatre company. They were looking for "tiny plays for Ireland". This proffered the two things that, for a journalist, the play in the drawer had lacked: a deadline and a word count. To be precise: six hundred words. What can you dramatise in six hundred words? One moment of decision. Might there be a moment of decision worth dramatising in recent Irish politics?

My tiny play, Guaranteed Irish, was duly staged by Fishamble alongside 24 others; together, they made for a moving, often comic, portrait of a country under stress, but resilient. But there was, I thought, a different quality to the laughter at my tiny satire. There was a grim recognition in it.

I suggested a full-length, serious treatment of the issue to Fishamble. I proposed to research the bank guarantee, as a journalist, and bring them a dossier; we would workshop the material with a director and cast and find a play in it. I submitted freedom of information requests, discretely contacted as many of the protagonists as I could, and started working my way through the official inquiries and the multiplying books by journalists and economists.

In the meantime, Fishamble got back in touch: they couldn't fund a week-long workshop, as I had suggested; we would just have two days. I ploughed on, starting to draft rough scenes based on the research material. Then Fishamble got in touch again: actually, the two days would just be one day.

We can't workshop a "dossier" in one day, I thought, all we can do is read it: I'm going to have to write the thing. That was the moment I became a playwright.

Fishamble hired director Conall Morrison; he recruited a crack cast, the reading went well, and Fishamble started to approach theatres offering a rehearsed reading of something that was so untypical of Irish theatre, we didn't know quite what to call it: we went with the ungainly strapline, "a dramatisation based on documentary sources", and put an exclamation mark in the otherwise dryly factual title, *Guaranteed!*, to suggest it mightn't be entirely po-faced.

This first cast — Peter Hanly, Darragh Kelly, Peter Daly, Caitríona Ní Mhurchú, Mark Lambert — were seminal in my training as a playwright. I would arrive for rehearsals sharp, early, laptop at the ready, primed to interrogate my script; Conall and the cast would amble in, make coffee, and chat. We had just *eight days* — how could they afford to spend so much of it so idly, even if the idle chat was often about bankers and politics?

But there was method in their indolence. What Conall was pursuing was an absolute understanding. He talked about theatre of *argument* – something he had learned from his work on Greek drama – and about the almost cathartic satisfaction an audience gets when something formerly opaque becomes suddenly clear. He and the cast were using rehearsals to do what I had used the research process to do: overcome the profoundly alienating experience of being an Irish citizen during the financial crisis. Accountant-turned-actor Peter Daly was a particular asset. 'Wait!', Conall would cry, his face crumpling in pain, mid-scene. 'Explain how shorting works *again*.'

And then, on the morning of our first performance, I awoke to hear the voice of David Drumm, the former boss of Anglo Irish Bank, on the radio. The Irish Independent newspaper had obtained leaked recordings from the Anglo internal phone system; these "Anglo tapes" captured Drumm and senior colleagues joking about their efforts to save the bank. One of them gloated that a request to the Central Bank for an emergency loan of seven billion euro had been picked "out of my arse".

Five years after the bank guarantee, as I worried that my play might be too after-the-fact, the guarantee was front-page news again. Our rehearsed reading was suddenly a hit. I tweaked a scene that featured David Drumm asking the Central Bank for seven billion euro, to now include the question to him: "Is that a precise figure David . . . where did you get it from?"

*

Guaranteed! finished with Brian Lenihan's line that the bank guarantee had been "the cheapest bailout in the world so far". As we by then knew, it hadn't. So the line begged the question, and Fishamble, with Pavilion Theatre, duly commissioned the sequel.

Bailed Out! was, I thought, a better play. Not merely had I learned from experience, but the material had an innate tragic momentum. A party steeped in the mythology of the fight for independence was fighting to avoid the loss of that independence, even as its two leading figures, Brian Cowen and Brian Lenihan, were themselves stalked by tragedy. Cowen's was the more prosaic: the self-harm of alleged excess drinking — an allegation vindicated, for many, by one catastrophic, apparently hung-over, early-morning interview. Lenihan, meanwhile, discovered he was fighting terminal cancer even as he was fighting the bond markets – something that, though it was initially revealed to the public with unseemly haste by TV3, was then almost entirely ignored by the media.

These personal tragedies posed a dramaturgical challenge, however. These were plays about public decisions, not private lives. They were about the argument. The cast sought to embody the characters with merely a hint of the real person behind them. Nobody in the Irish audience was in any doubt who these characters were, but I wanted to signal we were commenting on their lives in politics, in the public realm. The point was not that they were uniquely flawed; rather, they were everymen, in unique circumstances. What I was really trying to dramatise, to embody, was the systems around them.

*

By the time *Bailed Out!* came to the stage, it was seven years on from the bank guarantee, and almost two years since Ireland had exited the bailout. If *Guaranteed!* had played like a current affairs documentary, *Bailed Out!* — better play or no — played as a period piece. I decided to write a history play proper.

By then the country had entered what was being branded as the "decade of centenaries", with the looming centenary of the Easter Rising of 1916 the most pivotal. Pauric Dempsey, a friend then working at the Royal Irish Academy, facilitated an introduction to An Post, which runs the GPO as a corporate headquarters and working post office. We suggested a play about the Rising, to be staged inside the GPO on the centenary. To our surprise — and, I think, theirs — they said yes. We called it, simply, *Inside the GPO*.

But being in the cathedral of revolution on the centenary of that revolution creates a particular pressure. I worried that the occasion would overwhelm the play, turning it into pageantry. I thought of the astonishing precedent of Seán O'Casey, who — just *ten* years after the Rising — mocked it on the Abbey stage. I spoke to Catriona Crowe of the National Archives. "Our job is to complicate the narrative", she said. Gavin Kostick, dramaturg for Fishamble, asked how I wanted the play to make people feel. I answered: whatever your certainties coming into the play, I want you to leave uncomfortable about them. Perhaps I was echoing a line I had read by David Hare: if journalism is about certainty, drama is about ambiguity.

I had long been skeptical of the Rising. I thought it madness — and not glorious madness, as the O'Rahilly had it. A century on, its malign influence was still felt. Three years further on, in 2019, dissident republicans would shoot the journalist Lyra McKee dead at a riot in Derry. They drew their mandate from the Rising.

But reading, thinking, writing about these men and women made me

less comfortable in whatever certainty I had possessed. On the final night, as the audience dispersed, I noticed an elderly woman still sitting, upset. I approached her. "My father was here," she said. Her name was Mary Finlay; her father, Patrick J Hughes, had been a Volunteer in the GPO. I brought her backstage. She approached Daniel McDermott, still in his Volunteer uniform, who had led the singing of The Soldier's Song (later to become the national anthem) as they left the stage at the end of the play, replaying the evacuation. "My father told me about you," she said, "about how you sang." She turned to Aidan Kelly, who played James Connolly, still with his leg wrapped in a bloodied bandage. "And my father was shot with you," Mary said to him. "He told me how brave you were."

*

In February 1982, a young, socialist, working-class teacher, Tony Gregory, was elected to represent Dublin Central and found himself with the deciding vote in the contest for taoiseach. The two bourgeois party leaders, Garret FitzGerald of Fine Gael and Charles Haughey of Fianna Fáil, duly came courting, and (spoiler alert – but then, this is a history play) Haughey won out. The Gregory Deal, as the agreement between Gregory and Haughey became known, was either overdue social justice or outrageous clientelism, depending on your perspective. (Where I grew up, in the leafy suburbs of the Southside, it was more often seen as the latter.)

My friend Des Gunning had been a member of the Gregory group, the wider circle of activists around Gregory, and suggested I might find the deal fruitful material for a play. I was wary: there was an obvious dramaturgical problem. Plays are about disagreement, not agreement. From early on Haughey and Gregory had each wanted the same thing – a deal. But as I dug deeper, and came to know the people around Gregory — in particular Mick Rafferty and Fergus McCabe — I realised the drama lay in the disagreement within each side.

There was another problem: men. *Again* a play about *men* making decisions. Again, I used the device of fictionalising a female character to act as the chorus for the play. I had decided that the character of Gregory's secretary would fill this role, and hoped I could get away with the character being a bit flimsy. And then Janet Moran was cast, and I thought, *Janet's too good for such a flimsy role.* And so I went back to Pauline Kane, the woman who had been the secretary in the community project from which Gregory launched his political career. This time, I asked her more about her life and work, rather than about her memories of Gregory and his team in 1982. Thirty-five years on from when, as a teenager, without a Leaving Cert, she had joined the project as secretary, Pauline was now running the project descended from it; she was the defender of the legacy; she was the one still fighting the fight. Though the character is fictionalised in the play, as Eileen, much of Eileen's story belongs to Pauline, even as the story of the play — despite it being called *Haughey/Gregory* — belongs to Eileen.

*

The Treaty was another play that belonged to the secretaries. It was inspired by the Whitehall Diaries of Tom Jones, secretary to the British prime minister, David Lloyd George; when I discovered the memoir by one of the Irish secretariat, Kathleen McKenna, I found myself with joint narrators.

It was a centenary, again, that was the catalyst for the play. But I had learned that history plays are never just about the history, and as I researched and wrote *The Treaty*, it was a contemporary negotiation that was very much on my mind. In Brexit, there was a curious mirror image of the Irish separation from Britain, a hundred years earlier. In each case, an island was trying to take back control from the empire to its east — an empire, saddened, that believed they were stronger together. Tory diehards holding the government's feet to the fire; debate over customs areas and free trade agreements; Canada being held out as an exemplar; dispute over whether the Irish border should be on the island or in the sea. Most intriguing, though, was the resonance between Brexiteer aspirations and that of the Irish republicans of a century earlier. Again, I felt this should make its audience less comfortable with their prior certainties. British conservatives might be surprised to hear such "remainer" arguments from conservative icons like Winston Churchill and FE Smith; Irish nationalists, hostile to Brexit, might be surprised to hear their republican forbears anticipating the Brexiteers' arguments.

Again a play about men making decisions. Kathleen McKenna gave me a vital female voice, but (unlike Jones) she was not in the room where it happened. So we started to think about gender-neutral casting. Conall and I went through lists of actors, male and female, with a key question: could this person play this part? What would this cast look like if we simply cast the best actors, irrespective of gender? We duly cast the play half and half, male/female. The performances were vindication enough; still, it was nice that the Guardian's veteran critic, Michael Billington, judged it "some of the best gender-blind casting I have seen".

But the most daunting challenge facing a play in 2021 was less dramaturgical than epidemiological. Pandemic public health measures were still in place in Ireland: our audience capacity was tiny; everybody had to wear masks. After our run in Dublin, we were due to travel to London, to play a week at the Irish Embassy (with their ballroom standing in for the Downing Street cabinet room), to conclude on the centenary of the signing of the Treaty, December 6. Just as we were finishing in Dublin, we started to hear about a new variant of the virus coming from South Africa: Omicron.

Countries started to close their borders – we worried what Boris Johnson would do. On our final Saturday night in Dublin, with the crew due to travel the following morning, and our first London show on the Thursday, Johnson announced new public health measures: all arrivals into the country were to be tested at a centre and then self-isolate till receiving the all-clear – which could take up to 48 hours. Our short London run was suddenly in jeopardy. It was 1.30am that night when we got confirmation, via a tweet from the British Embassy in Dublin, that the new testing requirements would not apply to Ireland.

Safely in Britain, we found a different world: public and political opinion had turned against public health measures, which were still very much in vogue at home. In Ireland, masks were still being worn inside pubs; in London, when I wore a mask into a pub, I was told brusquely to take it off. (I was the only one who could be so adventurous: cast and crew couldn't run the risk of getting sick, and sloped off home after the show each night, in cars booked by Fishamble, to avoid the dangers of the Tube.)

Meanwhile, Ireland was getting nervous. The government announced that all arrivals into the country would have to have a certified negative test before departure. On the second last night of the London run, one of the crew happened to take one of these tests shortly before the show was due to go up. They tested positive.

PANIC! We had a case of Covid in the house; a crew and cast any one of whom might also have it; and an audience due to start walking in the doors any moment. The distraught crew member was bundled into makeshift quarantine in a commandeered embassy office, while the producer scoured the building for Covid tests. By 7.15, with the curtain due up at 7.30, and many of the audience already in their seats, crew and cast had all done their tests and were waiting nervously for those pregnancy-test-like lines to appear. One by one, people got the all-clear. And then two tests came back uncertain. PANIC! Producer scoured the building again; two fresh tests were unearthed; another 15-minute wait ensued.

I was sitting in the audience, oblivious to any of this but for the rather unavoidable fact that the show had not begun. Eventually, the lights went down and the cast entered, and I realised something had gone badly wrong: they looked frazzled; there were noticeable fluffs; everybody was on edge. And then something happened, and that energy became a part of the play, and the jeopardy, that night — as they argued about the "ensanguined hue" of the relationship between these islands — felt never greater.

*

These were the first words of mine spoken from the stage in a full-length play, in *Guaranteed!*:

"This play is based on a true story. Some of it is literally true. When you see us speaking at public events, our words are based closely on verbatim records, though sometimes different speeches and events have been combined. And some of it is invented. When you see us speaking in private – behind closed doors, as it were – those conversations are imagined, but based on some documentary record: internal documents, media reports, the official inquiries, or conversations with people involved in these events."

I can't quite believe I felt that level of caveat necessary, or tolerable (though on opening night we received a hand-delivered letter from the Director of Public

Prosecutions warning us of the danger of prejudicing any ongoing legal proceedings). Each of these plays traces its own fault line along the seam between fact and fiction; each time, for different reasons, I have been nervous about whether that fault line would crack open.

With *Guaranteed!* and *Bailed Out!*, there was the danger of compromising prosecutions, of being sued and, fearing these, of going too soft. With *Haughey|Gregory*, the danger was of doing hurt to people who had not lived lives in public, but whose lives I was putting on stage. But with each play, I grew more confident in the sophistication of the audience: they do not expect literal truth; they appreciate creative licence; they do not need the distinction spelled out.

By *Haughey|Gregory*, the unwieldy declaration at the start of *Guaranteed!* had been replaced with the line "based on a true story", projected onto the rear wall from an overhead projector. As the play started, the character Eileen approached this and added the word, "loosely".

In *Inside the GPO* and *The Treaty*, I took more liberties. These are simply history plays, rather than some form of documentary. I felt a need at the time to tease out how I had approached the recorded history, and so I have included these original notes as afterwords here below. Ironically, it was *The Treaty* – a play about people long dead, and politics long moot (in as much as that can ever be said) – that provoked a challenge to the integrity of my approach. I have elaborated on that in an addition to the afterword.

Three of these plays were first staged script-in-hand, as rehearsed readings, or "workshop" or "semi-staged" productions (another term we were never quite sure about). Making a virtue of necessity, the presence of the scripts served as an acknowledgement that these stories were not made up; the spiral-bound scripts were reminiscent of the documents the characters might have been carrying; as a journalist by trade, they were also, for me, reminiscent of newspapers. Like news reporting, these plays were a first draft of history, subject to change (and they did change), only as good as their sources. Looking over them now, though, I see that all five plays are "documentary" in a more literal sense; each is about a foundational document: the Proclamation; the Treaty; the Gregory Deal; the Guarantee; the Bailout.

*

I find, to my astonishment, that it is 20 years since the very first piece of work I did with Fishamble, an earlier short play, Dublin Noir, for a theatre "trail" they produced in Dublin's Temple Bar, called Whereabouts. In that time, the company has consolidated its position as the country's leading and most inventive producer of new writing. Their playwriting courses, and initiatives like their Tiny Plays for Ireland and the Show in a Bag and New Play Clinic supports for theatre makers, have provided the opportunity and the means for many a writer to convert their aspirations into practice. Their collaborations with other companies and organisations – such as our ongoing work with Larkin Community College in inner-city Dublin – have brought new plays into nooks and crannies of the city that theatre rarely penetrates. (A personal highlight was bringing *Haughey|Gregory* into Mountjoy Prison, where the audience consisted largely of men who had grown up on the streets outside, where the play was set.) Under the leadership of Jim Culleton and producers Marketa Puzman, first, and then Eva Scanlan, and with the deft guidance, always, of literary manager Gavin Kostick, they have been the backbone of my playwriting career.

Fishamble paired me with Conall Morrison for *Guaranteed!*; he has since directed another three of the plays here (the exception is *Inside the GPO*, directed by Jim Culleton) and, more recently, *The United States vs Ulysses* (published separately by Bloomsbury). I find it difficult to separate out his role as director from his contribution to their authorship. Conall runs a collaborative, questioning rehearsal room: the plays benefitted immeasurably from the insights and suggestions of their original casts. But not only have the plays been refined under his guidance in the room, we have spent countless hours, often over late-night takeaways, discussing, editing and reworking them. If the plays might not exist without Fishamble, they would be far the lesser without Conall.

*

Months after that theatre trail in 2006 – a visceral celebration of live theatre in the streets of Dublin – the iPhone came out. As Fishamble were working on Tiny Plays for Ireland, Snapchat launched. As we were producing *Guaranteed!*, Vine created the culture of vertical short-form video that TikTok would later perfect. As Bloomsbury has been working on this volume, I learned that some of my plays had been included in the dataset used to train Meta's AI model. AI can now write bad plays, credible essays and excellent blurbs. It will get better at essays; why should it not get better at plays also?

So playwriting — let alone history plays, let alone documentary theatre — can seem increasingly anachronistic. Certainly, our purchase on both the wider culture and the funding infrastructure feels increasingly precarious. So why do we do it?

When we first produced *Guaranteed!*, we followed it each night with a post-show discussion. One woman in the audience bravely told her own, grim story of her family's struggle with debt and the banks, and finished with a question: "What should we do?" I had no answer. But I think doing *this* is part of an answer. We — the writers and theatre makers — can and should do what journalists and the media also do: we should tell urgent political stories; we should hold a mirror up. But our mirror is different to that of the media. They speak truth to power; they hold their mirror up to the powerful. We hold our mirror up to the audience. In a culture ever more angry, ever more polarised, ever more judgemental, we invite the audience into an act of empathy with the characters on stage, in all their flaws. It's that David Hare line again: if journalism aspires to certainty, drama embraces ambiguity.

Something similar is at work in a history play. History, as we learn it in school — and as we often intuitively absorb it — appeared fixed in aspic. Things happened because they happened; they can hardly have been different. The job of the history play is to undo that certainty and take us back to a point when what we know will become fixed is still contingent; when actors who will become defined by their decisions have not yet made those decisions, and may yet make other ones, and be judged differently by history. The history play raises the question of the counterfactual: it allows us to imagine what the alternatives might have been.

Fundamentally, this is all about empathy. This is why we do it – and this is why, in a world growing ever more digital, theatre grows perhaps more necessary. To sit amongst an audience in a theatre at a play is the opposite of scrolling on a phone or talking to a chatbot. It is not an anachronism – it is an antidote. The paradox of the pandemic was that it both reminded us of this and, for many, it broke the habit.

The unfinished play is still in the drawer. The one-year-old, though, has made more progress. He is now 18. He is as digitally-native and as shaped by the pandemic as any other of his generation. And he is also writing plays.

Colin Murphy, October 2025

Inside the GPO

Inside the GPO was presented by Fishamble: The New Play Company in the round in the public hall of the General Post Office, Dublin, in March and April 2016, to mark the centenary of the Easter Rising, with the following cast:

Winnie Carney	Orla Fitzgerald
Mary Louisa Hamilton Norway	Karen Ardiff
Arthur Hamilton Norway / Tom Clarke	Michael Glenn Murphy
James Connolly	Aidan Kelly
Michael Collins / Volunteer Keogh	Gavin Fullam
The O'Rahilly	Don Wycherley
Sean MacDermott	Manus Halligan
Patrick Pearse	Ronan Leahy
Min Ryan	Liz FitzGibbon

And featuring an ensemble cast from the Gaiety School of Acting playing members of the Irish Volunteers and Cumann na mBan, and all other parts:

Murphy/Good	Louis Deslis
Separation Woman/Walsh	Carolyn Donnelly
British Officer/The Swede	Gavan O'Connor Duffy
Gahan/Fr Flanagan	Daniel McDermott
Byrne	Martha Dunlea
O'Sullivan	Desmond Eastwood
Duffy	Ali Hardiman
McLaughlin	Meg O'Brien
The Finn	Tom Duffy

Directed by	Jim Culleton
Dramaturgy by	Gavin Kostick
Set and costume designed by	Niamh Lunny
Lighting designed by	Mark Galione
Sound designed by	Carl Kennedy
Hair & make-up designed by	Val Sherlock
Movement direction by	Bryan Burroughs
Produced by	Eva Scanlan

Inside the GPO was presented in partnership with Fáilte Ireland, Dublin City Council, Ireland 2016, An Post, DublinTown and Arnotts. Fishamble is funded by the Arts Council and Dublin City Council.

The filmed production of *Inside the GPO* is available for teachers and students as part of Fishamble's Encore Programme: www.fishamble.com/encore.

Characters

Arthur Hamilton Norway, *Secretary of the Post Office in Ireland*
Mary Louisa Hamilton Norway, *his wife*
Winnie Carney, *secretary to James Connolly and adjutant in the Irish Citizen Army*
James Connolly, *Commandant-General of the Irish Citizen Army and Vice President of the Provisional Government of the Irish Republic*
Patrick Pearse, *Commander-in-Chief and President of the Provisional Government*
Tom Clarke, *member of the Military Committee of the Irish Republican Brotherhood, and of the Provisional Government*
Seán MacDermott, *member of the Military Committee and of the Provisional Government*
Min Ryan, *member of Cumann na mBan and girlfriend of MacDermott*
The O'Rahilly, *Director of Arms in the Irish Volunteers*
Michael Collins, *a junior officer*
Members *of the* **Irish Volunteers** *and of* **Cumann na mBan**
A Post Office official, a **Separation Woman** *(ie. the wife of British Army soldier)*, a **British Officer, Joseph Plunkett,** a **priest,** a **Swedish sailor,** a **Finnish sailor**

The surnames used for the Volunteers and Cumann members are typically drawn from Bureau of Military History witness statements or other sources but these are not intended to be historically accurate characters. These parts may be organised however best suits the production. 'Volunteer' on its own refers to both male and female.

* * * indicates a shift in the focus or location of the action on stage, without being a new scene per se.

Prologue

In the public hall, a sense of occasion, of celebration. It is March 1916. Post Office staff welcome the audience. **Arthur Hamilton Norway** *wanders amongst them, savouring it.*

From the balcony, **Winnie Carney** *watches over proceedings.*

At the first-floor window, **Mary Louisa Hamilton Norway** *stands in profile, reading a letter, in silhouette. At some point during the following, she will walk onto the balcony, at the opposite end to Carney, and take up position at a writing desk, with a lamp on it.*

A smartly-dressed **Post Office Official** *enters.*

Official   Ladies and Gentlemen, please be upstanding for the national anthem.

The audience stands, expecting Amhrán na bhFiann. Instead, God Save the King plays.

As it finishes, on the balcony, **Mary Louisa** *turns on her desk lamp and holds out the letter she is writing. She gives a polite cough.*

Carney (*to audience*)   Mary Louisa Hamilton Norway . . .

Mary Louisa (*to audience*)   To begin at the beginning.

Carney   an inveterate letter writer.

Mary Louisa *addresses the audience as if reciting her letter to her unseen correspondent.* **Carney**, *on the other hand, addresses them as narrator – knowing, somehow, they are a theatre audience. When other characters address the audience, they do so without such insight – they believe the audience to be part of their environment.*

Mary Louisa   The Sinn Féin movement has been in existence for years, but has always been looked on as a small body of cranks. It became known some months ago, in certain circles, that they were obtaining large quantities of arms and ammunition. Various persons did all they could to open the eyes of the authorities – including Arthur . . .

Down below, the Official re-enters.

Official (*announcing*)   The Secretary of the Post Office, Mr Arthur Hamilton Norway.

Carney   Mary Louisa's husband.

Arthur Hamilton Norway *takes the floor to applause.*

Arthur   Thank you.

Mary Louisa   but they wouldn't listen.

Arthur   Lord Lieutenant . . . Chief Secretary . . . Ladies and Gentlemen . . .

Carney   The 5th of March. 1916.

Arthur You are very welcome to the opening of this beautifully restored Public Office for the GPO . . . Tonight is a night to look back a hundred years . . .

He savours the expanse and beauty of the GPO.

Mary Louisa This has been the culmination of Arthur's career.

Arthur A century ago, this magnificent edifice was built to house the postal service in the second city of the Empire. But no longer is this just a postal service. This is the era of communications! The telegraph . . . telephony . . . perhaps soon also the wireless!

But these inventions all take space! My predecessors allowed this room become cluttered with back offices. So when I arrived here in Ireland, I decided to restore this public hall to its former glory – to make it a civic space worthy of this city. It is a privilege to be able to re-open it now, tonight.

I trust we shall do a better job of protecting it over the next one hundred years!

Mary Louisa Oh, we have been happy here, in Ireland. As happy as could be . . .

Arthur Now, I wish to pay tribute to one of our post men. – Mr J.F. Connell, who has been fighting for the rights of small nations in France, and has just been awarded the Distinguished Conduct Medal for valour in the field. Please join me in wishing that he will soon be able to return to his duties here after a victorious war.

Arthur *leads an applause.*

Mary Louisa And the boys were happy in Blackrock. It was so good to have the chance to rear them in the countryside!

Arthur We might take a moment now to remember those of our colleagues, our friends and . . .
(faltering)
our . . . families . . . who will not be returning.

He bows his head, privately upset.

Mary Louisa But after Fred –
(faltering)
After Fred was killed at the Front, last year . . .

Arthur's *moment of silence ends.*

Arthur Thank you.

He leaves. **Carney** *leaves the balcony.*

Mary Louisa the house was too full of memories . . . So we put our furniture in storage . . .

and we moved in to the Royal Hibernian Hotel, on Dawson Street. But we didn't want to bring our valuables . . . Fred's books . . . his sword . . . all his possessions . . . So we've stored them in Arthur's safe, in his office in the G.P.O.

Monday

Carney *has arrived downstairs, to a small desk with a typewriter on it, placed just off stage.*

Connolly *leads in the rebels.*

Carney   The 24th of April, 1916. Easter Monday.

Connolly *stops centre stage. He looks around. The men wait nervously for orders.*

Connolly   There's not as many of you as I'd hoped – but it'll have to do.

Carney   Shortly after midday.

Connolly   Get everybody out.

A pause and then the ensemble lurches into action, ferrying in supplies and munitions, preparing the GPO for siege.

Carney *sits down at her desk and sets up the typewriter. Volunteers arrive with messages, which she types up in memos for* **Connolly**.

Henceforth, scenes happen in different areas on stage, overlapping, so that the action is constant.

A volunteer jostles a woman across the stage.

Volunteer Murphy   You heard the man, m'am – everybody out!

Separation Woman   I'm not going anywhere till I've got my separation money.

Volunteer Murphy (*contemptuous*)   There'll be no money for British Army wives in the Irish Republic.

Separation Woman   I'd like to see you feed six children with an Irish bleedin republic.

The volunteer manhandles her out, as she abuses him.

Connolly   These women battered the peelers during the Lockout, lads – let's not make an enemy of them!

Carney   The General Post Office is to be the headquarters of a national rising . . .

Collins, *revolver out, grabs a* **British Officer** *who has been trying to slip out.*

Collins   What the fuck are you doing?

British Officer   Sending a telegram.

Collins   It's a different kind of telegram your family will be getting if you show any fucking cheek.

He bundles him off.

Carney   The first rising in almost 50 years.

Carney *produces a place a large map of Dublin, and makes notes on it.*

Connolly   Start barricading the doors.

Carney   Elsewhere in the city, other garrisons are taking strategic positions . . .

Connolly   And the windows – like you were taught! – break the glass out – or it'll turn into shrapnel.

Carney *adds a map of Ireland to the one of Dublin.*

Carney   Outside of Dublin – well, we don't know . . .

A volunteer carries in food supplies.

Volunteer Murphy   How long does this food need to last?

Connolly *thinks for a moment.*

Connolly   Three weeks.

Volunteer Murphy   Three weeks it is.

Carney   The forces in Dublin are led by James Connolly, founder of the Irish Citizen Army.

Connolly   If you can't find any more furniture for the barricades, use paper! Notebooks – letters – even books of stamps!

Volunteer Gahan (*skeptical*)   Paper?

Connolly   It slows bullets, man.

Carney   Alongside him is the well-known school principal, and polemicist, Patrick Pearse.

Pearse *stands in the centre of the stage, looking about him.*

Connolly   Well, Pearse. Here we are. A day late.

Pearse   What's one day in 750 years?

Connolly (*looking about him*)   The enemy's communications centre. Where better to start a revolution?

Pearse   But where will it end?

Carney   With them are some 200 men of the Irish Volunteers and Irish Citizen Army . . . Amongst them is The O'Rahilly . . .

O'Rahilly *enters.*

Connolly (*guarded*)   O'Rahilly . . . I thought you were against us.

O'Rahilly (*bitter*)   I helped to wind up the clock, didn't I. I may as well hear it strike.

They exit.

Carney   And they are joined by three other key figures in the planning of the Rising . . . Joseph Plunkett . . .

Plunkett *walks on weakly, coughing. He looks about him and smiles.*

Carney   . . . who is in the advanced stages of tuberculosis, and reliant on his young aide-de-camp . . .

Collins *rushes to help him.*

Collins   I've got you, General.

He leads **Plunkett** *off stage and calls another volunteer to find a mattress for him.*

Carney   and the legendary Fenian, Tom Clarke, and his protégé, Sean MacDermott . . .

Clarke *and* **MacDermott** *stand centre stage, surveying the scene.*

MacDermott   What's O'Rahilly doing here?

Clarke   Keep an eye on him . . . And make sure Pearse gets a desk and paper and sticks to the writing . . .

They exit.

Carney   And with these men, there is one woman . . . me.

Connolly   Miss Carney!

Carney   Winnie Carney.

Connolly   Where the hell is that woman?

Carney   Secretary to Mr Connolly – I came with him from Belfast, for my sins.

Connolly   For Christ's sake, *Carney*!

Carney (*calmly, behind him*)   Yes, sir.

Connolly   Oh! Ehm-
(*flustered*)
The Tricolour, Miss Carney, where is the Tricolour?

Carney   The flags were not my responsibility, sir.

Connolly   Blast it!

Carney   I suspect you've left them at Liberty Hall, sir.

Connolly   Bloody hell.
(*to another volunteer*)
You! Go back to Liberty Hall and get the blasted tricolour!

Carney   Mr Connolly?

Connolly (*irritable*)   What?

Carney   The Plough and the Stars.

Connolly (*after him*)   And the Starry Plough, man!

Volunteer   The Starry Plough?

Connolly   Let's not forget – we're fighting for the cause of labour *and* the nation. (*to Carney, sotto voce*)
They might not be the same cause for too long.

Glass breaks, off.

Volunteer Gahan (*Off*) (*angry*)   Hey! What the –

Cumann Byrne (*Off*) (*impatient*)   Get out of the *way*!

Carney (*pleased*)   Ah hah.

Catherine Byrne *enters, followed by Joe Gahan trying to stop her.*

Volunteer Gahan   Catherine!

Cumann Byrne   Oh! Joe!
  Sorry about that.

Carney   Make that *two* women – and counting.

Volunteer Gahan   What the hell are you doing here?

Cumann Byrne   I'm with Cumann na mBan! I'm reporting for duty.

Volunteer Gahan   Why couldn't you use the door?

Cumann Byrne   Paddy wouldn't let me in.

Volunteer Gahan   Oh Jesus, well don't tell him I did. Go and make yourself some use.

Cumann Byrne   I've brought some first aid materials.

She produces some materials, including torn-up sheets.

An explosion, off, followed by a burst of shouts and screams: 'What was that?' 'Jesus Christ!'

Volunteer Gahan   Looks like you've found your first patient.

Volunteer Murphy *carries a wounded volunteer onstage, his head bleeding profusely. Byrne runs over to tend to him.*

Cumann Byrne   Where's the medical station?

Volunteer Murphy   There isn't one, yet.

Cumann Byrne   Well this'll have to do.

Pearse *strides on, holding the Proclamation.*

Pearse (*exhilarated*)   Are they attacking? Was he shot?

Volunteer Murphy   He dropped one of his own bombs.

Pearse *gazes on, transfixed.*

Connolly *enters.*

Connolly   Miss Carney – have some of these put up, will you.

He hands her some copies of the Proclamation.

Connolly   Pearse! Are we launching this Republic or are we not?

Pearse   Of course.

They exit.

Carney *unrolls the Proclamation and reads.*

Carney   'The Republic guarantees religious and civil liberty, equal rights and equal opportunities to all its citizens, and declares its resolve to pursue the happiness and prosperity of the whole nation and all of its parts.'

As she reads, a volunteer enters carrying a silver platter with a whole salmon on it.

Volunteer Good (*calling*)   Where do I go with provisions?

Volunteer Murphy   What the hell is that?

Volunteer Good (*uncertain*)   A fish.

Pearse*'s voice drifts in from outside. It continues underneath their dialogue, barely audible.*

Pearse (*off*)   We place the cause of the Irish Republic under the protection of the Most High God . . . We pray that no one who serves that cause will dishonour it by cowardice, inhumanity, or rapine.
In this supreme hour . . .

Volunteer Murphy   Where did you get it, man?

Volunteer Good   I commandeered it from the Gresham.

Volunteer Murphy   Good work. Get it into the kitchen.

Carney *accompanies* **Pearse***'s reading.*

Pearse/Carney   . . . the Irish nation must, by its valour and discipline, and by the readiness of its children to sacrifice themselves for the common good, prove itself worthy of the august destiny to which it is called.

Cheers, off.

Carney   Well. Day one of the Irish Republic.

* * *

The leadership gathers: **Clarke**, **MacDermott**, **Pearse**. **Connolly** *approaches the map.*

Connolly   Miss Carney – is this up to date?

Carney Yes, sir.

Connolly Thank you.

He turns to the assembled leadership.

During **Connolly**'s *speech,* **Carney** *receives a dispatch and waits to approach* **Connolly** *at an opportune moment.*

Connolly Gentlemen . . . To the west, Commandant Ned Daly's battalion holds the Four Courts and is ready to repel an incursion from the Royal Barracks . . . To the south-west, Commandant Éamonn Ceannt's battalion has secured the South Dublin Union and is positioned to control Richmond Barracks . . . To the south, Thomas MacDonagh has taken Jacob's Biscuit Factory on Bishop Street, allowing him command the canal bridges giving access to the city from Portobello Barracks . . . And to the south-east, Éamon de Valera holds the area around Boland's Bakery, covering the barracks at Beggars Bush and the road and railway from Kingstown harbour.

Once we take the Telephone Exchange in Crown Alley, we will have total control of the city's communications – that will severely compromise the Castle's ability to respond, and should delay the arrival of reinforcements from across the water.

We know the British won't shell the city – capitalists will never willingly destroy capital. That means they'll send infantry against us – and we'll be waiting. When the country rises, these barracks will find themselves sandwiched between the forces in the city and those advancing from outside.

Clarke The country would be out now if it weren't for that turncoat MacNeill.

MacDermott What is O'Rahilly doing here?

Connolly He has a good military mind – we can use him.

MacDermott He was MacNeill's messenger boy for the countermand.

Pearse He's thrown his lot in with us now. That's what counts.

Clarke We should have gone ahead yesterday – there was more men turned out – despite MacNeill.

Connolly The confusion would have been worse.

Clarke We should have shot them.

Pearse They acted in good faith.

Clarke What do the British do to cowards, out in Flanders?

Connolly Let's wait till we've won this before we turn our guns on each other.

Carney (*interrupting*) Commandant General?

Connolly Try and get some sleep tonight – it'll be difficult enough when the heat comes on.

She hands him the dispatch.

Connolly   Should anyone need a sleeping draught – we have some opium.

He looks at the dispatch and calls after the others.

Connolly   Gentlemen. We have failed to take the Telephone Exchange at Crown Alley . . . We will have to be ready to repel an attack sooner than we had anticipated.

Pearse   I'll alert the other garrisons.

Connolly   I'll reinforce our outlying posts. We'll meet again in the morning.

The meeting breaks up.

* * *

Pearse *spots a nearby volunteer,* **Gerald Keogh**.

Pearse   Volunteer!

Volunteer Keogh   Sir!

Pearse *does a double-take.*

Pearse   Buachail ó Scoil Éanna? (You are a student from St Enda's?)

Volunteer Keogh *(flattered)*   Sea, a mhástéir. (Yes, sir.)

Pearse   Keogh, nach é? (Keogh, isn't it?)

Volunteer Keogh *(proudly)*   Sin é! Go díreach. (Yes! Exactly.)

Pearse   Tá áthas orm go bhfuil tú anseo linn. (I am happy that you are here with us.)

Volunteer Keogh   Níl fonn orm bheith in aon áit eile. (I wouldn't be anywhere else.)

Pearse   Weren't you one of our actors?

Volunteer Keogh   I was in The Boy-Deeds of Cúchulainn, sir.

Pearse *(suddenly alight)*   Ah – our first pageant! You know Mr Yeats was in the audience?

Volunteer Keogh   No!

Pearse   Yes! You performed for Yeats! Imagine that.

Volunteer Keogh *(reciting)*   'If I die, it shall be from the excess of love that I bear the Gael.'

Pearse   Ah, Colmcille . . . And Cúchulainn?

Volunteer Keogh   'I care not if I live but one day and one night if only my name and deeds live after me.'

Pearse *kisses him.*

Volunteer Keogh *(surprised)*   A mhástéir-

Pearse   Have you a bicycle?

Volunteer Keogh Yes, sir.

Pearse Are you fast?

Volunteer Keogh Very.

Pearse Take this to Commandant Mallin at the Stephen's Green garrison. If you are caught, eat it.

Keogh exits.

On The Balcony

Mary Louisa It was quiet this afternoon, so I went out to see what was happening on Sackville Street . . . Over the GPO floats a great green flag with the words 'Irish Republic' on it in large white letters . . . Arthur can't understand why the rebels have chosen to advertise their headquarters, instead of keeping themselves hidden . . .

Every window on the ground floor was smashed and barricaded – but I could see Arthur's room, on the first floor, and it appeared not to have been touched – so at least Fred's things are safe.

After they took the GPO, the rebels sent a unit to take the Telephone Exchange – but just as they were turning into Crown Alley an old woman rushed towards them, crying 'The place is crammed with soldiers!' So they turned back . . . But there weren't any soldiers there – it was unprotected.

Our boys arrived a few hours later, and now it's secure. Had the rebels taken the Exchange we would have been absolutely powerless – we would have been unable to send messages or telegrams for troops . . . We don't know who the woman was – whether she was on our side, or thought she *had* seen soldiers. But she may just have won this fight for us . . .

Tuesday

Carney *is at her desk, receiving and typing up dispatches.* **Pearse** *is writing, oblivious to all else.* **Connolly** *is asleep on a mattress.* **Clarke and MacDermott** *sit on a nearby mattress in low conversation.*

Carney Tuesday. Day two of the Irish Republic . . .

A volunteer walks quickly through carrying an old pail. Another volunteer spots her and approaches, keenly.

Cumann Byrne I'm parched. Is that tea?

Cumann McLoughlin (*grimly*) Toilet.

Carney More men and women have flocked to the GPO as word has spread about the Rising.

A young volunteer cycles a post office bike cautiously into the hall. He looks around – nobody senior is watching. He continues onto the stage. He pulls a wheelie.

A female volunteer approaches the first.

Cumann Duffy   What the blazes are you doing?

Volunteer Gahan   What the fuck does it look like I'm doing?

He pulls another wheelie.

Cumann Duffy   Where did you get that?

Volunteer Gahan   It's the Post Office – it's full of bikes!

Cumann Duffy   Shouldn't you be at your post?

Volunteer Gahan   Relax, would ye. The British have run scared. We're in charge now.

Another volunteer approaches carrying a crate of beer bottles and hands it over to Duffy.

Cumann Walsh (*to Duffy*)   We found these upstairs . . .

The cyclist realises she is carrying beer and rushes over.

Volunteer Gahan   A party!

Cumann Walsh   Would you pour them down the drain?

Cumann Duffy   Of course.

Volunteer Gahan   What?!

Cumann Walsh   No drinking in headquarters.

Volunteer Gahan   The whole city is boozing for free and we can't have a sup?

Cumann Walsh   Tom Clarke's orders.

Volunteer Gahan   Oh come on, nobody's going to notice a bottle.

Cumann Walsh   Oh alright – take one.

He goes to take a bottle.

Cumann Walsh   But make sure you enjoy it. Because when Clarke sees you, you'll be shot.

Volunteer Gahan   I'll help you get rid of them.

Meanwhile, another volunteer has entered the hall, concentrating on a very worn tennis ball, throwing it to himself, carefully.

He reaches an appropriate point and turns and throws the ball back into the depths of the hall.

British Officer (*off*)   No! Out of the *back* of the hand.

*The **British Officer** enters carrying a piece of salvaged wood, approximating a cricket bat, and the tennis ball.*

Volunteer Murphy   I *am* throwing it out of the back of my hand.

British Officer   Here.

He places the tennis ball in the other's hand and moulds the hand and fingers as he explains the move.

British Officer   At the point of release, the palm is open upwards, towards the sky. The back of your hand is facing the batsman. Your wrist is 180 degrees to the ground. And the seam of the ball is pointing towards fine leg.

It's your third finger that does the work. As you release, you turn the ball anti-clockwise.
(*demonstrating*)
See?

Volunteer Murphy (*befuddled*)   Show me again.

He gives the Officer the tennis ball and he demonstrates the bowl.

British Officer (*as he winds up*)   Remember – hide the ball, lad – never let him know your intentions – that why it's also called 'the wrong 'un'. Now – (*throwing*)
that's the googly –

O'Rahilly *enters, gun drawn, covering the Officer.*

O'Rahilly   What the hell is going on here –

British Officer   Don't shoot!

Volunteer Murphy   Sir! Don't shoot, sir!

O'Rahilly   An escaped prisoner throwing projectiles – why the hell wouldn't I shoot?

Volunteer Murphy   He hasn't escaped, sir!

O'Rahilly   Well what in God's name *is* he doing?

Volunteer Murphy   Bowling, sir.

O'Rahilly   Bowling?

British Officer   He asked me to –

O'Rahilly   Shut up!

Volunteer Murphy   We were talking cricket, sir –

O'Rahilly   Cricket?

Volunteer Murphy   And he mentioned he could bowl that new ball they're all talking about – the googly.

O'Rahilly   The googly?

Beat.

O'Rahilly   You can do it?

He nods.

O'Rahilly   They say the trick is to release out of the back of the hand . . .

British Officer   It feels unnatural at first, but you can get used to it . . .

O'Rahilly   Oh, I think my bowling days are behind me . . .

They leave together.

A volunteer delivers a newspaper to **Carney**.

Cumann McLaughlin   The Irish Times is out.

Carney *takes it.*

Carney (*eager*)   What do they say about us?
(*leafing through it*)

The Spring Show . . . The races at Fairyhouse . . . The D'Oyly Carte Opera at the Gaiety! Bourgeois nonsense!

She finds something on the Rising and reads – with growing disgust. **Connolly passes**.

Connolly   Is that our paper – the Irish War News?

Carney   It's the Times.

Connolly (*eager*)   What do they say about us?

Carney (*reads, sardonic*)   'This desperate episode in Irish history can have only one end . . .'

Connolly   That's why we're publishing our own paper.

Carney   We need to think further afield . . .

Connolly   London would just censor anything we put out over there anyway . . .

Carney (*looking around the GPO*)   Wireless . . .
(*beat*)
We could broadcast the proclamation –

Connolly   Broadcast?

Carney   Morse Code . . .

Connolly   To who?

Carney   To America.

A beat as it sinks in. Then he strides off, shouting to nearby volunteers.

Connolly Find me someone who can use a wireless machine!

Collins *enters.*

Cumann Byrne Sir!

Byrne *enters, followed by the* **Swede** *and the* **Finn**.

Cumann Byrne These men say they want to join us.

Collins Well, who are they?
(*to* **Finn**)
Who the hell are you?

The Finn Ah –

Collins Speak up, man!

The Swede He not speak the English.

Collins (*jibing*) Well what about Irish?

The Swede (*confused*) We are not Irish.

We sailors. We dock in Dublin yesterday. I am of Sweden. He Finland. We want join your fight.

Collins (*holding up his gun*) Can you use a weapon?

The Swede I can use a –
(*mimes, looking for word*)
rifle.

The **Finn** *mimes shooting fowl.*

The Swede My friend – he can use what you shoot the fowl with.

Collins A shotgun.
(*to* **Byrne**)
We'll need to get them guns.

Cumann Byrne Yes, sir.

Collins Welcome to the Republic.

He shakes their hands.

* * *

Meanwhile, **Pearse** *has risen from his desk, preparing to make his daily address to the volunteers. He takes some dispatches from* **Carney**'s *desk.*

Pearse Comrades! Soldiers and officers of the Irish Republic!

The men and women gather round. **Min Ryan** *enters during his speech.*

Pearse On this second day of the Republic, the Republican forces hold all their positions and the British forces have nowhere broken through. The casualties of the

enemy are much more numerous than ours. The populace of Dublin are plainly with the Republic. The officers and men are everywhere cheered as they march through the streets.
(*waving the dispatches*)
Reports to hand show that the country is rising.

Cheers.

* * *

Carney *notices* **Min Ryan**.

Carney   Can I help you?

Ryan   I need to see Seán –

Carney   'Seán'?

Ryan   MacDermott –

Carney   Who are you?

Ryan   Ryan – Máirín – Min Ryan.

Carney   What are you doing here?

Ryan   I'm with Cumann na mBan.

Carney   Which branch?

Ryan   Dawson Street . . . I was sent to Wexford with the order from MacNeill –

Carney   The countermand?

Ryan   I need to talk to MacDermott –

Carney   Is Wexford rising?

Ryan   I don't think so . . .

Carney   Have you a dispatch?

Ryan *delivers it.*

Ryan   They were confused by the countermand.

Carney *goes to the map and puts a line through Wexford on it.*

Ryan   Pearse said – the 'Republic' –

Carney   Haven't you seen the Proclamation?

Ryan   I just got here – he said they're cheering in the streets –

Carney   He did.

Ryan   There are dead horses in the streets.

Carney   There were dead bodies, too.

Ryan   And Clery's – they've broken into Clery's.

Carney   Aye.

Ryan   Why?

Carney   Because there's nobody to stop them.

Ryan   Somebody *should* stop them.

Carney (*contemptuous*)   How?

Ryan   You have guns – how else do you stop a mob?

Carney   The Irish Republic will never turn its guns upon the workers.

Ryan   Where's MacDermott?

Carney   Wait there.

Carney *leaves.* **Ryan** *waits.*

* * *

O'Rahilly *enters, troubled. Pearse is at his desk, writing.*

O'Rahilly   Pearse.

Pearse *glances up.*

Pearse   What would you think of a German prince – a Catholic one?

O'Rahilly   A what?

Pearse   As head of state –

O'Rahilly   Head –

Pearse   *Titular* head of state, I mean. To represent us at the peace conference –

O'Rahilly   What peace conference?

Pearse   After the war – the one to resolve the rights of small nations.

O'Rahilly   Pearse –

Pearse   A monarch would give us international standing.

O'Rahilly   It's not –

Pearse   It would be great for the language – a blow against the Saxon tongue.

O'Rahilly   It's not German *princes* we need. It's German *guns*.

Pearse   They didn't get through – Casement was caught.

O'Rahilly   You should have called it off.

Pearse   The men had been brought so far – we had to go forward . . . Besides, we'd shown our hand. They'd have arrested us all – disarmed the Volunteers. That would have killed off the movement for a generation.

O'Rahilly   What do you think *this* is going to do?

Pearse   We have proclaimed the Republic.

O'Rahilly   'The Republic' –

Pearse   We are broadcasting it to the world.

O'Rahilly   What *is* that? Is it socialist?

Pearse   It will be *separate* – then the people can decide. It's something to strike the world's imagination.

O'Rahilly   What use to us is that?

Pearse   This is a battle on the world stage, O'Rahilly.

O'Rahilly   This is a battle on the streets of Dublin – and it's a battle we're going to *lose*.

Pearse   We just have to last three days.

O'Rahilly   And then what?

Pearse   That will entitle us to representation at the peace conference – so we can make our case against the Empire.

O'Rahilly   Pearse – this is madness –

Pearse   The whole centre of Dublin is in our hands!

O'Rahilly   You believe your own propaganda?

Pearse   It's *true*! We have taken the city!

O'Rahilly   We have nothing outside the city! It's just a matter of time before they concentrate their forces on us.

Pearse   Just *three days*, O'Rahilly. We can last three days . . .

O'Rahilly   *How*?

He takes the map.

O'Rahilly   *Show me*. Show me how. Show me the strategy.

Pearse *hesitates. Then they fall to examining the map.*

* * *

Clarke *approaches* **MacDermott**.

Clarke   The girl, Seán –

MacDermott   I know.

Clarke   She took the countermand. She took it to Wexford.

MacDermott   She was given an order. She had no choice.

Clarke Did she know about our plans?

MacDermott Nothing.

Clarke Why is she here?

MacDermott For the same reason we are.

Clarke Why is she asking for you?

He doesn't answer.

Clarke We said our goodbyes, Seán – there's a reason we didn't bring our women.

MacDermott I've worked for this for 15 years, Tom.

Clarke I know.

MacDermott I'm not going anywhere.

Beat.

Clarke Do you trust her?

MacDermott With my life.

Clarke We need people we can trust – people who can organise . . . for afterwards . . . Do you want to talk to her?

MacDermott I can't.

Clarke I will.

* * *

O'Rahilly *despairs.*

O'Rahilly Three days? We won't last 36 hours!

He breaks away.

O'Rahilly I left five children at home, Pearse, and one more –

He falters.

Pearse You can leave, O'Rahilly. Honourably. No man will accuse you of cowardice.

O'Rahilly (*pointing to the GPO around him*) I recruited these men. Do you expect me to leave them to their deaths?

Pearse You may die with them.

O'Rahilly In *another* futile attempt against the Crown?

Pearse 'I care not if I live but one day and one night if only my name and deeds live after me.'

O'Rahilly What *is* that?

Pearse Cúchulainn.

O'Rahilly Great. Is he coming?

Pearse We are fighting for Ireland's honour, O'Rahilly. For the people's hearts.

O'Rahilly (*pointing outside*) Those people? The ones shouting abuse at your men? The ones marauding around Clery's?

Beat.

O'Rahilly What if your 'name' – your 'deeds' – are spat upon?

Pearse Then it is over.

O'Rahilly *What* is –

Pearse Everything.

Beat.

O'Rahilly So this –

He looks around at the GPO.

O'Rahilly The Post Office – This Rising – This is –

Pearse This is our last chance.

O'Rahilly For Ireland.

Beat.

Pearse Yes.

* * *

Clarke *approaches* **Ryan**.

Clarke (*gentle*) Miss Ryan.

Ryan Mr Clarke – I was hoping to see Mr Mac –

Clarke Seán is asleep. We none of us have slept much these past days. We need to keep our wits about us . . .

He is watching her closely.

Clarke For the fight ahead.

Beat.

Ryan Will we win?

Clarke You won't be here at the end – you will have work to do, outside, afterwards.

Ryan My work is here.

Clarke You work is where I say it will be.

Ryan I haven't given ten years to this movement to be sent home when it is finally –

Clarke I have waited my whole life for this! I was 16 years in British prisons. They beat us. Starved us. Froze us. They didn't let us talk. They didn't let us sleep. I thought I would go mad. But I didn't. One thing kept me sane. Kept me whole.

Memory. Our Fenian dead. The Manchester Martyrs. Emmet. Tone. Those before me who suffered the same – and worse.

We need people to remember. What we have done. What we have been through. That will be your role.

Ryan And Seán –

Clarke Seán is a member of the Provisional Government of the Irish Republic – his work is here, now.

Beat.

Clarke Clarke's tobacconist on Parnell Street. You'll find my wife there. I want you to bring this to her.

He hands her a rolled-up proclamation.

Clarke Seán's name is on it, with mine – you should be proud. Talk with Kathleen, my wife . . . After this, you will have to work together – to preserve the memory of it . . .

She nods, reluctantly.

Clarke Well. Come on. Walk with me. We'll talk some more.

* * *

As **Clarke** *and* **Ryan** *leave,* **Volunteer O'Sullivan** *carries in a bloodied and moaning young volunteer.*

Pearse *gravitates towards them to observe, without intervening.*

Volunteer O'Sullivan Where's the first aid station?

Cumann Duffy What happened to you?

Cumann Walsh Jesus, he's been shot. Get the nurse.

Carney Have you dispatches?

Volunteer O'Sullivan He was carrying it . . .

The nurse enters.

Cumann Byrne Oh Good God. Bring him here.

O'Sullivan *helps the injured man towards the first aid station.*

Volunteer O'Sullivan It's – it's in his breast pocket.

His breast area is bloodied. **O'Sullivan** *pauses, grimaces, then tries to find the message. The injured volunteer groans.*

Volunteer O'Sullivan   Sorry about this, pal.

He fishes out a bloodied dispatch and hands it to **Carney**, *who takes it, reads, and makes a note.*

Cumann Byrne   Put him down here.

She starts to care for him.

Carney   What happened?

Volunteer O'Sullivan (*dazed*)   Snipers . . .

Carney   Where?

Volunteer O'Sullivan   Passing Trinity . . .

Carney   Did you not know there were snipers there?

Pearse   It's alright Miss Carney.
(*to the volunteer*)
Tell me what happened, lad.

Volunteer O'Sullivan   Sir . . . We were coming back from the Green, sir, with dispatches from Commandant Mallin . . . They had details on British troop movements further west – reinforcements . . . We were crossing College Green . . . I heard shots . . . My bike went from under me. I heard a shout. He went down . . . I managed to get him behind some pillars. We managed to crawl away . . . eventually . . .

Pearse   You'll get a medal for this, lad. You saved his life.

Volunteer O'Sullivan   We had to leave the other fellow, sir.

Pearse   What other fellow?

Volunteer O'Sullivan   I'm surprised they got him – he was fast.

Pearse   Who?

Volunteer O'Sullivan   I didn't know him. He came with us from the Green.
(*remembering*)
He had a dispatch too – he gave it to me, before, before he –

He fishes it out of his pocket – very bloody – and hands it to **Pearse**.

Volunteer O'Sullivan   There was blood – It was coming out his mouth sir. He tried to say something . . . I think it was in Irish . . . I couldn't catch it . . .

Pearse   Keogh.

Volunteer O'Sullivan   I don't know, sir.

Pearse   Where is his body?

Volunteer O'Sullivan   I assume – I assume it's still there, sir . . .

Pearse   Where?!

Volunteer O'Sullivan   College Green. In front of the gates at Trinity.

Pearse (*to* **Carney**)   Can we –

Carney   It's too dangerous, sir. The Red Cross are collecting bodies. And –

Pearse   The British.

Carney   When they can.

Pearse *sags.*

Carney   He knew what he was doing, Mr Pearse.

Pearse   Yes . . . We taught him well . . .

Beat.

Pearse   The men will need a priest.

Pearse *attempts to return to his writing, but struggles.*

On The Balcony

Mary Louisa   When the shooting in Grafton Street was over, the mob appeared . . . At the corner of the Royal Hibernian Way is a high-class greengrocer, and they swarmed inside. Children ran out dragging great bunches of bananas by cords tied to the stalks. One woman was hanging out of an upper window dropping down apples and oranges to a friend – and she was shot through the head by a sniper . . . He was probably one of ours . . . Her body dropped into the street and the mob cleared. A few minutes later, a hand-cart appeared and gathered up the corpse . . . And, instantly, the mob swarmed back to continue their looting.

We hear the military have poured into the city, and are in the Shelbourne Hotel and Trinity College. The rebels have barricaded Sackville Street. It is expected to be very fierce fighting over the GPO.

We hear lots of strange things . . . That Sir Roger Casement has been shot in London . . . That Larkin was shot on the top of a house in St Stephen's Green . . . That three of the ringleaders were caught and executed . . . And we know nothing of what is going on in other parts of Ireland – just more rumours of insurrection, in the West and the South.

Wednesday

Sound of shelling, in the distance.

Everybody stops and looks up. Then they look to each other.

Carney Wednesday. Day three of the Irish Republic.

Pearse *approaches* **Carney's** *desk, takes some dispatches and addresses the volunteers.*

Pearse Our lines are everywhere intact and our positions of great strength . . . (*waves the dispatches*)
Reports to hand from the country show that Dublin's call is being responded to . . . Large areas in the West and South are now in Arms for the Irish Republic . . . The final achievement of Ireland's freedom is now, with God's help, only a matter of days . . .

* * *

The shelling continues.

Connolly *enters, carrying the map, with* **Collins**.

Connolly We believe the British have occupied Amiens Street station. We have units on the corners of North Earl Street – here and here – make sure they're well fortified. See if you can garrison the corners of Abbey Street as well.

Collins (*tracing route on map*) They could just march straight down to the quays . . .

Connolly Aye – that would leave our southern flank vulnerable . . . I'll post some men on Liffey Street.

O'Rahilly (*bursting in*) So much for your socialist claptrap that capitalists would never shell capital.

Connolly Don't you see? They are shelling us because they are afraid.

O'Rahilly (*dismissive*) Afraid of what?

Connolly Afraid of our *ideas* . . . That men should be equal and nations sovereign . . . Afraid that the mere mention of the Republic will serve as a beacon-light to the oppressed of every land.

O'Rahilly They are shelling us because we've made ourselves a sitting target. We can't stay here.

Connolly We have declared the Republic. Our flag is flying.

O'Rahilly Tis – telling them exactly where we are . . .

Explosion.

Connolly (*to* **Collins**) We need to strengthen our defences.

O'Rahilly We can't defend against that.

Connolly They'll use the artillery to soften us up. Then they'll send in infantry.

O'Rahilly You can't fight a revolutionary war from a static position – we should be *mobile*. Defence in depth – we need to prepare fall-back positions. Force them to come after us.

Connolly *dispatches* **Collins**.

O'Rahilly   We cannot hold the GPO.

Connolly   You said we wouldn't last 36 hours – and this is our third day.

O'Rahilly   It is against all the rules of warfare that we have.

Connolly   So stop worrying about the rules.

He takes out his revolver and inspects it, and makes to leave.

O'Rahilly (*disbelieving*)   Where are you going?

Connolly   Out. We need to garrison Liffey Street

O'Rahilly   Send somebody else. An officer should never fire his gun.

Connolly   I'm a soldier, O'Rahilly.

O'Rahilly   You're the Commandant General.

Connolly   Why do they call you *The* O'Rahilly, anyway?

O'Rahilly   It's – Ah – It's an old Gaelic title . . .

Connolly   Where I come from, O'Rahilly, it's what you do that counts – not your title.

* * *

As **Connolly** *leaves, a volunteer leads in a priest.*

Cumann Duffy   This way father.

Fr Flanagan (*to himself*)   These people are murderers . . .

Cumann Duffy (*to* **Clarke**)   I brought the priest.

Fr Flanagan   They should be left to burn to death.

Clarke (*droll*)   Are you here to excommunicate us, Father?

Fr Flanagan   I will administer the sacraments . . . But I will not be associated with your revolutionary project –

Clarke   Find him a room. Make sure they all have access to him

Fr Flanagan *begins hearing confessions from the volunteers, who take it in turns to approach him.*

* * *

A group of volunteers sit around by candlelight, smoking. They pass around a pail of tea, wincing as they sup it. Two of the men are trying to fix a damaged wireless telegraphy machine.

A particularly loud shell hits.

Volunteer Good   Blimey.

Silence.

Volunteer Good I hear they've already used artillery on our men at Fairview.

Volunteer O'Sullivan We don't stand a chance.

Cumann Byrne The Fairview men fought them off.

Volunteer Good I was in the British army . . . I've seen what their artillery can do.

Brooding silence.

Cumann Byrne When we get the German guns –

Ryan What German guns?

Cumann Duffy The ones that landed in Kildare!

Cumann McLaughlin There's ten thousand Germans marching down the Naas Road.

Volunteer Good How do you know?

Ryan Hang on –

Cumann Duffy There's some men just came in from Fingal. They said.

Ryan They can't have landed in Kildare –

Cumann McLaughlin They heard it on the road.

Ryan There's no coast in Kildare.

Cumann McLaughlin And there was a u-boat spotted in Dublin Bay.

Cumann Byrne They landed in Kerry –

Ryan (*to* **McLaughlin**) There was not –

Cumann McLaughlin Pearse said it.

Cumann Byrne They're sweeping up from the south. It should be just a matter of days.

Cumann Duffy What if the British attack before they get here?

Volunteer O'Sullivan Hey Blimey – can you send an SOS on that?

Volunteer Good (*working on machine*) We have to get it working, first.

Cumann Duffy We'll need guns – somehow –

Cumann McLaughlin (*remembering*) Oh! I've got a gun!

She pulls out a revolver and covers them, to consternation.

Volunteer Good Blimey!

Volunteer O'Sullivan Watch out!

Collins Put that down!

Ryan   Where did you get that?

Cumann McLaughlin (*waving it about*)   I found it. On the street. Taking a message for Mr Pearse.

Collins (*stern*)   Give it to me!

Volunteer Good   Is it British?

Cumann McLaughlin   I don't know.

She turns it around to examine it, alarming them further.

Collins   Give it to me, lass.

Cumann McLaughlin   I may need it.

Collins   That's an order!

He takes it and checks it.

Cumann McLaughlin   That's not fair.

He puts it away and looks at her more closely.

Collins   How old are you anyway?

Cumann McLaughlin (*proudly*)   Fifteen.

Ryan   You should be locked up at home.

Cumann McLaughlin   I was!

Collins   I suppose you shot your way out.

Cumann McLaughlin   I went home to see Mammy cause she hadn't seen me since this started and I was worried she'd be going up the walls – and doesn't she lock me in my room! 'You'll be safer there till this is over,' she says. And then she goes back down to the kitchen and I take out the gun and break the window and climb out – and here I am!

Walsh *enters.*

Collins   Some army.

Cumann Walsh   The priest is free.

Another volunteer slips out to confession.

MacDermott *appears in the background, watching.*

Cumann Byrne   I hope the Germans get here quick.

The Swede   Why you trust the Germans?

Cumann Byrne   The enemy of mine enemy . . .

The Swede   Germany is big country. Big countries fuck small countries.

Cumann Duffy   This is an Irish fight – what do you even know about it?

The Swede Sweden is small country too. Russia fuck Sweden. Russia is friend of England. England fuck Ireland. So you fight England – I fight with you.

Volunteer O'Sullivan Anybody who is willing to die with us can consider himself an Irishman.

The Swede Oh, I not die with you. I sail tomorrow. But perhaps I kill English before then.

Laughter. Then silence, again.

The Swede The people outside – Irish people – why they hate you?

Awkward *silence for a beat.* **MacDermott** *speaks up.*

MacDermott They have been colonised. That's why.

We are a subservient people. That is what colonisation does . . . Big countries do not 'fuck' small countries – they consume them . . . For hundreds of years, we have tried to fight that – to assert our birthright – a separate Irish nation. Every generation, we have risen – and we have failed – but we have kept the *idea* of the nation alive.

But now, in our time, that idea is nearly extinct. Our men volunteer for Kitchener's Army in their tens of thousands. Our 'nationalist' leaders boast of our sacrifice for Britain's war. They are doing what hundreds of years of colonisation failed to achieve . . . And the people accept this as natural and suitable – because they have no memory of anything else. They don't argue for what is *right* – they acquiesce . . .

Collins What he means is, we're turning into Scotland.

MacDermott This is the time of our final acquiescence.

Fr Flanagan *has entered.* **Ryan** *stands behind him.*

Fr Flanagan And that justifies murder.

MacDermott We are defending ourselves against a foreign invader.

Fr Flanagan Like James O'Brien –

Collins Who?

Fr Flanagan A policeman from Limerick – shot dead at Dublin Castle.

MacDermott In the uniform of the enemy –

Fr Flanagan Unarmed!

MacDermott He took the King's shilling.

Fr Flanagan Like the woman –

MacDermott What woman?

Fr Flanagan The 'separation woman' – shot at Jacob's Factory –

MacDermott There will be tragic accidents in war –

Fr Flanagan Shot in the *face* for throwing fruit at your comrades – because her husband was out in France.

Uncomfortable silence.

Fr Flanagan Is this what you are here for? Is it?

He looks around the room.

Fr Flanagan What *are* you here for?
(*to* **McLaughlin**)
You, child.

Cumann McLaughlin (*intimidated*) My brothers joined, Father.

Fr Flanagan And you?

Volunteer Good For Irish freedom.

Flanagan *looks to them, one by one.*

Cumann Byrne I am here for the vote.

Fr Flanagan You?

Volunteer O'Sullivan For the workers. I was locked out in 13 – I said never again . . . I don't remember the priests helping much then, either.

Fr Flanagan And –

Ryan We're here for Kate.

Fr Flanagan (*derisory*) Kate!

The Swede Who is Kate?

Volunteer Good Kathleen Ní Houlihan – it's their name for Ireland.

Fr Flanagan Which of these things you seek could not be achieved under Home Rule? A more Irish Ireland? A more equal Ireland? For a war to be *just*, violence must be the *last* resort.

Collins That many men are dying for your 'just' war, in Flanders, that there soon won't be any Ireland left.

Fr Flanagan What authority have you to declare war?

MacDermott We are the Provisional Government of the Irish Republic – that is our authority.

Fr Flanagan Who gave you that mandate?

MacDermott It is the mandate of history.

Fr Flanagan So let's say you win your 'republic' . . . What happens then when some rump group of disaffected decides to take up arms against it, and cites 'history' as a justification?

MacDermott When we enthrone the Republic, there will be no more justification for physical force.

Fr Flanagan You have lit a flame. It may be more difficult to quench than you think.

MacDermott (*leaving*) We will take responsibility for that, Father . . .
(*to Collins, sotto voce*)
Get him out of here.

Ryan *attempts to stop* **MacDermott** *as he leaves.*

Ryan Seán –

MacDermott (*brusque*) I can't, now, Mairín.

He leaves.

Collins Father . . . I think these people would value consolation.

The priest leads out another volunteer for confession.

Silence descends again, more sombre.

Volunteer O'Sullivan I had a nightmare . . . I was hanged, and after being hanged I could see myself, without any head, and my body suspended from a hood that went through my throat . . .

Cumann Walsh I wouldn't like to be hanged . . .

Volunteer O'Sullivan I'd prefer to be shot.

Cumann Byrne I'd prefer to be hanged.

One of the volunteers has been growing uncomfortable.

Collins (*dismissive*) I'd prefer not to be shot or hanged.

Volunteer Good They do love a good hanging, the English. Always have.

Volunteer O'Sullivan I hope they use firing squads . . .

Min Ryan *leaves in disgust.*

The volunteer grabs the pail and vomits into it.

Silence. The shelling intrudes.

A volunteer (perhaps **Byrne***) starts to sing Fáinne Geal an Lae.*

Volunteer (*singing*)   Maidin moch do ghabhas amach,
   Ar bruach Locha Léin;
   An Samhradh teacht's
   an chraobh len'ais,
   Is ionrach te ón ngréin,
   Ar thaisteal dom
   trí bhailte poirt

Is bánta
mine réidhe,
Cé a gheobhainn le máis
ach an chúileann deas,
Le fáinne geal an lae.

Ní raibh bróg ná stoca,
caidhp ná clóc;
Ar mo stóirin óg ón spéir,
Ach folt fionn órga sios go troigh,
Ag fás go barr an théir.
Bhí calán crúite aici ina glaic,
'S ar dhrúcht ba dheas a scéimh,
Do rug barr gean
ar Bhéineas deas,
Le fáinne geal an lae.

Do shuigh an bhrideog sios le m'ais,
Ar bhrinse glas den fhéar,
Ag magadh léi bhios dá maiomh go pras,
Mar mhnaoi nach scarfainn léi.
'S é dúirt í liomsa,
'imigh uaim,
Is scaoil ar siúl mé a réic',
Sin iad aneas
na soilse ag teacht,
Le fáinne geal an lae.

The Swede Your story – it sounds like a Greek tragedy.

Collins Too many poets – not enough guns. *That*'s our tragedy.

On the Balcony

Mary Louisa Arthur is more confident now . . . They have repaired the telegraph lines the rebels cut and, with the Telephone Exchange running, we have complete control of communications again.

It seems the Sinn Féiners were led to believe that they would have great German reinforcements, and that all they had to do was to hold the troops here for a couple of days while the Germans landed a big force on the west coast of Ireland.

We have now over 12,000 troops in Dublin . . . They have cut the rebel leadership off from their garrisons south of the river, and are tightening the cordon around the GPO.

We hear they are going to fire some 'gas' shells into the GPO and then rush it . . . Arthur says they will not raze it to the ground if they can help it . . . It has such valuable records . . . and the contents of the safes are so precious.

Thursday

Carney   Thursday. Day four of the Irish Republic . . .

Cumann Duffy   The glass in Clery's windows is melting!

Carney   The opposite side of Sackville Street is on fire . . .

Volunteer Gahan   The sandbags are smouldering!

Carney   The air in the GPO is thick with smoke and sparks.

Cumann McLaughlin   They could go up any time!

Cumann Walsh   Let's soak them with water – before they go up in flames!

A volunteer shouts.

Volunteer (*off*)   Commandant Connolly's been shot.

Carney *is shook.*

Carney   Is he –

Collins (*off*)   He's made it back into the building. He's losing blood.

Carney   What was he doing outside?

Volunteer Gahan   He was reviewing positions.

Cumann Duffy   He insisted on going himself.

Cumann Byrne   I'll go to him.

She leaves, carrying first aid materials. **Carney** *follows.*

Elsewhere:

Volunteer Murphy   Why won't they attack?!

Collins   Don't show yourself in the window! The snipers.

Volunteer Murphy   I can't even fuckin see them!

Volunteer Good   When you've got artillery, and machine guns – you don't need to attack.

* * *

Pearse *passes by* **Carney**'s *desk, and takes a typed dispatch from it.*

Pearse   Miss Ryan.

Ryan   Mr Pearse –
(*corrects herself*)
Commandant General.

Pearse   I have some dispatches.

Ryan I don't think we can get through the barricades any more, Sir.

Pearse You'll find a way, Miss Ryan.

He holds them out.

Pearse These are messages to the country –

Ryan (*confused*) To the *country* –

Pearse We are relying on them to continue the fight . . . You must get the word to them.

And this is for my mother. You know the house?

Pearse *moves on, leaving* **Ryan** *bemused.*

* * *

Connolly *is carried on stage by a* **volunteer and Carney***.*

Connolly (*weakly*) Winnie. Get me O'Rahilly.

She leaves. During the following, she returns with **O'Rahilly***, who kneels down to* **Connolly***, and they fall into conversation.*

* * *

MacDermott and Ryan *meet.*

Ryan Seán –

MacDermott Mairín –

Ryan Come with me, Seán.

MacDermott (*not understanding*) Where?

Ryan Out. Away from this.

MacDermott I'm needed here.

Ryan There's enough leaders with a death wish here.

MacDermott I gave my word.

Ryan You gave your word to me!

MacDermott There's nothing I can –

Ryan We could go to England – I have friends in London. Or America. Just till it all dies down – then we can come back. We just have to get out of here . . .

MacDermott (*dismissive*) How –

Ryan There's a tunnel – out the back – they're using it to run messages – you're not in uniform – we could slip out onto the streets – disappear –

MacDermott This is what I've *lived* for.

Ryan And me? What am I to you?

Beat.

Ryan It doesn't have to be one or the other – you don't have to choose – we can live for Ireland, together . . .

Ireland will get her sacrifice. But she'll need new leaders to build on it. A new generation.

MacDermott (*warning*) Mairín –

Ryan Who is that going to be? One of these youngsters? What if it were you? Can anybody else do what you've done, organising this?

She is getting through to him, despite himself.

Ryan The Castle don't know you.

Beat.

Ryan When the movement needs a new leader . . . You could be the one . . .

He breaks away.

Ryan Seán!

He stops.

Ryan Clarke was 16 years in jail – I can't wait 16 years –

MacDermott Min – I won't be in jail.

Beat.

Ryan I always thought we'd . . .

MacDermott I did too.

She leaves.

* * *

MacDermott *joins the leadership.* **Connolly** *lies on the mattress.* **Collins** *listens from the wings.* **O'Rahilly** *takes the meeting.* **Carney** *hands him various notes. All of them are dishevelled, exhausted.*

O'Rahilly *looks at the map of Dublin.*

Carney Gentlemen, the Commandant General has asked Captain O'Rahilly to update you.

O'Rahilly To the west, Commandant Ned Daly's 1st Battalion still holds the Four Courts. Their D Company, under Captain Seán Heuston, had occupied the Mendicity Institution on Usher's Quay. It was taken, yesterday – we believe with the loss of all lives . . .

Everyone (*blessing themselves*) The Lord have mercy on their souls. / Ar dheis Dé go raibh a hanam uasal.

O'Rahilly Our dispatch carriers can no longer get across the river – we have lost contact with the battalions to the south . . . As of yesterday, Commandant Éamonn Ceannt's battalion at the South Dublin Union was under siege . . . Commandant Thomas MacDonagh's battalion at Jacob's had seen no action at all . . . Commandant Éamon de Valera had withdrawn all his outposts into the garrison headquarters at Boland's Bakery . . . None of them have achieved anything more than slightly delay the advance of British troops into the city.

Connolly What about Malone?

O'Rahilly Lieutenant Michael Malone, de Valera's C Company, had some success. They held off a British battalion at Mount Street Bridge.

MacDermott Casualties?

O'Rahilly Reports said 200 British –

MacDermott Dead?

O'Rahilly Or injured.

Connolly And ours?

O'Rahilly Five killed.

MacDermott That's what we'll do to them when they attack here.

O'Rahilly Malone's men were defending against *infantry* – not artillery. The British will soon have our range, here. We need a new strategy. We need to prepare for evacuation.

Connolly What are our options?

O'Rahilly There's the soap factory, on Parnell Street – we could regroup there . . . Or the Four Courts – it's not as exposed as here . . . That could buy us time – time for the country to rise – or to get more support from Germany – or from Irish-America – or for the war to turn against Britain . . .

Carney But we're surrounded – how do we get there?

O'Rahilly The tunnels.

Clarke What tunnels?

O'Rahilly Out the back. The men have tunnelled through as far as Arnotts . . . That will take us past Moore Street, nearly onto Liffey Street.

MacDermott You want to move four hundred men . . . women . . . ammunition . . . supplies . . . through a tunnel *and* then out onto the streets across a battlefield?

O'Rahilly We'll have to leave the women.

Carney What do you mean, 'the women'?

O'Rahilly The front line is no place for a woman –

Carney   This is a revolution, comrade. The women are on the front lines already.

O'Rahilly   We cannot move a large number of unarmed people through a battle zone.

She holds up her revolver.

Carney   Who says we're unarmed?

Beat.

Connolly   I am not going anywhere without Winnie Carney.
(*wincing*)
Except perhaps the grave.

Clarke   None of us is going anywhere.
Our flag flies here. We will fight under it. To the end.

O'Rahilly   We could have *won* this – had we waited –

Clarke   We had waited long enough!

O'Rahilly   The time was coming! The British would have moved against us – or introduced conscription. That would have brought the people onside. We could have started in the country and moved in *slowly* towards the city. We should be fighting in Kerry, or Galway, or Donegal – they'd never defeat us!

Clarke   There would be fighting *now* in the country, had you not carried the countermand.

O'Rahilly   Fighting with *what*? There were no guns. They would have been annihilated. The only saving grace of this is that there are relatively few of us to be massacred now.

Clarke   If MacNeill thought the Rising should be postponed, he should have come to us and told us. And let us decide then. That would have been honourable. But to cancel it – behind our backs – that was treachery.

O'Rahilly   Treacherous – us? You ran a secret society within a secret society –

Connolly   We had no choice!
(*to* **O'Rahilly**)

We had to fight. If we had backed down – the shame would have been too great to bear.
(*to* **Clarke**)
But O'Rahilly is right. We have done what we can, here.

Clarke   We pledged our lives to the Republic.

Connolly   It's not an abstraction, Clarke – it's a republic of *people* –

Clarke   The shedding of blood has always raised the spirit of the people.

Connolly   It's difficult to see how having their city razed to the ground will raise their spirits. We have to be flexible now – no military strategy can afford to be set in stone.

Clarke This is not a military undertaking!

Connolly It is as long as I'm in charge.

He tries to get up but falls back.

Connolly O'Rahilly – tell the men to expect the order to evacuate in the morning.

Clarke I countermand that order.

Connolly On what authority?

Clarke On my authority as first signatory of the Proclamation and senior member of the Provisional Government.

Connolly The Provisional Government is not in session.

Clarke We are in continuous session –

MacDermott (*backing him up*) We have five members here –

O'Rahilly I can only take an order within the military command.

Collins (*entering*) I've had enough of this –

Carney You can't just barge in –

Clarke The Provisional Government has overall military command –

Connolly I am the Commandant General of the Dublin forces and in a combat situation I have authority over the men under my command –

Collins Who the hell is in charge?

Beat.

Pearse I am.

Beat.

Collins Because if you're planning a strategic retreat you want to effect it pretty soon –

MacDermott (*to Collins*) Who the hell are you –

Connolly This lad has seen more of Dublin this week than any of us – hear him out. What would you do, lad?

Collins Can we get out to the country?

O'Rahilly It's too late. We'd never get through the British lines.

Collins Disappear, then.

Connolly The G-Men know us. They'll hunt us down.

Collins Then we have to get mobile. Within the city. Before they choke us off.

Clarke We are ready for them here.

Collins We'll burn here!

Clarke If that is what it takes –

Collins And take the best of a generation with you? Where will that leave the cause of Irish freedom?

Clarke What do *you* know about Irish freedom?

Collins I know I want to live to see it!
Somebody has to be thinking about the *next* fight . . .

Clarke *This* is our fight – we nearly missed it. We won't abandon it now.

Pearse What do we achieve by leading more boys to the slaughter?

They look at **Pearse**.

Connolly Do you mean to surrender, Pearse?

O'Rahilly We cannot surrender by dark. They won't trust it. It could be a massacre.

Collins The men won't surrender – they want to fight.

Clarke We have proclaimed the Republic! To surrender would be to betray it!

'Bloodshed is a cleansing and sanctifying thing . . .' Your words, Pearse . . .

'The old heart of the earth needs to be warmed by the red wine of the battlefield. . .' Your words . . .

'The sea shall roll in red waves, and blood be poured out. . .' Your words.

You stood at O'Donovan Rossa's grave last August and you accepted the responsibility of carrying out the Fenian programme. 'Splendid and holy', you called him . . . Well
(*gesturing to the GPO*)

this is what is holy – the tradition we inherit – the physical force tradition – the tradition you said you would lead for a new generation . . .

Pearse (*to himself*) There can be no peace between the right and wrong.

Clarke If we retreat now, we risk wasting all we have sacrificed . . . These bombs that we're so afraid of – they will follow us – the British will destroy more of the city. Where do we go to – some factory on Parnell Street? To be burned out there? To crawl out and surrender then? This is the birthplace of the Republic. This is where we shall defend it.

Long beat.

Pearse Miss Carney. Call the men together.

O'Rahilly Pearse – what are we doing?

Pearse We defend the Republic. We stay.

The volunteers gather.

Pearse You have redeemed Dublin from her shame and made her name splendid among the names of cities . . . The Irish republic has been established by our actions and has attained the right to be at the peace table in Europe after the war . . . You deserve to win this fight, and win it you will, though you may win it in death . . .

Collins *and* **O'Rahilly** *make to leave.* **MacDermott** *catches them, quietly.*

MacDermott (*to* **O'Rahilly**) Make sure the tunnelling work continues. (*to* **Collins**)

See if it is possible to make it to the Four Courts . . . or the factory . . . just in case.

They leave.

On the Balcony

Mary Louisa We now have 30,000 troops and plenty of artillery and machine-guns. They have formed a huge semi-circle with the GPO as the centre. Starting from the river, they are driving the rebels back street by street, till eventually they will be in a small enclosure, when they will bombard it to pieces.

It seems as if the whole city is on fire. Above the roar of the fires, the whole air seems vibrating with the noise of the great guns and machine-guns. And when the roar of the guns ceases you can feel the silence.

If the main walls of the GPO remain standing maybe we shall find the safe in Arthur's room still intact. It was built into the wall. My jewel-case is in it. In it are three little brooches that Fred gave me when he was a boy . . . And a lock of his hair.

Friday

Connolly *lies on a mattress in the centre of the stage.* **Clarke** *and* **MacDermott** *confer, privately.* **Pearse** *paces.* **O'Rahilly** *and* **Collins** *are coordinating. There is constant motion – ferrying of orders, weapons, sandbags, the wounded, pails of water.*

Carney Friday. Day five of the Irish Republic . . .

Collins Stay back from the windows!

Volunteer Good I haven't received an order.

Collins There's machine gun fire coming in! You'll be killed.

Volunteer Good (*insistent*) I haven't received an order.

Collins *gives up on him in frustration.*

Volunteer Gahan (*from the balcony*) The roof's on fire!

Collins Get the hose up there!

O'Rahilly The water pressure's too weak!

Carney   The fire threatens to spread through the building . . .

Across the stage, another volunteer spots a separate problem.

Volunteer Murphy   The lift shaft's on fire!

* * *

Collins *approaches* **O'Rahilly**.

Collins   We're going to have to get people out. .

O'Rahilly   The women . . .

Collins   Anybody who's not fighting . . . The wounded . . .

O'Rahilly   The back way – through the tunnels. They can make for Jervis Street hospital. We can send some of the women with them.

Collins   What about Commandant Connolly?

Carney   He'll not go.

O'Rahilly   He's with us to the end.

Carney   And so am I.

* * *

O'Rahilly *confronts* **Pearse**.

O'Rahilly   Pearse! We have to send the women out. They will be killed if they stay any longer.

Pearse   They want to stay.

O'Rahilly   The only people we need now are people with guns.

Pearse   Is it safe to leave?

O'Rahilly   They can carry white flags.

Pearse   What guarantee is that?

O'Rahilly   At least it gives them a chance.

Cumann Walsh (*overhearing*)   We're not leaving.

Cumann Duffy   What's wrong?

Cumann McLaughlin   They want us to go.

Cumann Duffy   We're here till the end.

O'Rahilly   There's enough will die here. Ireland doesn't need your deaths as well.

Cumann Walsh   We won't be the first to die for the vote!

Cumann Byrne   You told us we were equal!

Cumann Duffy   We are not second-class soldiers!

O'Rahilly (*to* **Pearse**)   You'll have to order them out – or they won't go.

Cumann Walsh   We'll not follow any unjust order!

Pearse   Your presence has inspired the men – their heroism pales before the devotion and duty of the women of Cumann na mBan –

Cumann Walsh (*over him*)   Our *duty* is *here*!

Pearse (*faltering*)   May God give you the strength to carry on the fight.

Cumann Duffy   We'll fight on *here*.

Cumann Byrne   'The Republic guarantees equal rights and equal opportunities to *all* its citizens'.

Cumann McLaughlin   That includes the right to fight alongside you.

MacDermott   Pearse – there's no forcing them – let them make their own minds up.

Cumann McLaughlin   Yes!

Cumann Duffy   We'll decide for ourselves!

O'Rahilly (*to* **MacDermott**)   Don't confuse the orders!
(*to* **Pearse**)

If we don't order them, they won't go – and if they don't go, more will die!

Pearse *prevaricates.*

Collins *runs on.*

Collins   The fire is reaching this floor!

Pearse *gives O'Rahilly his assent.*

Pearse   The order stands.

O'Rahilly (*shouting*)   The women are to evacuate. Men – if you have a last message for your loved ones, give it to the women now.
(*to the women*)

But don't burden yourselves – you'll need to be able to run – fast.

The women take messages and mementoes from the men. One of them prepares a white flag from old sheets.

MacDermott *takes something from a pocket and presses it into the hands of one of the women.*

MacDermott   Give this to Mairín Ryan.

O'Rahilly   It's time to go!

Collins   Come on! Move it!

The women start to leave.

O'Rahilly   Where's their flag?

Collins   They'll be shot!

O'Rahilly (*calling after them*)   The white flag!

One of the remaining women unfolds it.

Cumann Byrne   I have it –

O'Rahilly   Get out in *front* with it, woman!

She runs after the others.

* * *

MacDermott *enters from fire fighting.*

Collins   The basement! The bombs!

MacDermott   What bombs?

Collins   We've stored the bombs in the basement. If the fire reaches them, we'll be blown to pieces.

MacDermott   Get them out into the yard.

Collins   I don't have any spare men – they're all fighting the fire.

MacDermott   We can use the prisoners!

Collins   It's pitch black down there. If anyone falls . . .

MacDermott   Put people on the stairs with lights – the prisoners can carry the bombs.

Collins *leaves.*

* * *

O'Rahilly *arrives in to* **Connolly, Clarke** *and* **MacDermott**.

O'Rahilly   The position is no longer defensible.

Clarke   We could build barricades in here.

O'Rahilly   For what?

Clarke   For when they storm it.

Connolly   They're not storming it, Clarke. They're burning us out. Like rats.

Clarke   I'm not leaving the Post Office!

O'Rahilly   As soon as a spark from that fire reaches the bombs, we're going to blow ourselves up.

Clarke   The bombs are being moved.

O'Rahilly   Moving them's nearly as risky as leaving them.

He finds **Pearse**.

O'Rahilly   Pearse –

Pearse *is dazed.*

O'Rahilly   We have to evacuate.

Pearse   It's – it's chaos –

O'Rahilly   That's why we need you.

O'Rahilly *clutches him.*

O'Rahilly   Command.

You have to order it.

Pearse *doesn't seem to register.*

O'Rahilly   I'll make a sally. Try and open up a route to the factory on Parnell Street.

He turns to the others.

O'Rahilly   Ready yourselves to leave.

Clarke (*taking out his gun*)   I'll not leave the post office alive.

O'Rahilly *draws his gun surreptitiously.* **Collins** *observes.*

Clarke   This is what I have *lived* for – to stand in a free Ireland. I'm not leaving.

MacDermott   It's time, Tom.

Clarke   I'll not surrender.

MacDermott   There may be life in this rebellion yet. And if there isn't, there's another generation with us that will strike again – soon.

Pearse   We have done what we came to do, Clarke . . . Let the Provisional Government not divide, now . . .

Clarke *relents.* **O'Rahilly** *looks around the room. Nobody is objecting – the evacuation is going ahead.*

O'Rahilly   We'll send a messenger back as soon as we have regrouped.

* * *

Connolly *finishes dictating to* **Carney**, *who is writing in a notebook. She finishes and tears the sheet out of the notebook and gives it to him.*

Connolly (*shouting*)   Bring the men in!
(*to* **Carney**)
Get me propped up over there.

Carney *looks for help.*

Carney   Captain O'Rahilly?

He rushes to help.

O'Rahilly   What are you doing?

Connolly   We need to raise the men's spirits.

They prop him up.

Connolly (*weak, but determined*)   For the first time in seven hundred years, the flag of a free country floats above our heads . . . Despite my wounds, I will have my bed pushed into the firing line . . . and with the assistance of our officers, I will be just as useful to you as ever . . .

He is overcome by pain. **O'Rahilly** *takes the sheet from him. He looks down at.* **Connolly**. *He continues.*

O'Rahilly (*reading*)   Courage boys, we –
(*faltering*)
We are winning . . .
(*quietly*)

Never had man or woman a grander cause, never was a cause more grandly served.

Connolly   Did we do it, O'Rahilly?

O'Rahilly   Do what?

Connolly   Did we prove that Irishmen will die for Irish freedom – not just Belgian freedom.

O'Rahilly   You're a bull-headed Scot, Connolly.

Connolly   The odds were a thousand to one against us.

O'Rahilly   It's been a good fight. Never dreamed it would last as long.

Connolly   It was madness.

O'Rahilly   Glorious madness. I'll send a messenger back as soon as we regroup. Ready the men.

O'Rahilly *leaves, calling men to him.*

Pearse   We shall wait for the signal from O'Rahilly's men. When it comes, go out and face the machine guns as though you were on parade.

Silence.

Shots.

Shelling.

Collins *runs in, blackened from the fire.*

Collins   We can't stop the fire spreading any more. We have to leave – now.

MacDermott   We're waiting for O'Rahilly.

Collins   For what?

MacDermott To open a route –

Collins To where?

MacDermott The soap factory – on Parnell Street.

Collins But that's madness. I've been out there. It's in the hands of the British. I thought we were aiming for the Four Courts.

Pearse He has just left.

Collins He'll be fucking killed. It is certain death. What way did he go?

MacDermott Out that way – Henry Place.

Collins I'll try and warn him.

Collins *runs out after him.*

Connolly (*very weak*) What now, Pearse?

Pearse We wait.

Carney He'll be back. We wait.

Connolly Winnie.

She leans in to him.

Connolly The city's burning, Winnie. Why did we do this? What have we done?

Carney We fought, James. That was all we could do.

They wait.

A single voice starts to sing. He continues under **Carney** *and the others.*

Volunteer (*singing*) We'll sing a song . . . a soldier's song . . .
   With cheering, rousing chorus
   As round our blazing fires we throng
   The starry heavens o'er us
   Impatient for the coming fight
   And as we await the morning's light
   Here in the silence of the night
   We'll chant a soldier's song.

Carney And so we wait.

Cumann Duffy The roof is starting to fall!

Connolly Where's the young fellow?

Volunteer O'Sullivan He hasn't come back.

Cumann Walsh What about the back route?

Volunteer Murphy They're stuck at Arnotts – they can't get any further.

Volunteer Good The O'Rahilly is lost.

Gradually, the volunteers pick up the song.

During this, **Mary Louisa** *leaves the balcony.*

As they sing, the men start to move. They do not do so hurriedly, as if evacuating, but do so solemnly, in an anticipatory 'echo' of the surrender that will soon come.

Volunteers Soldiers are we,
whose lives are pledged to Ireland,
Some have come
from a land beyond the wave,
Sworn to be free,
no more our ancient sireland,
Shall shelter the despot or the slave.
Tonight we man the bearna bhaoil,
In Erin's cause, come woe or weal,
Mid cannon's roar and rifles' peal,
We'll chant a soldier's song.

Carney And then, we can wait no longer.

The men are ordered out onto Henry Street, in the hope of making it to Moore Lane . . . Commandant Connolly is carried on a stretcher – I try to shield him as best I can . . .

The song continues, **Carney** *speaking over it.*

Volunteer In valley green, on towering crag
Our fathers fought before us
And conquered 'neath the same old flag
That's proudly floating o'er us
We're children of a fighting race
That never yet has known disgrace
And as we march, the foe to face
We'll chant a soldier's song.

Carney I turn for a last look, and can just see the Tricolour through the smoke . . .

And across the road, the Plough and the Stars still hangs above the Imperial Hotel – just out of reach of the flames.
We have no plan, now . . .
We have just each other. For what its worth.

Pearse *leads the last of them out.*

Mary Louisa *arrives onto the stage.*

Mary Louisa The rebels have surrendered unconditionally . . . So I walked out to look on the wreck and desolation of this great city . . . Eason's Library and all the shops and buildings between O'Connell Bridge and the GPO on both sides of

Sackville Street are gone. Behind the GPO was the Coliseum Theatre . . . A shell. On the other side of the street was the Freeman's Journal . . . The printing machines are lying among the débris, all twisted and distorted. Behind that was a great riding school . . . All the horses were burnt to death. And of the GPO . . . nothing remains but the four main walls and the great portico.

Arthur's room was on the first floor. When the whole place fell in, Arthur's room fell through into the room below, and a portion of that fell through to the cellars . . . So everything belonging to Fred has gone.

I am not thankful to have escaped. No thankfulness at all. I don't understand it; but so it is.

So ends, we hope, the days of horror and slaughter – this appalling chapter in the history of Ireland.

Epilogue

Pearse *re-enters, carrying a large notebook, in which he has been working on the Proclamation. He reads it as if trying it out, testing it on his audience, still considering the words.*

Pearse   Poblacht na hÉireann.
The Provisional government of the Irish Republic to the People of Ireland.

Irishmen and Irishwomen:

In the name of God and of the dead generations from which she receives her old tradition of nationhood, Ireland, through us, summons her children to her flag and strikes for her freedom.

Having organised and trained her manhood through her secret revolutionary organisation, the Irish Republican Brotherhood, and through her open military organisations, the Irish Volunteers and the Irish Citizen Army, having patiently perfected her discipline, having resolutely waited for the right moment to reveal itself, she now seizes that moment, and, supported by her exiled children in America and by gallant allies in Europe, but relying in the first on her own strength, she strikes in full confidence of victory.

We declare the right of the people of Ireland to the ownership of Ireland, and to the unfettered control of Irish destinies, to be sovereign and indefeasible. The long usurpation of that right by a foreign people and government has not extinguished the right, nor can it ever be extinguished except by the destruction of the Irish people.

In every generation the Irish people have asserted their right to national freedom and sovereignty; six times during the last three hundred years they have asserted it in arms. Standing on that fundamental right and again asserting it in arms in the face of the world, we hereby proclaim the Irish Republic as a Sovereign Independent State, and we pledge our lives and the lives of our comrades-in-arms to the cause of its freedom, of its welfare, and of its exaltation among the nations.

The Irish Republic is entitled to, and hereby claims, the allegiance of every Irishman and Irishwoman. The Republic guarantees religious and civil liberty, equal rights and equal opportunities to all its citizens, and declares its resolve to pursue the happiness and prosperity of the whole nation and all of its parts, cherishing all of the children of the nation equally and oblivious of the differences carefully fostered by an alien government, which have divided a minority from the majority in the past.

Until our arms have brought the opportune moment for the establishment of a permanent National Government, representative of the whole people of Ireland and elected by the suffrages of all her men and women, the Provisional Government, hereby constituted, will administer the civil and military affairs of the Republic in trust for the people.

We place the cause of the Irish Republic under the protection of the Most High God. Whose blessing we invoke upon our arms, and we pray that no one who serves that cause will dishonour it by cowardice, in humanity, or rapine.

Connolly *enters, with* **Clarke and Carney**.

Pearse   In this supreme hour the Irish nation must, by its valour and discipline and by the readiness of its children to sacrifice themselves for the common good, prove itself worthy of the august destiny to which it is called.

Connolly   Pearse.

Pearse *is still enraptured.*

Connolly   Pearse!

Pearse *turns to him.*

Connolly   Are we launching this Republic or are we not?

Blackout.

The following was written as a programme note for the original production of Inside the GPO.

A note on historical inaccuracy

Is this *documentary* theatre? The answer may depend on who is asking.

To the historians: No. I have taken huge licence with the historical record; and where that record is silent, I have imagined it.

To the non-historians: Perhaps. I have started with the documentary record, hewn pretty carefully to the chronology, noted many of the key developments during Easter Week, and portrayed some of the key figures in the GPO, based on evidence as to their actions and opinions.

But there is a problem with that evidence. It is factually incomplete: there is no authoritative record of how the Rising was planned; and there is little record of what the leaders thought as the Rising progressed.

And it is emotionally incomplete: the various memoirs, and the witness statements in the Bureau of Military History – taken 30–40 years after the events – tend to portray those involved as almost unfailingly stoic, and the leadership as resolutely calm.

Yet there are plenty of factual details that appear to contradict this: Pearse unable to sleep; Clarke waving his gun in the air, refusing to evacuate; people injured by guns mistakenly discharged and bombs dropped; the threats to shoot protestors and looters – and the killing of at least one of the former.

The O'Rahilly is a useful case study. Generally portrayed as an unflappable and enthusiastic contributor to the Rising throughout the week, he had, the previous weekend, believed he was likely to be kidnapped (or worse), had drawn his gun on Pearse, and had then travelled across the country for 24 hours, trying to stop the Rising. Is it credible to think he carried none of the emotional baggage of that into the GPO?

Countess Markievicz was reported to have said, after Eoin MacNeill's countermand, that he should have been shot. If she meant pre-emptively (rather than as retribution), then, in military terms at least, she was right: the failure to take MacNeill out was an extraordinary omission, comparable to Dublin Castle's failure to act on intelligence that a Rising was imminent.

That omission may speak to an innate decency – or naivety – in the leadership of the Rising, but it seems hardly credible to think that there cannot have been regrets, later on, at something that had such catastrophic consequences for the Rising.

My job has been to sift through these records and try and tell a story that is true to the jeopardy these people faced and the emotional conflict they felt, while showing a basic respect to the documentary record.

The challenge of documentary is that you are restricted to telling such a story based only on the evidence. The joy, and the liberation, of drama, is that you get to use your own imagination – and that of the director, actors and designers – to fill in the blanks.

That means taking liberties. I take the characters in a certain direction; the director, actors and designers take them further along that direction, or may take them in another direction. Somewhere along that journey, real people – people with famous names – become fictionalised; but they become fictionalised in the quest to bring them to life again.

I have perhaps taken most liberty with the character of Min Ryan. Her very rich witness statement gives no indication that she had doubts about the wisdom of the Rising. I have chosen to portray her differently, in pursuit of a broader dramatic truth. By virtue of the facts that she arrived into the GPO late, after the start of the Rising, and that she had a relationship with one of the leaders, she presented the opportunity to confront the leadership – and therefore the audience – with a different vision for the future. This was something we only fully discovered in rehearsal, and we thought it true to the play to pursue it, even if not necessarily true to the historical character.

A further liberty is the decision not to include Joseph Plunkett, other than in passing mention. Plunkett was an influential member of the leadership and, despite severe illness, was active at times during the five days in the GPO. We are constrained by resources and by the needs of the drama. The latter, I felt, demanded the inclusion of The O'Rahilly, bringing a perspective from outside the narrow leadership circle; in turn, I had to sacrifice a character — Plunkett lost out. I also needed a character who would speak to a more pragmatic sense of the future of the movement. In the original production, I referred to him simply as a young officer, for he was fictionalised, but I was always clear who he was inspired by. Having written a further play in which that source of inspiration became the lead, it seems unnecessarily coy not to name him here, as Michael Collins.

Selected Bibliography

Primary Sources

Brennan-Whitmore, W. J. *Dublin Burning: The Easter Rising from Behind the Barricades.* Dublin: Gill & Macmillan, 2013.
Collins, Michael. *The Path to Freedom.* Corpus of Electronic Texts Edition. celt.ucc.ie.
FitzGerald, Desmond. *Desmond's Rising: Memoirs 1913 to Easter 1916.* Dublin: Liberties Press, 2006.
Good, Joe. *Inside the GPO 1916: A First-hand Account.* Dublin: The O'Brien Press, 2015.
Norway, Mary Louisa, and Arthur Hamilton Norway. *The Sinn Féin Rebellion as They Saw It.* Edited by Keith Jeffery. Dublin: Irish Academic Press, 1999.
Pearse, Patrick H. *Fragment of Autobiography.* Manuscript. The Pearse Museum, St Enda's, Dublin. (Also available in *The Home Life of Pádraig Pearse*, edited by Mary Brigid Pearse, published online by An Chartlann at cartlann.org.)
Ryan, Desmond. *The Man Called Pearse.* Dublin: Maunsel & Co., 1919.
The Irish Times Newspaper Archive. irishtimes.com.
The Military Archives. Bureau of Military History. Witness Statements. www.militaryarchives.ie.

Secondary Sources

Caulfield, Max. *The Easter Rebellion.* Dublin: Gill & Macmillan, 1995.
Coogan, Tim Pat. *Michael Collins: A Biography.* London: Arrow Books, 1991.
Crowley, Brian. *Patrick Pearse: A Life in Pictures.* Cork: Mercier Press, 2013.
Edwards, Ruth Dudley. *Patrick Pearse: The Triumph of Failure.* Dublin: Poolbeg Press, 1990.
Enright, Seán. *Easter Rising 1916: The Trials.* Sallins: Merrion Press, 2014.
Feeney, Brian. *Seán MacDiarmada: 16Lives.* Dublin: O'Brien Press, 2014.
Ferguson, Stephen. *GPO Staff in 1916: Business as Usual.* Cork: Mercier Press, 2012.

Foy, Michael T. *Tom Clarke: The True Leader of the Easter Rising*. Dublin: The History Press Ireland, 2014.
Foy, Michael T., and Brian Barton. *The Easter Rising*. Stroud: Sutton Publishing, 1999.
Hart, Peter. *Mick: The Real Michael Collins*. New York: Viking, 2006.
Jeffery, Keith. *The GPO and the Easter Rising*. Dublin: Irish Academic Press, 2006.
Joye, Lar. "A Military Analysis of the Easter Rising." Lecture, National Museum of Ireland, 11 February 2016.
Keogh, Raymond M. "Well Dressed and from a Respectable Street." History Ireland 17, no. 2 (2009): 32–33.
Kiberd, Declan. "The Ideas of 1916." Lecture, RTÉ Road to the Rising at The Abbey Theatre, 6 April 2015.
Matthews, Ann. *Renegades: Irish Republican Women 1900–1922*. Cork: Mercier Press, 2010.
McDiarmid, Lucy. *At Home in the Revolution: What Women Said and Did in 1916*. Dublin: Royal Irish Academy, 2015.
McGarry, Fearghal. *Rebels: Voices from the Easter Rising*. Dublin: Penguin Ireland, 2011.
Nevin, Donal. *James Connolly: A Full Life*. Dublin: Gill & Macmillan, 2005.
O'Rahilly, Aodogán. *The O'Rahilly: A Secret History of the Rebellion of 1916*. Dublin: Lilliput Press, 2016.
Sisson, Elaine. *Pearse's Patriots: St Enda's and the Cult of Boyhood*. Cork: Cork University Press, 2005.
Townsend, Charles. *Easter 1916: The Irish Rebellion*. London: Penguin Books, 2006.
Wills, Clair. *Dublin 1916: The Siege of the GPO*. Cambridge, London: Profile Books, 2009.
Woggon, Helga. *Silent Radical: Winifred Carney, 1887–1943*. Dublin: SIPTU in association with the Irish Labour History Society, 2000.

Michael Glenn Murphy as Tom Clarke, clutching a copy of the Proclamation, in *Inside the GPO*. ©Photo by Pat Redmond

The Treaty

The Treaty was first presented by Fishamble: The New Play Company in the Kevin Barry room at the National Concert Hall, Dublin (where the Dáil debates on the Treaty were held) and at the Embassy of Ireland, London, in November and December 2021, to mark the centenary of the signing of the Treaty, with the following cast:

Arthur Griffith	Karen Ardiff
Éamon de Valera	Jane Brennan
Cathal Brugha/Emmet Dalton	John Cronin
Robert Barton	Shadaan Felfeli
Micheal Collins	Patrick Moy
Lady Lavery	Caitríona Ní Mhurchú
Tom Jones	Simon O'Gorman
Winston Churchill	Camille Lucy Ross
Kathleen McKenna	Kate Stanley Brennan
Erskine Childers	Ian Toner
Lord Birkenhead (FE Smith)	Ali White
David Lloyd George	Jonathan White

Directed by	Conall Morrison
Set and Lighting designed by	Paul Keogan
Costume designed by	Catherine Fay
Composer & Sound designed by	Denis Clohessy
Dramaturgy by	Gavin Kostick
AV design by	Neil O'Driscoll
Hair & make-up designed by	Val Sherlock
Produced by	Eva Scanlan

The Treaty was co-commissioned by Fishamble and Pavilion Theatre. The production was part of the Department of Tourism, Culture, Arts, Gaeltacht, Sport & Media's Decade of Centenaries programme, and was supported by that Department and by Culture Ireland, National Concert Hall, Irish Embassy London, Department of Foreign Affairs and British Irish Chamber of Commerce.

An education pack to accompany this production is available for teachers on request. Contact info@fishamble.com for details. The filmed production of *The Treaty* is also available for teachers and students as part of Fishamble's Encore Programme: www.fishamble.com/encore.

Characters

The Irish

Kathleen McKenna, *24, one of the secretariat*
Arthur Griffith, *50, Minister for Foreign Affairs, chairman of delegation*
Michael Collins, *30, Minister for Finance, President of the Irish Republican Brotherhood*
Robert Barton, *40, Minister for Economic Affairs*
Erskine Childers, *51, secretary to the delegation*
Éamon de Valera, *39, President of Dáil Éireann, the parliament of the Irish Republic*
Cathal Brugha, *47, Minister for Defence*
Emmet Dalton, *23, IRA officer, member of the Irish Republican Brotherhood*
Ernie O'Malley, *24, IRA officer*

The British

Tom Jones, *51, Deputy Secretary to the Cabinet*
David Lloyd George, *58, Prime Minister, Liberal Party*
Winston Churchill, *46, Secretary of State for the Colonies, Liberal Party*
Lord Birkenhead (FE Smith), *49, Lord Chancellor, Conservative and Unionist Party*
General Sir Nevil Macready, *59, General Officer Commanding-in-Chief, the Forces in Ireland*

Also

Lady Lavery, *41, Chicago-born London society hostess*
Sir James Craig, *50, Prime Minister of Northern Ireland*
Priest, waiters, aides, butlers, *as required*

Setting

London, Chequers and Dublin, October–December 1921

Prologue

A large table denotes the Downing Street Cabinet Room; above it hangs a large map of the world; the British Empire, covering two thirds of it, is coloured in red. Some simple furnishings denote the Irish HQ at Hans Place in Knightsbridge. A separate area consists of a small, plain desk with a typewriter. This is **Erskine Childers'** *office: whenever possible, he remains here, watching the action and typing. The staging is fluid; other locations are conjured up as necessary.*

Glasnevin Cemetery

Rain.

Kathleen McKenna *enters, opening a black umbrella. She and* **Tom Jones** *will be our guides.*

McKenna   August. 1922. Glasnevin Cemetery, Dublin.

She stands in the rain, watching the (offstage) burial ceremony. The drone of the rite drifts in.

McKenna   So many funerals.

She looks around her at the size of the crowd.

McKenna   Each one bigger than the last . . . If this keeps going, some day all Ireland will be at one big funeral.

(*Wry.*)

Or we'll all be dead.

She returns to the rite.

Tom Jones *enters, and deftly makes his way to her side.*

Jones   Miss McKenna.

McKenna   Mr Jones. Thank you for coming.

Jones   I bring the condolences of the British Government.

McKenna   You are here on business, then.

Jones   Ah.

(*He considers.*) No, Miss McKenna. This is personal. Mr Collins. . . .

He tails off. They listen to the rite.

Jones   Not quite a year since we first met. Who could have known it would turn out like this?

McKenna   Oh, we knew, Mr Jones. We knew it in our bones.

Priest (*off*)   In nomine Patris et Filii . . .

McKenna *blesses herself.* **Jones** *bows slightly.*

Priest (*off*)   et Spiritus Sancti . . .

Jones *leaves her, turning to the audience as he walks.*

Jones   A year earlier.

Act One

One

Downing Street

Jones *arrives at the Cabinet table, now carrying a sheaf of documents. He places one at each place setting.*

Jones June, 1921. Downing Street, London.

Churchill, **Birkenhead**, **Macready** *enter.*

Jones India is on the verge of revolt. In Iraq we've just defeated a revolt. In Egypt, we are staving off revolt. But most of the Cabinet's time is taken up with –

Lloyd George (*entering*) Bloody Ireland!

Birkenhead Not another outrage?

Churchill Another constable shot in cold blood.

Birkenhead But that must be –

Macready Five hundred and one members of our forces since January last year.

Lloyd George I swear, General, if this new policy doesn't have the band of murderers by the throat within weeks, I will take every man we have out of Mesopotamia and I will drop them on Ireland and lay waste to it.

Macready (*tapping the paper*) It's all there, Prime Minister. As you requested.

Birkenhead General. This new policy . . . 'Coercion' . . . You suggest we try the rebel leaders for treason.

Macready Yes.

Birkenhead Which ones?

Macready Well, de Valera, obviously.

Churchill Never mind de Valera – it's Collins runs the murder gang.

Birkenhead They can't *catch* Collins.

Birkenhead What about Childers?

Lloyd George Can we really hang the author of *The Riddle of the Sands*?

Birkenhead Such a dreary novel. We should have hanged him for that.

Churchill Why stop at the leaders – *every* Sinn Féin MP who takes his seat in this 'Dáil' –

Every one of them should hang.

Lloyd George Isn't that a little bloodthirsty, Winston?

Birkenhead There is some precedent that suggests that executing Irish rebels may not be the most effective strategy for winning over the Irish public.

Churchill So what should we do with them? Imprison them and they just go on hunger strike and martyr themselves slowly.

Macready My preference would be for transportation . . .

Lloyd George But we haven't transported convicts for fifty years!

Churchill There isn't anywhere far enough to transport the Irish. We used send them to Van Diemen's Land – they kept coming back!

Lloyd George General, some of the other measures proposed here could appear somewhat . . . indiscriminate . . . We don't want another 'Bloody Sunday' on the front page of the *New York Times*.

Macready That was unfortunate. But I must be clear. This policy means that dreadful things must happen. When I commit my men, I need to know that His Majesty's Government will not resile from it. When you hear of our shooting a hundred men a week, will you stay the course?

Lloyd George Thank you, General. And Northern Ireland?

Macready Some hiccups – it can be difficult to restrain the 'B-Specials' from carrying out reprisals. But partition seems to be having the desired effect.

Lloyd George (*dismissing them*) Gentlemen.

The meeting disperses. **Lloyd George** *remains at the table as* **Jones** *gathers up the papers.*

Lloyd George Well, TJ?

Jones *looks at him skeptically.*

Jones 'Coercion', PM?

Lloyd George They have no uniforms, no rules of engagement, no Hague Convention. They shoot men in their beds, in front of their wives. They're not an army, TJ – they're murderers.

Jones They're *Celts*, Prime Minister. They've been at it for 700 years. They'll happily keep going for 700 more.

Beat.

Jones *leaves.* **Lloyd George** *looks after him, thinking, then leaves.*

Hans Place

McKenna *leads* **Griffith, Barton** *and* **Childers** *in.*

McKenna   Four months later – October, 1921. Hans Place, Knightsbridge. A truce has been agreed; the Irish have been invited to London for peace talks.

The men admire their surroundings.

McKenna   Well, Mr Griffith, Mr Barton, Mr Childers. I hope you find the accommodation appropriate to plenipotentiaries of Dáil Éireann.

Griffith   Thank you, Miss McKenna. I'm sure it will be more than adequate.

Childers   And where is Mr Collins?

A man enters and observes them, unseen, from the shadows.

Griffith   . . . Mr Collins thought it better he had his own . . . team . . . around him, Erskine.

Childers (*with derision*)   His 'brotherhood', no doubt.

Griffith   His security needs are somewhat more acute than ours.

McKenna   Mr Collins is lodging nearby. I'll show you to your rooms, gentlemen.

They leave.

Outside

Michael Collins *enters. The man in the shadows steps out and places a gun against his back.* **Collins** *freezes. The man leans in towards* **Collins**'s *ear.*

Dalton (*mock Cork accent*)   Bang bang.

Collins *whirls and pushes him.*

Collins   You little fucker, Emmet. You'll pay for that, boy.

Collins *coils.*

Collins   Let's have a bit of ear.

He pounces.

Dalton   Careful! It's loaded.

Collins So it should be.

They wrestle, wildly. **Dalton** *bests him.*

Dalton Jesus, Mick, you're out of shape.

Collins *looks around with disdain.*

Collins I'm out of my fucking element, is what I am.

They get their breath back.

Dalton I don't like it, Mick.

Collins Did I have any choice?

Dalton There's a bay window in your room. Garden lined with trees and hedges. Multiple access points. They have men everywhere.

Collins If the Brits wanted me dead, they'd have shot me by now. It's not their men I'm worried about.

Dalton The Brotherhood is with you, Mick. We have control of the Army.

Collins For now. We're here to compromise, Emmet. The Army's not ready for compromise.

Dalton You're the Big Fella. The men will follow you anywhere.

Collins Just keep a close eye on Childers, will you?

Dalton (*laughing*) What kind of a threat is Childers?

Collins He has the zeal of the convert. There's no greater threat than that.

Dalton *disappears back into the shadows.*

Hans Place / Downing Street

Collins *arrives at Hans Place.*

McKenna Good morning, Mr Collins.

Collins Kathy, for Christ's sake, it's *Mick*! There's enough about this place already would put a poker up a man's arse.

Griffith, **Barton** *and* **Childers** *enter and greet* **Collins**.

Griffith Gentlemen. Before we meet the British, I'd like to review our instructions from President de Valera one last time.

Griffith *produces a letter, and* **Éamon de Valera** *appears.*

De Valera A chairde dhil.

Your objective is to secure recognition of the Irish Republic by the government of the United Kingdom, and the support of that government for the reversal of partition and the unity of Ireland.

You have been appointed plenipotentiaries of Dáil Éireann, with full decision-making authority. But you will refer back to the Cabinet in Dublin before making any decisions.

You should expect that your movements and your communications will be monitored constantly. All communications with Dublin are to be by courier only. Under no circumstance is the telephone to be used.

You will accept no hospitality.

I advise that you start with the smaller issues. Avoid the issues of the Republic and Ulster for now. I am working on a proposal that I intend will resolve these. An entirely new device in international relations. I will send on details presently.

Brugha *appears behind* **de Valera**.

Brugha   'An entirely new device', Chief?

De Valera   Something new is needed, Cathal.

Brugha   Is the Republic not enough for you?

De Valera   We were never Republican doctrinaires, Cathal.

Brugha   You should have gone with them, Chief.

De Valera   There will be time enough for that, Cathal. I am busy here for now.

De Valera *and* **Brugha** *disappear.* **Griffith** *puts away the letter. The delegation falls into discussion.*

Churchill *and* **Birkenhead** *have meanwhile entered;* **Birkenhead** *peers out the window of the Cabinet Room.*

Birkenhead   Did you come in the front door, Winston?

Churchill   The crowds! Damn Irish! I had to come round the back.

Birkenhead   What the devil are they doing on their knees?

Churchill   I think they're praying.

Birkenhead   Well thank God for Henry the Eighth.

Lloyd George *enters, followed by* **Jones**.

Birkenhead   A splendid place to meet a group of anarchic gunmen, Prime Minister.

Lloyd George   The Irish question has haunted us for 700 years, gentlemen. It is the key to all politics: India; Iraq; a trade deal with the United States; even the future of our own coalition. Let us not be squeamish about solving it.

Churchill   To allow the Irish a 'republic' would give succour to every insurrectionary rabble across the Empire. It would fatally undermine the Crown. Any government that facilitated it would be smashed to atoms.

If there must be compromise, it must be on something else.

Lloyd George   Ulster.

Jones (*to audience*)   Ah yes. Ulster.

Birkenhead   We are committed to Ulster.

Jones (*to audience*)   Perhaps I should clarify. Since the Government of Ireland Act of 1920, Ireland has been partitoned. Sir James Craig is the first Prime Minister of Northern Ireland.

Birkenhead   We have pledged to Craig that we will not coerce Ulster into a united Ireland. My party will not tolerate any weakening of that pledge.

Lloyd George   But a Southern Ireland that abandons its claim to the status of 'republic' – that gives its allegiance to the Crown – is one that poses no threat to Northern Ireland.

Churchill (*following his logic*)   So if we can persuade the Irish to give allegiance to the Crown. . .

Lloyd George   . . . we can persuade the Unionists to reunite with the South.

Birkenhead   And should the Irish refuse to give allegiance to the Crown?

Lloyd George   The alternative is clear.

Churchill   War.

Lloyd George   TJ, remind us who the Irish have sent to represent them, would you?

Griffith (*in parallel*)   Mr Childers – would you brief us on the British delegates?

Jones   Surprisingly, the Irish are being led *not* by their so-called president, Éamon de Valera, but by the founder of Sinn Féin, Arthur Griffith. His party was originally a non-violent movement, but we mistakenly blamed it for the 1916 'Rising' – so the gunmen all joined it.

Childers   The British delegation is being led by the Prime Minister himself – the 'Welsh Wizard', David Lloyd George. I sought some advice on negotiating with him. 'Better to write to him,' I was told: 'After all, a letter cannot be mesmerised.'

Jones   Second in command for the Irish is their, em, 'Finance Minister', Michael Collins –

Birkenhead (*astonished*)   They sent Collins?

Churchill   At least now we'll know what he looks like.

Jones   Not a subtle man, by reputation. We think he is the real force in the delegation.

Birkenhead Can we shoot him?

Churchill Not yet, Freddie.

Childers Lloyd George's fellow Liberal on the British delegation is Winston Churchill. He defected from the Tories about fifteen years ago – as a result, he's not really trusted by anyone.

Collins Nobody trusts a defector.

Childers (*ignoring* **Collins**) His reputation never quite recovered from the disaster of the Gallipoli campaign. In my opinion, he's a spent force.

Jones The economic expert on the Irish delegation is Robert Barton. Anglo-Irish. A veteran – Royal Dublin Fusiliers. He was stationed in Dublin during their 'Rising', when some of the leaders were imprisoned in his barracks, and he came under their influence – and joined them.

Childers The lawyer on the British delegation is F.E. Smith – Lord Birkenhead. He leads the Unionist wing of the Conservative Party – so he is key to keeping the Unionists on board.

Jones And lastly, the secretary to the Irish delegation . . . a certain Erskine Childers. His mother was Irish – he is a first cousin of Robert Barton. Had a distinguished record of service but then we sent him to Dublin in 1917, and he came under the influence of the nationalists . . .

Birkenhead This seems to be rather a pattern.

Jones He is not, however, universally trusted in Ireland.

Birkenhead (*eyeing* **Churchill**) Turncoats rarely are.

Griffith And your opposite man, Childers – the secretary to the British?

Childers A civil servant, Thomas Jones. Welsh, I believe. Close to Lloyd George. I'm afraid we don't know much else about him.

Griffith Well, gentlemen, we shall be greeting them / very shortly . . .

Lloyd George We expect them any moment, / gentlemen . . .

Collins Wasn't Birkenhead the counsel who had Casement hanged?

Childers He led the prosecution, yes.

Collins I'll be damned before I'll shake that hand.

The Irish delegation erupts.

Griffith Michael, we can hardly start with hostility.

Childers I think there are more important things at stake here.

Barton Arthur I think the chairman should decide.

Birkenhead   Well I'll be damned if I'll shake hands in this room with any traitor or murderer.

The British delegation erupts.

Lloyd George   That kind of atitude is unhelpful, FE.

Churchill   Freddie, don't be so disagreeable.

Jones   Prime Minister?

He switches to Welsh for private conversation.

Ma' da fi syniad. Dodwch eich cydweithwyr y tu ôl i'r bwrdd cyn i'r Gwyddelod ddod mewn – wedi 'nny, fydd dim cyfle i ysgwyd llaw. (I have an idea. Place your colleagues behind the table before the Irish enter – there will be no opportunity to shake hands.)

Lloyd George   Syniad ardderchog, TJ. (That is inspired.)

Lloyd George *directs* **Churchill** *and* **Birkenhead** *to their places on one side of the table as* **Jones** *brings the Irish in.*

Lloyd George (*shaking his hand*)   Mr Griffith! You are welcome to Downing Street.

He ushers **Griffith** *along the opposite side of the table.* **Griffith** *goes to shake hands across it but realises he can't.*

Lloyd George   Gentlemen.

He ushers **Collins**, **Barton** *and* **Childers** *along after* **Griffith**.

The two delegations face off across the table.

Lloyd George (*motioning to sit*)   Please.

He chooses his words very carefully.

We are here to discuss how the . . . *association* . . . of Ireland with the . . . *community of nations* known as the British Empire . . . may best be . . . *reconciled* . . . with Irish . . . national *aspirations* . . .

He pauses to check that no offence has yet been taken.

Let us begin.

Two

McKenna   And so it starts.

The men fall into impassioned dumb show of the negotiations. A whirl of movement and documents – memos, newspapers, scrawled notes.

Jones   The first country in the British Empire to negotiate for its independence.

McKenna The first country to fight the British Empire to a stalemate.

Lloyd George If you turn to page four of our proposals, I think you'll find a very generous concession.

Jones Hours . . .

McKenna . . . days . . .

Jones . . . weeks . . .

Griffith The Irish nation is wary of the outstretched hand of the Empire.

McKenna . . . months to come, of talking . . .

Jones . . . positioning . . .

Barton Our right to naval defence is non-negotiable.

McKenna . . . arguing . . .

Jones . . . jousting . . .

Churchill It is time to put aside your historic grudges

Birkenhead You can't afford your naval defence!

McKenna . . . lecturing the opposing side . . .

Childers The thing you have to understand about the British is . . .

Jones . . . lecturing one's own side . . .

McKenna . . . statements to the press . . .

Lloyd George The negotiations with the Irish representatives are making good progress . . .

Jones . . . leaks. . .

Collins Call off your attack dogs in the Tory press!

McKenna . . . rumours.

Jones They have plenary conferences at Downing Street in the morning, then –

Lloyd George Let me accompany you to lunch, Mr Griffith.

Griffith I'm afraid we are under instructions to accept no hospitality. We will lunch at our lodgings.

McKenna They come back to Hans Place to eat . . .

Jones Then back in for an afternoon session . . .

McKenna And then delegation meetings . . .

Jones . . . and Cabinet . . .

McKenna . . . and memos to be written . . .

Jones . . . and Red Boxes . . .

McKenna   . . . and correspondence . . . into the small hours . . .

Jones   The PM has laid out an agenda, but . . .

McKenna   We avoid the big issues, for now.

Jones   . . . the Irish won't engage on the big issues.

Lloyd George   The question of *allegiance*, Mr Griffith. The oath to the King. Ireland's relationship to the British Empire.

Griffith   Of critical importance. But first we'd like to look at some of the detail of your proposals on tariffs, here (*Picking up a document.*) on page, eh . . .

Later.

Churchill   But what will be the position of Ireland *within* the British Empire?

Collins   A crucial issue, but we need some certainty first on the issue of pensions. If you look at page, eh . . .

Jones   It's almost as if they are delaying, for some reason.

Aside, with the Irish only.

Collins   We're in there talking shite like fucking eejits.

Griffith   Is there nothing yet from Dublin?

Collins   Where the fuck are the proposals from Dev?

McKenna   We've nothing yet.

Collins   We're supposed to be plenipotentiaries!

Childers   Would you like me to remind your of your instructions, Mr Collins?

Aside, with the British only.

Lloyd George   Pensions! At least this should be straightforward.

Birkenhead   I wouldn't be so sure.

Lloyd George   They can't object to paying the pensions of Crown servants whose careers have been spent in Ireland.

Birkenhead   I have a hunch it could be a little tricky to get the Irish to pay the pensions of the Black and Tans.

Jones   Nobody could say it is going well . . .

Jones *receives a document.*

Jones   Ah.

His mood darkens. He passes it to **Lloyd George**.

McKenna   But it is still going . . .

Lloyd George *rises, furious.*

Lloyd George   Gentlemen!

McKenna   . . . for now.

Lloyd George   We have taken you as men of your word, negotiating in good faith on the basis of the truce agreed between us. The German authorities have seized a consignment of weapons being carried on board a German merchant cargo ship, bound for Dublin. For your 'Irish Republican Army'.

Birkenhead (*rising*)   What?

Churchill (*rising*)   A breach of the truce!

Birkenhead   A breach of your commitments!

Barton (*rising*)   It's a lie.

Lloyd George   A breach of integrity.

Collins (*rising*)   How dare you question our integrity!

Churchill   While you smuggle arms for another cowardly atrocity?

Collins   Who the hell are you calling cowardly?

Birkenhead   A breach of the truce is a declaration of war.

Lloyd George   This calls the entire premise of these negotiations into question.

A cacophony. All are standing except **Griffith**.

Griffith   Mr Lloyd George. You have weapons factories here in Britain.

This cuts through.

Churchill   We have the greatest weapons factories / in the world!

Griffith   Have they gone silent?

Churchill *blusters.*

Griffith   You have armed men in barracks all over Ireland. Are we to understand that these barracks are no longer being provisioned?

More bluster.

Griffith   My conception of the Truce is not such that *your* military forces should use it to prepare for the end of it – and ours should not.

The mutual remonstration bursts out again – but they all remain at the table.

Hans Place

McKenna *takes delivery of a letter and hands it to* **Griffith**.

McKenna   Finally, the full detail of President de Valera's proposals arrives.

Griffith *opens it and reads.* **De Valera** *reappears.*

De Valera A chairde dhil.

He has an acetate projector which beams onto the wall.

De Valera This is the British Empire.

He draws a large circle.

De Valera And, from the British perspective, this is Ireland.

He draws a small circle at the centre of the large one.

De Valera *Within* the Empire. At the *heart* of the Empire. In a *union* with Britain herself.

But at Easter 1916, we proclaimed a Republic – a Republic free of allegiance to a foreign crown – a Republic we have sworn to uphold. And since then, in fact, *this* is Ireland.

He draws a small circle apart from the large circle.

De Valera Entirely independent of the Empire . . . The problem is that *this* (*Pointing at the second small circle.*) is intolerable to the British . . . and *this* (*Pointing at the first small circle.*) is intolerable to us.

So the question is, is there a political form that can move this (*The first.*) closer to this (*The second.*)?

Is there a way that this (*The second.*) can be *associated* with this (*The large circle.*), without violating the integrity of either?

He pauses.

De Valera This will be a *new* form of association, Gentlemen. Something not yet tried amongst the community of nations . . .

He draws a third small circle, touching the large one, and writes 'EXTERNAL ASSOCIATION' above it.

De Valera So this is your task. To move the British from here (*The first.*) to here (*The third.*). If you can achieve that, I believe we can succeed in moving our people from here (*The second.*) to meet the British there (*The third.*).

Griffith So that, gentlemen, is President de Valera's proposal.

He looks at the diagram.

Beat.

Barton Has he a term for this new form of association?

Griffith (*checking the letter*) He calls it 'External Association'.

Collins It would be difficult to get that into a ballad.

Childers So we are to sacrifice the name of the Republic?

Collins Who gives a fuck about the name, Erskine?

Griffith A rose by any other name would smell so sweet.

Barton Men died for the Republic.

Collins Don't tell me what my men died for, Bob.

Barton They didn't die for a Venn diagram.

Griffith Gentlemen, some compromise was inevitable. This has merit.

Collins It would be good if we could explain it without a blackboard.

Griffith We shall have to choose our moment carefully.

Brugha *appears with* **de Valera**.

Brugha We took an oath to the Republic.

De Valera And this respects that oath.

Brugha It comes almighty close to entering the Empire.

De Valera But it doesn't enter it. That's the point.

Downing Street / Hans Place

McKenna The negotiations continue.

Jones October 17th.

Birkenhead You will of course be left with certain legacy debts and obligations. We estimate the bill for your departure to be two hundred and thirty million pounds.

Barton We would like to lodge a counter claim.

Birkenhead For how much?

Barton Approximately three thousand nine hundred and forty million pounds.

Birkenhead When does that date from – the time of Brian Boru?

General outburst. Through this sequence, **Griffith** *and* **Collins** *worry at the uncompromising approach of* **Barton** *and* **Childers**.

Jones October 21st.

Childers Ireland is an island. If you deny her the right to defend her sea border, with a navy, you deny her existence as a nation.

Churchill Mr Childers, I think from your experience with the British Navy, you know well we simply must have free use of the Irish coasts for Imperial defence.

Childers   As I know well from experience, Mr Churchill, 'Imperial defence' is too often a euphemism for colonial expropriation.

General outburst.

McKenna   October 24th.

Barton   The right to impose trade tariffs is a key element of sovereignty.

Churchill   You export nine-tenths of your produce to us. Why would you want to place a customs barrier in the Irish Sea?

Barton   When we have taken back control of our trade policy, we will be free to trade globally – we will no longer be so reliant on you.

Birkenhead   You can't boost your trade by withdrawing from your largest market – that's economically illiterate.

General outburst.

McKenna   While they talk all day, I type up the minutes and memos of the previous day, for relaying back to Dublin, by hand.

She hands **Griffith** *some memos which he quickly reviews, initials, and returns.*

McKenna   Mr Childers does his own typing, late into the night . . .

Childers *hands her an envelope.*

McKenna   . . . and in the mornings he hands me sealed envelopes addressed to President de Valera.

Collins   Have I ever told you how angelic you look after mass of a morning, Kathy?

McKenna   By God but the effect of mass doesn't be long wearing off you, Mick.

Collins   The usual post this morning?

McKenna   Sealed, to the President.

Collins   And if it ever happens to not be sealed, you'll let me know?

McKenna   You'll get me into trouble, Mick.

Collins   All in the name of the Republic, Kathleen, a stór.

McKenna   What are you so afraid of, Mick?

Collins   All I'm afraid of is the things I don't know.

Jones   But for all the industry, progress is imperceptible.

Lloyd George (*with* **Jones**)   This isn't working, TJ.

Collins (*with* **Griffith**)   We're going round in fucking circles, Arthur.

Jones   It does seem to be rather stuck, PM.

Griffith   What can we do about it?

Lloyd George Griffith – I sense a moderate spirit. Collins – a man who wants to get things done.

Collins I can't move with Childers breathing down my neck. And writing secretly to Dev every night.

Jones Mr Childers would appear to be something of a straitjacket.

Collins We have to get him out of the room.

Lloyd George Can we get rid of him?

Collins Barton also.

Jones Leave it with me, PM.

Griffith They'll smell a rat.

Collins What if the Brits proposed something?

McKenna Mr Griffith? Mr Jones is here to see you.

Griffith Mr Jones!

Jones The PM feels we're not making as much progress as we could . . . I was wondering – The PM was wondering . . . if perhaps it might be expedient to have a sub-conference meeting to expedite some of the more procedural issues that may be holding us back . . .

Griffith 'Sub' conference?

Jones Purely the leadership – no secretaries – I wouldn't want my good self to be getting in the way . . .

Act Two

One

Downing Street

Lloyd George, Churchill, Collins and **Griffith** *approach the table.* **Griffith** *distributes a document. The diagram appears.*

Jones And so the negotiations move into sub-conference format.

McKenna Mr Griffith decides now is the time to present President de Valera's proposal for 'external association'.

Griffith *does so in dumb show,* **Jones** *speaking over him.*

Jones The Irish have a natural appreciation of the rich ambiguity of the English language . . . But I confess, even the Celt in me flounders amidst the finessing they bring to the question of 'association'.

Griffith *has finished. Silence around the table. The British look at each other and at the document.*

Lloyd George Mr Griffith. Will you. Take. An oath. To the Crown?

Griffith We will . . . *accept* the Crown as the . . . *bond* of association.

Lloyd George The 'bond' of association?

Griffith We will . . . *adhere* to the Commonwealth.

Churchill What do you mean by 'adhering'?

Lloyd George You mean membership? Allegiance?

Collins Not quite.

Griffith We should be *associated* with the Commonwealth – outside of that, we would be a free people.

Lloyd George I wish you to be a free people –

Griffith Excellent. We are / agreed then . . .

Lloyd George and to freely choose to enter the Empire.

Collins It's not a free choice if the alternative is war.

Churchill The alternative to a truce is always war.

Lloyd George So you do not accept the link with the Crown?

Griffith We would accept it as head of the association.

Churchill As mere 'allies'?

The Treaty 89

Griffith More than that –

Collins *Permanent* allies, not temporary.

Lloyd George But not as members of the Empire?

Collins No.

Griffith But we would have representation at the Imperial Conference and would accept its decision in matters of common concern.

Churchill So you would not be a member of the Empire but would attend the Empire's conference and accept its decisions?

Griffith In matters of common concern.

Lloyd George What are matters of 'common concern'?

Griffith Large matters.

Churchill War?

Collins And peace.

Griffith Trade.

Lloyd George So you want to leave the trade association that is the Commonwealth, but accept its rules on trade.

Griffith Well, that would be the / essence of our proposal.

Churchill It sounds to me rather like you want to have your cake and eat it.

Griffith I confess, I've never quite understood that saying: surely, by definition, you have to have cake in order to eat it?

Jones I believe the phrase used be 'eat your cake and have it' – in the sense of 'have' meaning to keep.

Collins Ní thig a bheith ag feadaíl agus ag ithe mine.

Lloyd George What?

Griffith In Irish. 'You can't whistle and eat porridge'.

Jones Ah! That's like the Welsh proverb –

Churchill I think we are losing sight of the problem –

Collins Here's the problem: you people came to our country, and you *stole* all our fucking cake.

Lloyd George We digress. (*Addressing the document.*) Can you change 'free partnership *with* the British Commonwealth' to 'free partnership with*in* the British Commonwealth'?

Griffith But that would mean Ireland being prepared to *enter* the Commonwealth – we are prepared to *associate* with it, not enter it.

Lloyd George Can you change '*a* recognition of the Crown' to 'recognition of the Crown'?

Griffith But that would imply *allegiance* – we are offering simply a form of *recognition*.

Churchill (*impatient*) You mean to say you will go to war over an indefinite article?

Collins (*irritated*) Will you?

Tea is brought in.

Lloyd George Ah, a timely interlude, I think.

Griffith No, thank you.

Lloyd George Mr Collins.

Collins No. Thank you.

Lloyd George But / you don't mean to say that you're still bound by …

Griffith We can't.

Lloyd George I realise that the delegation has instructions / from Dublin …

Griffith We have undertaken to accept *no* hospitality while in Britain.

Churchill It's a cup of tea!

Lloyd George Perhaps we should have offered you cake.

Griffith We are not here as your guests. We are here / as plenipotentiaries.

Lloyd George Mr Griffith, for 700 years our nations have been enmeshed. / You don't mean to tell

Griffith I think 'enmeshed' is rather a euphemism.

Lloyd George Well let us spell it out then.

Beat.

Invasion.

Churchill Prime Minister?

Collins War.

Lloyd George Plantation.

Griffith Deportation.

Collins Enslavement.

Churchill Prime Minister?

Lloyd George Coercion.

Griffith Murder.

Collins Massacre.

Churchill Prime Minister!

Lloyd George Gentlemen! We have done far worse than offer you tea!

Griffith We have our instructions.

Lloyd George I was under the impression I was negotiating with plenipotentiaries of the Dáil Éireann.

(*To* **Churchill**.) These men are not even plenipotentiaries of their own breakfast.

Griffith We agreed to be bound by this stricture. It is a trivial inconvenience in the context of our historic struggle.

Lloyd George We are trying to end a war. Centuries of conflict, of spite, of distrust. We each of us take our careers, our reputations, in our hands.

Collins We take our lives in ours.

Lloyd George We have to learn to *trust* each other. We cannot do that from opposite sides of a bare table.

They break up.

Two

Hans Place

Collins It's not working, Kathy.

McKenna You're giving your all, Mick.

Collins It's not about effort. Lloyd George is right – it's about trust.

McKenna Lloyd George is the last person you can trust.

Collins I'm going to have to trust him at some point. But it's all too formal. Too fucking English. We can't even have a cup of tea with them.

McKenna No hospitality.

Collins Exactly.

McKenna No *British* hospitality.

Collins Right.

McKenna What about *Irish* hospitality?

Collins Bring them *here*?

McKenna Neutral ground.

Collins In London?

McKenna The Laverys'.

Collins   The painter?

McKenna   He's Irish. His wife is a society hostess. Irish-American. They're intimates of half the British cabinet. They throw parties. Perhaps that environment might be more conducive to . . . frankness.

Collins *leaves.* **Griffith** *enters.* **McKenna** *hands him a card.*

Griffith   An invitation?

McKenna   Lady Lavery is famous / for her parties.

Griffith   I have a meeting with the Prime Minister, at Chequers.

McKenna   But Mr Collins –

Griffith   If Mr Collins wishes to venture into the Laverys' den, he has my blessing.

Griffith *leaves.* **Collins** *appears in formal wear, struggling with his bow tie.*

Collins   What the fuck do I look like?

McKenna (*tying his tie*)   The lesser-spotted West Cork king penguin? (*Curtseying.*) Your cab awaits, m'lord. But at midnight, it turns into a pumpkin.

Collins   And do these turn back into rags? Jesus, I'd be only delighted.

They leave.

The Laverys'

A party. **Churchill** *and* **Birkenhead** *enter.*

Birkenhead   Winston!

Churchill   Freddie!

Birkenhead   You know who I met at the last one of these – old Phillimore.

Churchill   Judge Phillimore – still going strong!

Birkenhead   He wanted some advice on a tricky sentencing question – a sodomy case.

Churchill   Ah.

Birkenhead   'Smith!' he cried. 'What do you think one ought to give a man who allows himself to be buggered?'

'Oh', I replied. 'Thirty shillings, two pounds – whatever you happen to have on you.'

Lady Lavery *enters amidst their laughter.*

Lavery   Gentlemen.

Birkenhead   Lady Lavery! / I didn't mean to cause any offence.

Churchill Lady Lavery! / Please excuse my right honourable friend.

Lavery How are the negotiations with the Irish going, Winston? I expect you find it terribly boring – all this talking, not fighting.

Birkenhead Winston's only truly happy when he's got something to shoot – or someone's shooting at him.

Churchill Did I ever tell you about the time I was in my dug-out in France, having a nightcap, when a piece of shrapnel / shattered the glass in my hand?

Birkenhead (*anticipating him, in chorus*) . . . 'piece of shrapnel shattered the glass in my hand'

Lavery (*as above*) . . . 'piece of shrapnel shattered the glass in my hand'

Birkenhead You might have told us that one, Winston.

Lavery Once or twice.

She glides on to greet **Collins** *as he enters, uncomfortable.*

Lavery Mícheál Ó Coileáin.

Collins (*taken aback*)   Lady Lavery.

Lavery Hazel, please.

Collins Mick.

Lavery You dress up rather well, Mick.

Collins You are . . . a picture, Lady Lavery.

Lavery Don't mount me on the wall just yet, Mick.

She brings **Churchill** *and* **Birkenhead** *in.*

Lavery I think you know my good friend, Winston?

A **Waiter** *appears with a tray of drinks.*

Churchill Whiskey, Mr Collins?

Collins *hesitates.* **Lady Lavery** *takes one off the tray.*

Lavery *Irish* whiskey, Mick.

He takes it.

Lavery And, of course, Lord Birkenhead.

Birkenhead Actually, even before we met, Mr Collins and I had a mutual acquaintance.

Lavery How nice.

Birkenhead But I think Mr Casement is rather persona non grata in polite company, these days.

Collins I have to hand it to your intelligence service – they were very good at their jobs. Until we caught them.

Birkenhead Why you / jumped-up, murdering . . .

Lavery (*steering* **Birkenhead** *away*) Freddie, John's portrait of you is exquisite – the line of your face! You look ravishing . . .

Churchill and **Collins** are left alone.

Churchill (*gesturing outside*) Lavery's gardens are rather fine. Shall we?

They walk outside.

Chequers

Lloyd George *has entered meanwhile and set up a chess board.* **Griffith** *enters.*

Lloyd George A drink, Mr Griffith?

Griffith *demurs.*

Lloyd George (*apologetically*) Of course – 'hospitality'. You play chess?

Griffith I used play with some friends in a little cafe on O'Connell Street . . .

Lloyd George Very good.

Griffith Until it was shelled during the Rising.

Lloyd George Ah. So you're out of practice.

Griffith I managed to find some time again more recently . . .

Lloyd George Excellent.

Griffith . . . while at his Majesty's pleasure.

Lloyd George I apologise if having you released cut short your return to form. (*Producing a sovereign.*) Heads or tails?

Griffith Need you ask?

Lloyd George *tosses.*

Lloyd George George V it is. I'll play White, Mr Griffith.

Griffith Of course.

The Laverys'

As they drink.

Churchill You don't trust me, Mr Collins.

Collins You spent the last two years trying to kill me, Mr Churchill. You put a price on my head.

Churchill £5,000! A damn good price! When the Boers were hunting me, they offered just twenty-five quid.

Chequers

As they play.

Griffith This is a fine room.

Lloyd George It's the Cromwell Room.

Griffith Ah.

Lloyd George That's his sword on the mantlepiece – would you like to hold it?

Griffith Eh –

Lloyd George The great republican.

Griffith That's not quite how we think of him in Ireland.

Lloyd George Yes, his republicanism did perhaps prove a little extreme. Perhaps we can agree that beheading the king is not always the best guarantee of moderate government. If you win, I'll show you his death mask.

*

Churchill The Boers were magnificent fighters. As were those who fought against them – many of them your countrymen. You remember the Siege of Ladysmith, in '99?

Collins I was nine.

Churchill Didn't you learn about it in school?

Collins Have you ever been to West Cork, Mr Churchill?

Churchill The Boers were dug in on the Tugela Heights. It was the Irish led the assault – the Dublins and the Inniskilling Fusiliers. I watched them through my field glasses. They set off at dusk. Up the bare, grassy hill. The setting sun glinting on their bayonets. But we didn't know the Boers had guns hidden in the hills. Sixty of them. Boom. Boom. Boom. The men slowed. The guns kept pounding. The men dwindled. It was dark now, the only light coming from the shells as they fell amongst our men. Eventually, the men just disappeared into the hillside.

(*Pause*) Twelve hundred men took part in the assault. Six hundred fell.

Collins What a waste.

Churchill And yet, today, the Boer prime minister is a partner in the imperial conference, and helps design policy for the Empire.

*

Lloyd George I confess, I don't know this strategy, Mr Griffith.

Griffith It's called the King's Indian.

Lloyd George To glance at that board, anyone would think I was dominant.

Griffith It is a slow-burning strategy.

Lloyd George The long game.

*

Churchill I am sure you would rather have led from the front, in the field, instead of . . .

Collins Instead of what?

Churchill Sending boys out to shoot men in their beds.

Collins We fought in the field in '16 – you destroyed our city and executed our leaders. How the hell would you have had me lead this fight?

*

Lloyd George I read your study of the Austro-Hungarian Empire, Mr Griffith – you appreciate the unifying force of a king shared between two countries . . .

Griffith I once thought it offered a solution.

Lloyd George There is a German term you may have come across in your studies . . . Realpolitik . . .

*

Churchill It will be different next time – if these talks fail, if we have to go back to war. You have declared yourselves on the world stage. Your international supporters will not stand for you returning to your guerrilla tactics. You will have to fight in the field. Like you did in '16.

*

Lloyd George I lead the minority party in a coalition. The Tory die-hards know little about Ireland, and care less. But they will fight to keep Ireland in the Empire – not merely "associated" with it. So whatever I concede, I must keep Ireland within the Empire . . .

Griffith And I must return Ulster to Ireland.

*

Collins After we surrendered, your men marched us to O'Connell Street. There's a patch of green in front of the Rotunda Hospital there – a small patch, mind. They kept us there for the night. But there wasn't room for us all. So they made us lie on top of each other. Not allowed move – not even to take a shite. Anyone who so much as stretches himself gets a rifle butt to his skull. There's a district inspector in charge, a fellow called Lea-Wilson. He recognises Tom Clarke, and pulls him out in front of everyone.

Churchill Clarke – one of the leaders.

Collins That's right. Clarke's in his 50s, mind. Survived 15 years' hard labour. Lea-Wilson has his men strip off Clarke's trousers. The lot, like. All above us, at the hospital windows, the nurses are looking out. They keep him there. Standing. Bollock naked. Mocking him. For hours. And a week later, you shot him.

Beat.

Churchill That was unnecessary.

*

Lloyd George Think of what you gain from the Empire. Access to your greatest market. Influence in the greatest community of nations in the world. A seat alongside other proud, independent nations. South Africa. Australia. Canada.

Griffith Canada is three thousand miles away – the Crown has no practical authority there. We are sixty miles away – if you disagree with our interpretation of the Imperial constitution, you can have gunboats up the Liffey in a matter of hours. Again.

*

Churchill I envy Lavery his gardens. Such endless inspiration for painting.

Collins Sure where would the likes of us get time to be painting?

Churchill You're not married, Mr Collins, children?

Collins demurs.

Churchill You need something in your life other than war. Or politics.

Beat.

When the black dog descends . . . One needs something one can lose oneself in.

*

Griffith is pondering his move. **Lloyd George** *is thinking.*

Lloyd George You are correct . . . Canada does have more freedom in practice than it does in law, because of its distance . . .

Beat.

Lloyd George You Irish are masters of the English language – come up with the form of words that will codify in law the freedoms that Canada has in practice, and claim them for Ireland.

Griffith *moves.*

Lloyd George That, Mr Griffith, would be a constitutional revolution. An entirely new device in imperial relations.

Griffith Check.

*

Collins (*hesitant*) I am sorry for your recent loss, Mr Churchill.

Churchill Her birthday is next month. She will be— She would have been three.

(*pause*) I have seen men cut to death, clubbed to death, blown to smithereens. I thought I was inured to death. But this one . . .

Beat.

You and I, Mr Collins, we have known the power of life and death. But when we most need it, we have no power at all.

Collins I do not want any more death between us, Mr Churchill.

*

Lloyd George Don't you see, Mr Griffith, this is the path to Irish unity. A Southern Ireland that remains within the Empire – that gives its allegiance to the Crown – is one that Northern Ireland must be content to join with. If they refuse, I will go to the country on it, and the country will back me. I will not return to war with an Ireland that accepts the Crown.

*

Churchill We want you with us, Mr Collins. Free to govern yourselves but united in friendship within the Empire. The natural genius of our two nations collaborating on the world stage.

*

Griffith *moves.* **Lloyd George** *studies the board. He is beaten.*

Lloyd George It appears you are about to take my king.

Griffith The long game.

Lloyd George *concedes, offering his hand.* **Griffith** *shakes.*

Lloyd George The death mask?

Griffith I think not.

*

Churchill What happened to the district inspector? The one who stripped Clarke.

Collins Lea-Wilson? We found him.

Beat.

Churchill No quarter.

Hans Place

Childers *speaks from his typewriter – he is writing to* **de Valera**. **De Valera** *reappears.*

Childers Griffith and Collins are weak on the Republic, Chief.

De Valera I sent them to London in full knowledge of their predilections.

Childers We don't know what they're agreeing in these 'sub-conferences'.

De Valera Their pliancy will lure Lloyd George in. Assure him of our bona fides. Move him towards External Association.

Childers They may give too much away. What if they sacrifice the Republic entirely?

De Valera They cannot give anything away without our consent.

Childers But if things go too far –

De Valera We will rein them in in Dublin.

Brugha *has appeared.*

Brugha There's rumours, Dev.

De Valera I put no stock in rumours, Cathal.

Brugha Collins is going rogue. The Army are restive. GHQ are all in his secret society.

De Valera We have control of the government, Cathal. Have no fear. We will impose ourselves when they come home.

De Valera *and* **Brugha** *disappear.*

Three

Downing Street

Jones At last, there appears to be some momentum.

McKenna The British appear impressed with the subtlety of Dev's concept of 'association'.

Jones The Irish appear willing to come into the Empire – under the fig-leaf of 'association'.

McKenna Lloyd George has promised Mr Griffith that he will deliver Irish unity.

Jones The question of unity, though, is not entirely in the Prime Minister's hands.

McKenna All that remains is to get the endorsement of –

Jones Sir James Craig, Prime Minister.

Craig *enters.* **Lloyd George** *pours them both whiskeys.*

McKenna Leader of Ulster's Unionists.

Lloyd George Sir James.

Lloyd George *presses a drink on* **Craig**, *who protests.*

Jones Prime Minister of Northern Ireland.

Craig But it's ten in the morning!

Craig *takes it.*

Lloyd George We are on the cusp of resolving the eternal Irish question. The Irish will come into the Empire.

Craig I'm afraid I don't see quite what that has to do with Northern Ireland. What happens in the South is a matter between you and them.

Lloyd George You share a small island, Sir James. An island too small to have a boundary run through it. With the South settled in loyalty to the Crown, there can be no need for continued separation of the Six Counties.

Craig *goes to interrupt but* **Lloyd George** *powers on.*

Lloyd George You may prefer, of course, to retain your current status . . .

Craig *goes to interrupt but* **Lloyd George** *powers on.*

Lloyd George However, in that case, you are likely to face a customs border in your trade with Southern Ireland.

Craig goes to interrupt but Lloyd George powers on.

Lloyd George And it is difficult to see how the subsidies you currently receive could continue . . . I fear the tax burden on your people would be likely to rise very substantially.

Beat.

You might send me your response in due course, Sir James. We should conclude this process in time for the opening of the new session of your parliament.

Craig *knocks back his drink and leaves.* **Jones**, **Churchill** *and* **Birkenhead** *enter.*

Lloyd George (*triumphant*) I know the Presbyterians, gentlemen – my wife is one. They have their hands on their hearts all the time, but if you try to touch their pockets they shove their hands in them.

Laughter.

Lloyd George Craig will come in to an all-Ireland parliament. When he does . . .

Churchill (*congratulatory*) Ireland will come into the Empire.

Lloyd George Fill your glasses, gentlemen. Gladstone failed –

Birkenhead Asquith failed.

Lloyd George We are nearly there.

He raises his glass.

Lloyd George To peace in Ireland.

Birkenhead Peace in Ireland.

Churchill Peace in Ireland.

Craig *enters.*

Craig Prime Minister.

The others melt away.

Lloyd George Sir James! I trust you have given my proposal due consideration.

Craig I have, Prime Minister.

Lloyd George And found it favourable.

Craig I have not, Prime Minister.

Lloyd George But the Irish have all but conceded. They will come into the Empire – I am sure of it.

Craig Prime Minister, for three hundred years my people have tilled the soils of Ulster. Every stone wall in those counties affirms our faith in the Reformed Church and our loyalty to the Crown. Five hundred thousand of us pledged to resist any attempt to force us under an all-Ireland parliament. Thousands of our sons made the supreme sacrifice at the Somme, in testament to that faith and that loyalty. And now you expect me to go to every village – to every kirk – and tell them I have thrown off the protection of the Crown – for an alliance with the conspirators of republicanism and of Rome?

Lloyd George They will pledge allegiance to the Crown.

Craig And you would trust them on their pledges? They will abandon that allegiance as soon as suits them.

Lloyd George But I have given Sinn Féin assurances that, if they come into the Empire, the Six Counties will enter the all-Ireland parliament.

Craig I think you know the Presbyterians, Prime Minister – we place great store in God's gift of free will. If we are ever to enter an all-Ireland parliament, we will do so of our own free will.

Lloyd George (*disbelieving*) The negotiations will collapse. I gave Arthur Griffith my word I would resign rather than resume the war.

Craig Is it not extraordinary how many great men have come to grief over the eternal Irish question.

Lloyd George But you risk war on the island.

Craig   What we have, we hold, Prime Minister. Our answer is no.

Craig *leaves.* **Jones** *and* **Churchill** *return.*

Lloyd George (*devastated*)   I thought the logic of it was unassailable.

Churchill   We broke rebellion in Ireland before. When all we had was pikes and muskets. We are vastly more powerful now.

Lloyd George   I promised Griffith I would not coerce the South.

Churchill   Our first loyalty is to Ulster.

Lloyd George   The talks will collapse. The truce will be over.

Churchill   We must be ready.

Lloyd George   I will resign. I will go to the country. The country will back me.

Churchill   You *can't* go to the country – you haven't the numbers. The Tory die-hards won't give you an election. They'll just put their own man in as PM.

Lloyd George   I gave my word I would not return to war in Ireland. If war is ahead, I have no option but to resign.

Churchill   Coward.

Lloyd George   It is the only honourable option left.

Churchill   It would be the essence of dishonour.

Birkenhead   It would be an abdication of responsibility.

Lloyd George   Either Ulster must be coerced into a United Ireland, or the South must be coerced into Empire. But I cannot lead that coercion. Not any more. Let whoever replaces me repair the Irish problem.

Churchill   You give up too early.

Lloyd George   But all is lost!

Jones   If you'll excuse me, PM – I have an idea.

Hans Place

Jones *arrives to meet* **Griffith**.

Griffith   Mr Jones.

Jones   There is a problem, Mr Griffith. The Unionists are . . . surprisingly resistant to our entreaties . . .

Griffith   Your prime minister gave me his word he would resign rather than endorse the continued partitioning of our country.

Jones   That is precisely what he is contemplating.

Beat.

But what will happen then?

Griffith   An election. He will bring it to the country. The country will back him. That is / what he said.

Jones   There won't be an election. The Tories have the numbers on their own. They will abandon the coalition and form a Conservative and Unionist government – a militarist government. They will set to and coerce Ireland.

Griffith   That will mean war.

Jones   And they will relish it.

Silence.

Griffith   What can we do?

Jones   Craig doesn't trust you. The Unionists won't come in under an all-Ireland parliament. We cannot force them. We need another strategy.

Griffith   Their farmers, their businessmen – the border will cripple them – they don't want it.

Jones   Perhaps there could be a mechanism to review the border –

Griffith   Review?

Jones   Should it prove to be the case that – for now – we cannot get rid of it altogether . . .

Beat.

Griffith   We have always recognised that elements amongst Unionism may prove implacable, in the short term . . . Provided the principle of Irish unity is accepted – essential unity – we may be prepared to let individual counties in Ulster vote themselves out. That would reduce Northern Ireland to a rump in the north-east. In time, economic pressure would compel them to join us.

Jones   Yes, yes . . . But a vote . . . Would you really want the entirety of the province convulsed by a poll on the border?

Griffith   How else would we review it?

Jones   Perhaps some kind of expert body. A commission.

Griffith *advances to meet* **Lloyd George**.

Downing Street

Griffith   If you wish to propose such a commission, we will in due course consider it.

Lloyd George   I don't need you to support it. I just need you not to denounce it.

Griffith I will have to consult with my colleagues, and with Dublin.

Lloyd George I am not asking for a commitment from Dublin, Mr Griffith – I am asking you to hold your fire. If I fly this kite of a boundary commission with Craig, do not shoot it down. Do not draw attention to its defects.

Griffith But Craig will reject it.

Lloyd George The current border is indefensible. If Craig were to reject a reasonable proposal to review the border, he would lose crucial support in Westminster. Were he to accept it, it would shrink his state to the point where it would be barely viable. In the circumstances, he may come to consider an all-Ireland parliament the lesser evil.

Beat.

Griffith We will not denounce it. You have my word.

Hans Place

A party is underway. A man appears outside, and stands waiting – this is **Ernie O'Malley**. *Another man,* **O'Malley**'s *sidekick, appears behind him, and stands off, watching. In his room,* **Childers** *types on.*

McKenna (*arriving with a cake*) Where's the birthday boy gone?

Barton Let's have a song!

McKenna Mr Griffith – a ballad!

Griffith Well now, it would hardly be a party without a song.

He is bashful at first, but grows in confidence.

Griffith
  Of all the money that e'er I had
  I spent it in good company
  And all the harm I've ever done
  Alas it was to none but me
  And all I've done for want of wit
  To mem'ry now I can't recall

They join in for the chorus – **McKenna**'s *voice standing out.*

All
  So fill to me the parting glass
  Good night and joy be to you all.

Griffith
  So fill to me the parting glass
  And drink a health whate'er befall,
  And gently rise and softly call

Collins *arrives in, carrying a drink, and joins in.*

All Good night and joy be to you all.

Griffith
  Of all the comrades that e'er I had
  They're sorry for my going away
  And all the sweethearts that e'er I had
  They'd wish me one more day to stay.
  But since it fell unto my lot
  That I should rise and you should not
  I gently rise and softly call

All Good night and joy be to you all.

By unspoken agreement, **McKenna** *takes over.*

McKenna
  But since it has so ought to be
  By a time to rise and a time to fall
  Come fill to me the parting glass

All Good night and joy be with you all.

Silence.

Collins Your health, Arthur.

Barton What is it, Mick – forty?

McKenna Ah he's not a day over thirty-five!

Collins Bugger off the lot of you. I'm feeling old enough at thirty-one.

All Happy birthday, Mick.

Breithlá shona, a Mhicheál.

*

Dalton *steps outside to confront* **O'Malley**.

Dalton What has you in London, O'Malley – business or pleasure?

O'Malley I hear there's no shortage of pleasure, anyway.

Dalton There's a truce. You got orders. You shouldn't be here.

O'Malley The truce will end.

Dalton I hear there's some as wants to bring it to an end.

O'Malley There may be that.

Dalton What do you want?

O'Malley To talk to the Big Fella.

Dalton I have orders. He's seeing no one. The talks are at a sensitive phase.

O'Malley I hear they're going well.

Dalton Perhaps.

O'Malley I hear the Big Fella's enjoying them. Going down a storm with the Brits, they say. The papers are full of it. A real hit.

Dalton There's many over here as don't want these talks to work, O'Malley. You'd do well to pay less attention to misinformation.

O'Malley Just so he knows we're keeping an eye.

Dalton That's it?

O'Malley There might be talk of some action.

Dalton What kind of action?

O'Malley The kind of action that isn't talk.

Dalton Here?

O'Malley Where it hurts them most.

Dalton You know what it would mean to defy orders?

O'Malley We took an oath, Dalton. Before God. To the Republic. That supersedes orders.

Dalton I'll tell him you called, O'Malley. Be going on home, now. And don't be hanging around here – there's all sorts of dangerous people out there. With guns.

O'Malley There's more than just the Brotherhood in this fight, Dalton. Some of us have no need of secret societies.

Dalton *has produced his pistol and carries it low at his side.*

O'Malley We'll be watching, Dalton.

O'Malley *backs away, watching* **Dalton** *all the while. He and his comrade disappear.*

*

Back at the party.

Barton A song from the Big Fellow!

Collins Ah no.

McKenna Ah go on, Mick. Something from Cork. A ballad.

Collins A traditional number, is it?

McKenna To make us homesick.

Collins *thinks for a moment. He starts off as if it were a sean nós song – drawing out the note.*

Collins He . . .

He is delaying the punchline.

Collins　is an . . . Englishman!

And the song takes off, with boisterous support.

Collins
>For he himself has said it,
>And it's greatly to his credit,
>That he is an Englishman!

All　That he is an Englishman!

Collins
>For he might have been a Roosian,
>A French, or Turk, or Proosian,
>Or perhaps Itali-an!

All　Or perhaps Itali-an!

Jones *arrives at Hans Place.* **McKenna** *is called out to meet him.*

Collins
>But in spite of all temptations
>To belong to other nations,
>He remains an Englishman!
>He remains an Englishman!

All
>But in spite of all temptations
>To belong to other nations,
>He remains an Englishman!
>He remains an Englishman!

They toast and drink. Meanwhile:

McKenna　Mr Jones!

Jones　Miss McKenna. So sorry to disturb – You appear to be celebrating –

McKenna　It's Mr Collins's birthday – won't you come in?

Jones　No, I –

McKenna　Come in, Mr Jones!

Jones　Honestly, I / just wanted to speak to Mr Griffith.

McKenna (*ushering him in*)　Mr Jones, you know how the Irish take offence when hospitality is refused.

Jones　I don't think I – Isn't that a little / ironic?

McKenna　Something to oil the vocal cords?

Jones No! Thank you –

Collins Mr Jones! What a surprise. A song!

All A song!

Jones No, really, I / don't think I should.

Collins You know the rules, Mr Jones – you can't come to an Irish party without a song.

Jones But I wasn't coming to a party –

Griffith If music be the food of love, Mr Jones – play on.

An expectant pause. **Jones** *gives in.*

Jones Perhaps a little song from the valleys.

Griffith Ciúnas, le bhur thoil.

Jones
(*singing* Land of My Fathers)
Mae hen wlad fy nhadau yn annwyl i mi,
Gwlad beirdd a chantorion, enwogion o fri;
Ei gwrol ryfelwyr, gwladgarwyr tra mad,
Tros ryddid collasant eu gwaed.

During the chorus, **Collins** *joins him.*

Jones/Collins
Gwlad, gwlad, pleidiol wyf i'm gwlad.
Tra môr yn fur i'r bur hoff bau,
O bydded i'r heniaith barhau.

They finish. A moment's silence and then cheers.

Jones You are quite the man of surprises, Mr Collins.

Collins One of the benefits of spending a little time in a prisoner of war camp in Wales, Mr Jones.

Jones Mr Griffith – a moment?

They step away from the party.

Jones The idea of a boundary commission – that you discussed with the PM . . .

Griffith I said we wouldn't shoot it down.

Jones I wrote up a memo on it, for the record. You know how it is – civil service. Would you review it?

Griffith Of course. (*Scanning it.*) That seems to be the essence of it, Mr Jones.

Jones Would you mind signing it? Just a matter of protocol.

Griffith *pauses for a brief moment.*

Griffith Of course.

Jones *produces a pen and* **Griffith** *signs.*

Jones Thank you.

Griffith You'll stay for a drink?

Jones I shouldn't, Mr Griffith. Thank you. Good night now.

Griffith Good night, Mr Jones.

He watches after him for a moment.

McKenna All well, Mr Griffith?

Griffith Yes, Miss McKenna, yes. Let us return to the party. We have earned it.

As **Griffith** *returns,* **McKenna** *turns back to the audience.*

McKenna Over the following weeks, the British flesh out their offer, in a draft Treaty: a boundary commission, to ensure essential unity; and 'dominion' status, with a guarantee that Ireland will have the same rights as the other dominions have in practice as well as in law.

Griffith It's good, Michael.

Collins It's not the Republic.

Griffith It was never going to be the Republic. Dev knew that. Even Brugha must. It's time to bring it home.

Act Three

One

The Mansion House, Dublin

The Irish Cabinet gathers around the table: **de Valera, Brugha, Griffith, Barton**. **Childers**, *attending as secretary, confers quietly with* **de Valera**, *distributes copies of the draft Treaty, then stands off. They read in silence.*

McKenna   Mr Collins leaves London last, on the evening of December 2nd, taking the night train and mailboat – but, in the middle of the night, in the middle of the Irish Sea, the boat collides with a fishing trawler. Three fishermen are lost; Mick – Mr Collins is involved in the rescue.

As **Collins** *enters, a bucket of water is thrown at him.*

McKenna   The mailboat eventually arrives at Dun Laoghaire at 10 a.m. Mr Collins goes straight to the Mansion House, where the Cabinet is meeting.

Collins *slips* **McKenna** *a document and whispers something, then joins the Cabinet. A man emerges from the shadows and takes the document from* **McKenna**.

De Valera   An eventful night, Mr Collins?

Collins   A little more than usual.

The silence resumes as they study page by careful page. **Collins** *and* **Griffith** *exchange glances, hopeful. Eventually:*

De Valera   The question that confronts us, it seems to me, is this: can this document be the basis for further discussions? Or does it suggest that further discussions are pointless?

Griffith   But we have made great progress –

Collins   This is practically external / association.

Brugha   What have you been doing, spending all your time at the theatre?

Griffith   How dare you / Cathal.

Barton   The delegation has been working hard –

Griffith   Night and day.

Brugha   I hear there's been a lot of work at night / alright.

Collins   What the hell is that supposed to mean?

Brugha   Ní ormsa an locht má chuireann am fhírinne fearg.

Collins   Abair amach é Brugha. Anything you want to say about me, say it.

Brugha What is the point of continuing discussions with the British when there is no difference between the line the British pursue and the one that our people pursue?

Collins And what do you mean by that?

Brugha I mean the British chose their men.

Griffith That is an outrage!

De Valera I think Mr Brugha may have spoken intemperately.

Collins You think I am in their pay?

Brugha *glances to* **Childers**. **Collins** *sees it.*

Brugha The talks, Mr Childers – have they been conducted by the delegation as a whole, with you documenting them, as Secretary?

Childers For the past six weeks, the talks have been conducted to the exclusion of Minister Barton and myself, in 'sub-conference' format.

Brugha 'Sub-conference'?

Griffith Myself and Mr Collins. But we have always reported back thoroughly to the delegation and to Dublin.

Brugha And did the British object at any point to this sub-conference idea?

Griffith No / they did not.

Childers The idea came from the British.

Brugha Of course it did – because Lloyd George spotted you were weak on the Republic – he wanted to peel you off.

Collins I do not take my opinions from Mr Lloyd George. I am Michael Collins.

Brugha 'The Big Fella.' So easily seduced. And not just by Lloyd George, I hear.

Griffith You are out of / order, Cathal.

Collins Repeat that outside this room, Brugha / and so help me God I will . . .

De Valera Nobody is acting in bad faith here. Our differences are honest differences of opinion. But if we are intolerant of those differences – if we let them spread to the country – that would mean disaster.

They stand down.

De Valera Perhaps the delegation chairman would take us through some of the thinking behind this document.

Griffith We believe the British have made a number of substantial concessions . . . On trade . . . on defence . . . on the oath . . . on Ulster. If you turn to page five, I'll talk you through their proposal of a boundary commission, which will ensure essential unity . . .

McKenna The debate goes on all day. But it keeps coming back to one core issue.

Brugha The Republic means the Republic. Sovereign and separate.

Collins The Republic is a work in progress.

Brugha It was established in blood. And ratified by the votes of the people.

Griffith The people did not vote for the precise content of a republic. They voted simply for freedom from Britain.

Brugha Absolute freedom.

Collins This Treaty will give us the freedom to achieve that final freedom.

De Valera I proposed a solution to balance our freedom with association with their Empire.

Collins They rejected it.

Griffith The difference was merely one of emphasis – you were seeking an association with the Empire, they are offering an association within it.

Brugha That is the difference between keeping our oath to the Republic, and violating it.

Griffith We took an oath to do our best for Ireland.

Brugha We took an oath to overthrow the King – and now you want us to take an oath to the King?

Griffith Read the oath!

Brugha I will not read that aloud in this room.

Collins *grabs it.*

Collins 'I do solemnly swear to bear true faith and allegiance to the Constitution of the Irish Free State—'

Brugha Go on.

Collins *doesn't continue.* **Griffith** *picks it up.*

Griffith 'To the Community of Nations known as the British Empire; and to the King as head of the State and of the Empire.' It is an oath to the Irish constitution first – to the King as an afterthought.

Brugha An afterthought!

Childers Any Irishman who took that oath would be acting a lie.

Barton It is the principle of it! That oath creates a position that is not true – a false position.

Griffith The principle that I have stood on all my life is the principle of Ireland for the Irish people. If I could get that with a Republic I would have a Republic; if I could get that with External Association, I would have External Association; and if I can get that with a monarchy, now, I will have a monarchy.

Brugha   Do you think Tom Clarke died for a monarchy? Pearse? Plunkett? Ceannt? Do you remember Éamonn Ceannt's last words for us? Never treat with the enemy, never surrender to his mercy, but fight to a finish – his last words before they shot him.

Griffith   Is there to be no living Irish nation? Must we always live by the demands of the dead?

Brugha   If I were our last man . . . if my last cartridge had been fired . . . if I were lying on the ground, and our enemies standing over me with their bayonets raised, and they said to me, 'Now, will you take an oath to our King?' I would say, 'No! I will not'.

Beat.

Brugha   If you sign this Treaty you will split Ireland from stem to stern.

Silence.

De Valera   I propose that the delegation return to London to continue to pursue an association with the Empire.

Collins   You should go, Dev.

De Valera   I am needed here.

Griffith   Our best man should be at the negotiating table.

De Valera   Not until we have their final offer.

Barton   This is not London's final word.

Collins   You haven't been in the room, Bob!

Barton   And why is that?

Collins   If you think there's a better offer to get, Dev, you should be over there getting it. Lloyd George is leading his people in the negotiations –

Griffith   Craig has been in London, leading his.

Collins   Why is our Chief not leading us?

De Valera   I may have to lead our people back to war! That will be difficult if I am seen to have been bartering with the enemy.

Collins   And how do you think I look?

De Valera   I am the symbol of the Irish republic. It is vital to keep that symbol pure.

Griffith   I will lead the delegation back. We will seek further concessions. But I will not risk war by repudiating an offer that I think is honourable. I will not break off negotiations on the issue of the Crown and Empire.

De Valera Do not break on the Crown. That would damage us internationally. The world will not understand our objection on principle to staying within the Empire. If you cannot secure External Association, and a breakdown appears inevitable, switch the focus to Ulster. Object to the boundary commission. Make the negotiations break down on that. That will damage Britain internationally. They will find it hard to justify a threat of war over our refusal to accept their partition of our country.

Griffith But should they offer External Association, we are prepared to work with the Boundary Commission?

Brugha It's not unity, Chief.

Griffith It would be essential unity.

De Valera We can work with it.

Griffith *looks uneasily at* **Collins**.

De Valera If they offer new terms, bring them home. Do not sign in London.

Griffith *nods.*

Hans Place

McKenna The delegation arrives back in London the following morning.

Collins I'm not going back in, Arthur.

Griffith Michael –

Collins I can't.

Griffith But the Cabinet / gave us instructions.

Collins For Jesus' sake, Arthur. I have done what was asked of me. I have come here and acted like a fucking politician. And we got something. And if it's not enough for them, so be it. But I will not go back into that room and pretend that I think I can get something better.

Downing Street

Griffith, **Barton** *and* **Childers** *advance to meet with* **Lloyd George**, **Churchill**, **Birkenhead** *and* **Jones**.

Jones At 5 p.m. on Sunday, December the 4th, the Irish return to Downing Street – for what we hope will be the final time.

McKenna Mr Griffith leads a last attempt to secure a British concession on Empire . . .

Griffith Our proposal of External Association would do nothing whatsoever to undermine the Empire.

Lloyd George   We cannot open this up again!

McKenna   . . . or force a break on the issue of Ulster.

Griffith   But the *main* difficulty is Ulster – we can agree to nothing without a guarantee of unity.

Lloyd George (*exasperated*)   Our boundary commission will address this.

Churchill   By staying within the Empire, you will ensure essential unity, in time.

Barton (*frustrated*)   For God's sake, we cannot stay within the Empire!

He realises his mistake as he says it.

Birkenhead   Ah.

Churchill   So.

Lloyd George   Plainly spoken. I thank you. For two months, we have sought a simple answer to our essential question: would Ireland plot its future *within* the Empire, or *against* it? You have procrastinated, proposed ambiguities to avoid the question, and subtleties to obscure it. But now it is clear. There is no prospect of reconciliation. I suggest you send us your formal rejection of our proposals tomorrow and we can jointly announce the end of the conference. And of the truce.

The Irish leave.

The Laverys'

Collins *stalks the room, anguished.*

Collins   I was going to get married.

Lavery   I've asked you not to talk of her.

Collins   A young lad – to play in Croke Park some day.

Lavery   You've time.

Collins   It's too late.

Lavery   Don't be / ridiculous.

Collins   There's going to be war, again.

Lavery   Stay here.

Collins   This isn't a life.

Lavery   Make it your life. You're good at it. You've earned their respect.

Collins   What do I care for their fucking respect? I'm no politician.

Lavery   Ugh, such petulance.

Collins   I'm just a trumped up foot-soldier.

Lavery   What are you afraid of, Micheál?

Collins   I won't do what Pearse did – lead men to their deaths. I won't lead this.

Lavery   Good!

Collins   But I'll fight. I'll go back to Cork. Fight amongst my own. We might last longer down there.

Lavery   Madness.

Collins   Glorious madness, that's what we called it, once.

Lavery   Oh God, now you sound like Winston. The man's addicted to war.

Collins   War disgusts me.

Lavery   Then don't go back to it.

Collins   What choice have I got? The Chief is rejecting / their offer.

Lavery   Your Chief isn't even here! Don't you see? That makes *you* the Chief.

Downing Street

Lloyd George   We will have to institute Crown Colony Government in the South.

Churchill   They will resist.

Birkenhead   Martial law?

Churchill   As soon as the shooting starts.

Lloyd George   What will we need?

Churchill   About a hundred thousand troops.

Lloyd George   Do we have them?

Churchill   Not immediately. It will take a few months.

Birkenhead   When do we revoke the Truce?

Churchill   As soon as they've left.

Birkenhead   Can we arrest Collins?

Jones   Where *is* Collins?

Lloyd George (*shrugging*)   He's given up.

Jones   Why?

Lloyd George   Because he's surrounded by a bunch of die-hards who'd rather he died for their cause than did anything to resolve it.

Jones (*puzzled*)   They kept coming back to the issue of Northern Ireland.

Birkenhead They were trying to engineer a break on Ulster – it would play better for them internationally.

Jones But they can't break on Ulster – Mr Griffith gave you his word he'd support a boundary commission.

Churchill Collins is the real force anyway.

Birkenhead Didn't you put that in writing?

Lloyd George What?

Birkenhead The boundary commission.

Lloyd George Did I?

Jones (*remembering*) I wrote a memo.

Lloyd George Of course you did.

Jones And Mr Griffith signed it.

Lloyd George Well, where is it?

Jones I gave it to you!

Lloyd George You *know* not to give anything important to me!

Jones Try your pockets.

Lloyd George I *am* trying my pockets!

Jones I'll try your other suits. That's where we usually find them.

Lloyd George Get word to Collins. See if he can be persuaded to meet me. If there's a deal to be made, he's the one to make it. And find that blasted memo.

The street

Collins *emerges from the* **Laverys'** *to be met by* **Dalton**.

Dalton Lloyd George wants to meet you.

Collins Is there any point, Emmet?

Dalton Yesterday was a disaster. You weren't there.

Collins When?

Dalton You're late.

Collins Have you the reports from the Brotherhood?

Dalton *produces two documents. He hands one over.*

Dalton Their report on the Army.

Collins And?

Dalton Discipline's collapsed.

Collins How many men – *reliable* men?

Dalton Less than 2,000.

Collins Guns?

Dalton One per man.

Collins Ammunition?

Dalton About a round per gun. And – the Brotherhood's response to the draft Treaty.

He hands it over.

Dalton They think it's toxic.

Collins Fuck.

Dalton But it can be made acceptable. Changes on defence, the boundary commission, the oath – they've suggested a new wording.

Collins And with those changes . . . ?

Dalton The Brotherhood will back it.

Collins And the Army?

Dalton We have control of the leadership. After that, who knows. The men spent two years getting shot at for the Republic – they mightn't appreciate the subtleties involved in staying in the Empire.

Collins If there's a split – will they fight?

Dalton That will depend on Dev.

Downing Street

Collins *arrives to find* **Lloyd George**, **Churchill**, **Birkenhead** *and* **Jones** *waiting for him.*

Lloyd George What do you need, Mr Collins?

Collins Ulster.

Churchill You know we can't give you that.

Collins You put the northernmost part of Ireland in the South. Your boundary makes no sense.

Lloyd George The boundary commission will fix that. It will give you back at least two counties –

Churchill The dreary steeples of Fermanagh and Tyrone.

Lloyd George maybe three.

Birkenhead Half of Down. The cities of Londonderry and Newry.

Churchill We don't want them – but we can't be seen to give them away.

Lloyd George After the boundary commission transfers them to you, and the reality dawns on Craig, Belfast will come in under the Dublin parliament.

Collins When?

Birkenhead Sooner rather than later.

Lloyd George They will be forced to join you.

Collins Forced?

Lloyd George The force of economics.

Collins Not if you keep subsidising them.

Lloyd George We have pledged not to coerce them. But that does not oblige us to endlessly pour money down their throats.

Collins I need something more tangible.

Churchill If we force the Six Counties into a united Ireland, they will fight you. You will have civil war. What alternative is there to partition at this present moment? But Ireland will soon be united.

Lloyd George The unity of Ireland is an historical inevitability. If you and the Unionists can put your differences behind you, they will come in. But we cannot say anything publicly – the Tory die-hards would revolt.

Collins *hands him a document.*

Lloyd George What's this?

Collins A wording for the oath.

Lloyd George We have stretched the Empire as far as it will go.

Collins I've stretched the Republic till it snapped. I need you to bring the Empire almost to that point.

Lloyd George Am I to understand this has the backing of the delegation?

Collins It has the backing of the people who most count. I suggest you propose it.

Birkenhead *takes it.*

Birkenhead 'I do solemnly swear true faith and allegiance to the Constitution of the Irish State . . . and that I will be *faithful* to His Majesty . . .'

Lloyd George This is allegiance.

Collins You might call it allegiance. I might call it faithfulness.

Birkenhead '... in virtue of the common citizenship of Ireland with Great Britain and her adherence to and membership of the group of nations forming the British Empire.'

Collins 'Group of nations' helps take the sting out of the 'Empire' bit.

Birkenhead Why not leave out 'Empire' altogether?

Churchill What?

Birkenhead We could say 'Commonwealth of Nations'.

Beat.

Lloyd George Bring Griffith back this afternoon.

Collins If we can't bring Barton on board now, we never will.

Lloyd George Will Barton sign?

Collins Nobody will sign, here. We'll have to bring it back to Dublin –

Lloyd George Of course.

Collins ... but with this oath, we can win the argument there.

Jones At 3 p.m. on Monday, the Irish delegation returns to Downing Street.

Griffith We are close to agreement on many articles. But a gulf remains on the questions of allegiance and of Ulster.

Lloyd George On Ulster, you have our terms. You have not objected to them.

Griffith We have not accepted them.

Churchill We have given Mr Collins undertakings on the workings of the commission.

Collins It will give us back Fermanagh, Tyrone, half of Derry.

Lloyd George How the boundary commission will work, and how we will have to say it will work, are two different things.

Griffith That is a difficult thing for me to explain to the Irish people.

Childers This is a Treaty we are discussing – and you expect us to take your word for how it will be implemented?

Birkenhead This is not the real obstacle. The obstacle is your refusal to come into the Empire. You are merely trying to use the Ulster question to force the collapse of these talks so you can win a moral victory.

Griffith How dare you question our integrity!

Barton We are here in good faith!

Lloyd George Well, let us see ... Mr Griffith, you gave me your word that you would not repudiate the boundary commission proposal.

Barton What?

Griffith We discussed it, briefly.

Lloyd George Ges di hyd iddo fo? (Did you find it?)

Jones Mae e 'da fi fan hyn. (I have it here.)

Jones *produces the document and hands it to* **Griffith**.

Lloyd George Is that your signature?

Barton (*to* **Collins**) What is this letter?

Collins I don't know what the hell it is.

Lloyd George Mr Griffith?

Griffith It is.

Lloyd George There are other matters outstanding. I believe naval defence is one . . .

Childers Naval defence is inseparable from / Irish sovereignty.

Churchill I am willing to concede on the principle of defence sovereignty. We will, of course, need to retain some access to key ports – I think those details can be ironed out.

Lloyd George I believe trade policy is another outstanding issue . . .

Barton The right to an independent trade policy is a / fundamental component of sovereignty.

Birkenhead We are willing to concede your right to strike your own trade deals. We hope that you will conclude that a free trade deal with the United Kingdom is in your best interests, but you will be free to refuse.

Childers That would not alter the fact that you require us to swear an oath of allegiance to your king. That we cannot / do.

Lloyd George Ah yes. The oath. We have done some further reconsideration of that. This new draft of the Treaty incorporates the concessions we have mentioned and a new formula for the oath.

Jones *distributes copies.* **Collins** *glances at it to confirm that it is his proposal from earlier.* **Barton** *and* **Griffith** *consider it closely.* **Childers** *studies and then dismisses it.*

Griffith This is, indeed, better.

Childers It is still an oath to an English king.

Birkenhead It is far less of an oath to the King than that which you once took, Mr Childers.

Griffith There is room for some studied ambiguity.

Lloyd George You in Ireland often bring against us in England the charge of breach of faith, gentlemen. Now it is for you to show that Irishmen know how to keep faith. Let us end 700 years of conflict.

He takes out a pen. Silence.

Childers They can't sign here – they haven't the authority.

Lloyd George We have been talking to you for two months on the basis that you were plenipotentiaries.

Beat.

Lloyd George I told Sir James Craig I would send him the conclusions of the negotiations tonight, in time for the opening session of the Northern Irish parliament tomorrow.

Barton That's hardly a fixed / deadline . . .

Lloyd George I gave him my word, Mr Barton.

Silence.

Griffith I will sign.

Lloyd George For yourself or for the delegation?

Griffith I speak only for myself.

Lloyd George Though everyone else refuses, you will nevertheless agree to sign?

Griffith That is so.

Beat.

Lloyd George That is not enough. We shall sign as a delegation. We stake the life of the Government on our signature. Are you prepared to do the same?

Barton *shifts uneasily.*

Lloyd George *fixes on* **Barton**.

Lloyd George Those who do not sign must take the full responsibility for the war that will immediately follow.

Barton Immediately? But / that's completely unreasonable . . .

Lloyd George *has removed two letters from an inside pocket.*

Lloyd George (*in his right hand*) This letter encloses this Treaty that we propose now to sign. (*In his left hand.*) This letter says that the Irish plenipotentiaries refused to come within the Empire, and that the negotiations are thus at an end, and war beckons.

Whichever letter you choose travels, tonight, by special train to Holyhead, and by destroyer to Belfast. The train is waiting with steam up at Euston. If it is to reach Sir James Craig by the morning we must have your answer by 10 p.m. You have until then, but no longer, to decide which letter I will send. If I send this letter, it is war – and war within three days.

Collins (*standing up*) Why you / lying scoundrel . . .

Griffith *restrains him with a hand on his arm.* **Barton** *and* **Childers** *stand.*

Barton This is brinkmanship.

Childers This is a breach of international law.

Griffith *stands.*

Griffith You will have our answer.

The Irish leave.

Two

Hans Place

Silence. **Griffith** *is waiting.* **Collins** *is brooding.* **Childers** *and* **Barton** *exchange nervous glances.*

Collins I will sign.

Barton But your oath!

Collins What have we got for Ireland? Something she has wanted these past 700 fucking years. Will anyone be satisfied at the bargain? No. But this, this is the first real step.

Barton I will not violate my oath to the Republic – the most sacred bond on earth.

Collins We knew, coming here, that there would be compromise, Bob. What else is a negotiation for?

Barton Compromise – not outright surrender.

Griffith We have won on defence, on trade. A major concession on the oath. A boundary commission that will reduce Northern Ireland to a rump state – essential unity.

Barton You'd trust a British Prime Minister on a promise to Ireland?

Collins 'War in three days,' Bob! Do you distrust him on that?

Barton We fought before.

Collins I have one round of ammunition per soldier. I cannot send men out to fight on those terms.

Barton They will go willingly.

Collins You're not the one asking them.

Barton I will happily serve.

Collins Bob, you spent the war in jail – you didn't see what it was like. You have no idea what you are bringing on the people.

Griffith It will be on you if we go back to war now, Barton. All on you.

Collins Bob, if you cause a new war, you'll be hanged from a lamp post in the streets of Dublin.

Childers Traitors both.

Griffith I will not take that from an Englishman!

Childers I am by birth, domicile and deliberate choice an Irishman.

Griffith You are English by rearing and by culture.

Childers I am not alone in this room in having moved from my former views. (*Re.* **Collins**.) Some have moved very far indeed.

Collins Childers is merely secretary to the delegation. He has no vote here.

Childers I have my voice. I have a mandate / to be here.

Collins I propose that the delegation now meets in private conclave to decide whether we will sign this Treaty.

Griffith I second / that.

Barton I wish to speak to my cousin first.

Collins It's too late for that.

Griffith You may have a moment.

Griffith *and* **Collins** *withdraw.*

Barton All the dead fought for is lost, Erskine.

Childers No, Bob! They died to prevent surrender.

Barton Can we sustain the war?

Childers If we had asked that at the start, we would never have fought. This is the betrayal of everything we fought for. All the sacrifice. All the women widowed and children orphaned.

Barton War will widow more of them, Erskine.

Childers You alone can stop this, Bob.

Barton That means I alone bring war upon us.

Childers Refuse to sign. We shall bring the offer home, to Dev. Let him rally the people against it.

Barton There's no time!

Childers We've taken this journey together, Bob – we haven't taken it to end in surrender.

He clasps **Barton**.

Childers 'Trust thyself,' Bob – 'every heart vibrates to that iron string.'

Downing Street

The Irish return to the Cabinet table. The British are still there. Silence. **Jones** *enters with two copies of the Treaty. He places them in front of* **Lloyd George**, *who signs* *both, and then* **Jones** *places them before* **Churchill, Birkenhead, Griffith, Collins,** *who sign them. Finally, he comes to* **Barton**. **Barton** *doesn't react. He looks at* **Childers**. *Then at the others. He signs.* **Childers** *leaves, returning to his room. The rest all look at the documents. They look across the table. Then* **Churchill** *and* **Birkenhead** *surge forward around the table to shake the Irish hands.* **Jones** *retrieves a tray with whiskey. The British are exhilarated. The Irish are exhausted.* **Childers** *starts typing.*

Birkenhead   You know, Mr Collins, I think I may have just signed my political death warrant.

Collins   I have just signed my actual death warrant.

Birkenhead   More romantic than drinking yourself to death, I suppose.

Churchill   You are not in celebratory mood, Mr Barton.

Barton   I fear history will never forgive us.

Churchill   Oh, history will be kind to me. Because I intend to write it.

Lloyd George   What now, Mr Griffith?

Griffith   We go home.

Lloyd George   To build a State.

Griffith   To build a garden. I promised my wife I'd retire by next August. 'Tis an unweeded garden, That grows to seed,' as your poet said. Mine is very unweeded.

Lloyd George   What of Mr de Valera?

Griffith   There will be no surprise for him in this. It's the wild men behind him we have to fear.

Epilogue

De Valera *appears, with* **Brugha** *behind him. The others step forward to listen, one by one.* **Childers** *remains at his desk, alternately listening to* **de Valera** *and typing furiously.* **Jones** *passes through the group with a tray, collecting their glasses.* **Birkenhead** *does not relinquish his.*

De Valera   If the government and the people accept this Treaty, and if the Volunteers of the future try to complete the work the Volunteers of the last four years have been attempting, they will have to complete it, not over the bodies of foreign soldiers, but over the dead bodies of their own countrymen.

McKenna   In January, 1922, after a prolonged and bitter debate, the Treaty is approved by Dáil Éireann, and Arthur Griffith replaces Éamon de Valera as President.

Barton *exits (to join* **de Valera**). **Collins** *watches him.*

De Valera They will have to wade through Irish blood, through the blood of the soldiers of the Irish government and through, perhaps, the blood of some of the members of the government in order to get Irish freedom.

De Valera *and* **Brugha** *leave.* **Collins** *and* **Griffith** *look to each other.*

McKenna By June, the country has fallen into civil war. Arthur Griffith never gets to his garden. On the 12th of August, 1922, he collapses with a brain haemorrhage, and dies.

Griffith *exits.*

Jones Lord Birkenhead is proved right. The Tory die-hards never forgive him for the Irish Treaty. In October, 1922, they reject their own leadership, and bring down the government. Lord Birkenhead's career will never recover – he will drink himself to death eight years later.

Birkenhead *knocks back his drink, and exits.*

McKenna Erskine Childers keeps fighting for the Republic at his typewriter, long into the night, in a succession of ever more precarious offices and hideouts, on the run. In November, 1922,

Childers *stands up.*

McKenna he is captured by Free State soldiers at the Barton home in Wicklow, and executed for possession of a small pistol – which had been given to him as a present by Michael Collins.

Childers *exits.* **Jones** *surveys the remaining British.*

Jones Lloyd George resigns with the collapse of his government. The Welsh Wizard will never hold office again. Nor will the Liberal Party.

Lloyd George *exits.* **Churchill** *watches him, with a mild smirk. He takes out a cigar and lights it.*

Jones And Winston Churchill – well, as he promised, he will write his own story.

Churchill *arches an eyebrow and exits. Just* **Collins** *is left.*

It starts to rain. **McKenna** *and* **Jones** *open umbrellas.*

McKenna Ten days after the death of Mr Griffith, Michael Collins, now chairman of the Provisional Government of the Irish Free State, goes to visit army units in his home place, West Cork. His convoy is caught in a republican ambush, and he is shot.

Collins *exits.*

McKenna The Boundary Commission, which he believed would deliver 'essential' unity, will be postponed because of the Civil War, and eventually abandoned. The border will remain unchanged.

Rain. **Jones** *joins* **McKenna**, *now at Glasnevin Cemetery again.*

Jones I am so sorry for your loss.

McKenna Our losses, Mr Jones.

Jones Indeed.

McKenna When sorrows come, they come not single spies . . .

Jones But in battalions. Forgive me, Miss McKenna, but it has sometimes struck me that for a people so determined to throw off the shackles of the English, you are rather fond of quoting Shakespeare.

McKenna We never said we didn't *like* the English, Mr Jones. We just said we didn't like being ruled by you.

Jones I'm Welsh, Miss McKenna.

McKenna So perhaps you know what I mean.

Jones Ah.

McKenna Mick – Mr Collins – he liked to say . . . 'To go for a drink is one thing. To be driven to it is another.'

McKenna *holds out her hand.* **Jones** *takes it.*

Jones I hope we meet again, Miss McKenna.

McKenna In happier times.

Jones *leaves.* **De Valera***'s voice rings out again.* **McKenna** *looks up.*

De Valera Soldiers of the Republic.

McKenna Nine bloody months later.

De Valera The Republic can no longer be defended successfully by your arms.

McKenna May 1923.

De Valera Further sacrifice of life would now be in vain. Military victory must be allowed to rest – for the moment – with those who have destroyed the Republic.

It stops raining. **McKenna** *looks up at the sky. She closes her umbrella and makes to leave.*

McKenna The wars are over. But we do not celebrate. There are friends to be mourned, and work to be done.

As she leaves, she sings, softly, sadly.

McKenna
   But since it has so ought to be
   By a time to rise and a time to fall
   Come fill to me the parting glass
   Good night and joy be to you all.

She is gone.

Blackout.

The following was written as an afterword to the first published edition of The Treaty. I have updated it here.

A note on travesties and anachronisms

The negotiations that led to the Anglo-Irish Treaty of 1921 consisted of seven plenary conferences, 24 sub-conferences and meetings of various committees, between October 11 and December 6. There were five men in the Irish delegation, supported by a staff estimated at more than 70; the British delegation consisted of seven, with the entire architecture of State to call on in support. The British also had the constant business of everyday politics and governance to contend with, and the negotiations were punctuated with various domestic British political events, while the Irish returned home for consultations on a number of occasions.

Compressing all of this into an eighty-minute play with a cast of twelve will inevitably involve elision, invention and, at times, distortion. The Cabinet committee that discussed General Macready's plan for "coercion" in Ireland in June 1921 was the Irish Situation Committee; it was chaired by Austen Chamberlain, not the Prime Minister. In substance, though, the debate on stage here follows closely Tom Jones's diary note of the meeting. Birkenhead, a legendary drinker, was in fact on the dry during 1921, for a bet: he broke it to toast the signing of the Treaty. The room at Chequers that houses a famous Cromwell collection is known as the Long Room, not the Cromwell Room. Judge Phillimore had retired by 1921, though the story about him was recorded by Evelyn Waugh in his diary for 1924. Michael Collins's birthday, which the delegation did celebrate with a party, was on October 15, slightly earlier than suited my purposes.

There are anachronisms as well as travesties ("Venn diagram" may be one; "kite-flying" is not), but these liberties pale beside the liberty of putting words in people's mouths and, by implication, thoughts in their heads. Where possible, I like to use a historical character's actual recorded words, but where the choice is between mangling the words or mangling the drama, I will default to the former.

The historian Catriona Crowe has observed that the Irish revolution must be one of the best documented anywhere; yet there remain various enigmas about the Treaty negotiations. Did Michael Collins have an affair with Hazel Lavery (and does it matter)? Lavery certainly gave to believe that they did; and the mores of our time make it difficult to believe that a 31-year-old man of such energy and charisma, under such pressure, would have passed up on that opportunity. But Collins – along with many in the revolutionary movement – was a devout Catholic, attending mass at Brompton Oratory early every morning during the negotiations; perhaps their physical relationship was merely wishful thinking.

Of greater significance is the political role that Lavery may have played, as a go-between for the Irish and British negotiators and as an influencer in favour of a settlement. John Lavery recorded that Collins visited them on the final Sunday night, where his wife attempted to convince Collins to do a deal. "Eventually, after hours of persuasion, Hazel prevailed", John Lavery wrote (as recounted in Sinead McCoole's biography, *Hazel*). "She took him to Downing Street in her car that last evening, and he gave in." This sequence is backed up by the diary of CP Scott, but Frank Pakenham and

Tom Jones (as well as Collins's own memo) place the meeting on the following morning, with the telling detail that Collins arrived 15 minutes late. Hazel and John may have been exaggerating her influence, but so too may be those who see Hazel as simply the unwitting agent of Empire, a charge which falls a little too neatly into the misogynistic trope of the femme fatale.

Of greater significance still, yet typically attracting less comment, is Collins's role as President of the Irish Republican Brotherhood. Did Collins believe, as per the IRB constitution, that he was the de jure president of the Republic of Ireland? Was his loyalty to the IRB such as to make his loyalty to the Dáil, and subsequently to the Free State, suspect? He staffed his team and house in London with IRB men, had his key aide, army officer Emmet Dalton, inducted into the IRB shortly before bringing him to London, met with the IRB supreme council on return trips to Dublin, gave them sight of the draft Treaty simultaneous with the Cabinet's discussion of it, and acted consistent with their recommendations – and not those of the Cabinet – upon returning to London for the final negotiation. Perhaps Collins's only real loyalty was to Ireland, and the IRB was simply one more tool, alongside the army and politics, for advancing Irish freedom; but it is not difficult to make a case that, at the very least, Collins violated the trust of the Dáil and Cabinet. Whether any such violation was for the greater good is another question, perhaps the most important one of all.

A further enigma surrounds the position during the talks of James Craig, leader of the Ulster Unionists. Craig visited Downing Street on a Saturday in early November; Frances Stevenson, Lloyd George's secretary, lover and later his wife, recorded in her diary that Lloyd George had persuaded Craig to accept an all-Ireland parliament. But Craig returned to Downing Street on the Monday implacably opposed to any such concession. Had Craig really been on the verge of endorsing a form of Irish unity, or did the Welsh Wizard hopelessly misread him? In the optimism of Lloyd George after that first meeting lies an intriguing glimpse of an entirely different – and less tragic – history of 20th century Ireland.

Frank Pakenham's 1935 page-turner, *Peace by Ordeal*, for which he had access to a number of the protagonists, is the unrivalled account of the negotiations. His biases have been challenged, but it has not been surpassed for detail or atmosphere. Tom Jones's *Whitehall Diary*, the third and final volume of which is devoted to Ireland (an indication of the prominence of Ireland within British governance of the period) is a gold mine of insights into the negotiations, the protagonists and the business of politics. Between them, those two sources gave me the architecture of the play. T Ryle Dwyer's *I Signed My Death Warrant: Michael Collins and the Treaty* was also particularly useful.

Coincident with the original production of *The Treaty*, the journalist and historian Colum Kenny published a significant new work, *Midnight in London: The Anglo-Irish Treaty Crisis 1921*. In the archives of the Houses of Parliament, Kenny had discovered a memo about the boundary commission idea that appears to be the memo long referred to in accounts of the negotiations as having been signed by Arthur Griffith. In doing so, according the narrative traced by Kenny to Pakenham, Griffith purportedly gave away a crucial Irish position – the possibility of a "break on Ulster".

But the memo that Kenny unearthed had not been signed by Griffith. Kenny argued that the story that Griffith had signed it was a calumny, used to portray Griffith as hapless and Lloyd George as deviously clever.

The signing of the memo features in the play. Kenny saw the play in Dublin in preview, and corresponded with me about it. It was unfair to Griffith, he wrote: he asked me to rewrite it; I declined to do so. I leave it to the reader to assess the relative merits of the play and Kenny's fuller, and potentially more accurate, account.

Selected Bibliography

Barton, Robert. *The Truth about the Treaty and Document No. 2: A Reply to Michael Collins*. Pamphlet, 1921.
Bew, Paul. *Churchill and Ireland*. Oxford: Oxford University Press, 2016.
Bowman, John. *De Valera and the Ulster Question, 1917–1973*. Oxford: Clarendon Press, 1982.
Boyne, Seán. *Emmet Dalton: Somme Soldier, Irish General, Film Pioneer*. Dublin: Merrion Press, 2014.
Campbell, John. *F. E. Smith: First Earl of Birkenhead*. London: Faber & Faber, 2013.
Churchill, Winston S. *My Early Life: A Roving Commission*. London: Thornton Butterworth, 1930.
Churchill, Winston S. *The Aftermath*. London: Thornton Butterworth, 1929.
Churchill, Winston S. *Thoughts and Adventures*. London: Thornton Butterworth, 1932.
Collins, Michael. *The Path to Freedom*. Corpus of Electronic Texts Edition. celt.ucc.ie.
Colum, Padraic. *Arthur Griffith*. Dublin: Browne & Nolan 1959.
Coogan, Tim Pat. *Michael Collins: A Biography*. London: Arrow Books, 1991.
Curran, Joseph M. *The Birth of the Irish Free State, 1921–1923*. Tuscaloosa: University of Alabama Press, 1980.
Department of Foreign Affairs. *Documents on Irish Foreign Policy, Volume I: 1919–1922*. Dublin: Royal Irish Academy, 1998.
Dolan, Anne, and William Murphy. *Michael Collins: The Man and the Revolution*. Dublin: Collins Press, 2018.
Dwyer, T. Ryle. *I Signed My Death Warrant: Michael Collins and the Treaty*. Cork: Mercier Press, 2006.
Ellis, E.L. *T.J.: A Life of Dr Thomas Jones, CH*. Cardiff: University of Wales Press, 1992.
Ervine, St John. *Craigavon: Ulsterman*. London: George Allen & Unwin, 1949.
Fanning, Ronan. *Fatal Path: British Government and Irish Revolution, 1910–1922*. London: Faber & Faber, 2013.
Forester, Margery. *Michael Collins: The Lost Leader*. London: Sphere Books, 1972.
Halle, Kay. *The Irrepressible Churchill: Winston's World, Wars and Wit*. London: Conway, 2010.
Hart, Peter. *Mick: The Real Michael Collins*. New York: Viking, 2006.
Hattersley, Roy. *David Lloyd George: The Great Outsider*. London: Little, Brown, 2010.
Hopkinson, Michael. *Green Against Green: The Irish Civil War*. Dublin: Gill & Macmillan, 1988.
Jenkins, Roy. *Churchill*. London: Pan Books, 2002.
Jones, Thomas. *Whitehall Diary, Volume 3: Ireland, 1921–1926*. Edited by Keith Middlemas. London: Oxford University Press, 1985.
Kenny, Colum. *The Enigma of Arthur Griffith: 'Father of Us All'*. Dublin: Merrion Press, 2020.
Lee, J. J. *Ireland, 1912–1985: Politics and Society*. Cambridge: Cambridge University Press, 1989.
McCoole, Sinéad. *Hazel: A Life of Lady Lavery, 1880–1935*. Dublin: Lilliput Press, 1996.
McCullagh, David. *De Valera: Rise, 1882–1932*. Dublin: Gill Books, 2017.

MacDowell, Vincent. *Michael Collins and the Irish Republican Brotherhood.* Dublin: Blackhall Publishing, 1997.
McKenna, Kathleen Napoli. *A Dáil Girl's Revolutionary Recollections.* Dublin: Original Writing Ltd, 2014.
Maher, Jim. *The Oath is Dead and Gone.* Dublin: Londubh Books, 2011.
Murphy, Brian P. *John Chartres: Mystery Man of the Treaty.* Dublin: Irish Academic Press, 1995.
Ó Broin, Leon. *In Great Haste: The Letters of Michael Collins and Kitty Kiernan.* Dublin: Gill & Macmillan, 1984.
Ó Broin, Leon. *Revolutionary Underground: The Story of the Irish Republican Brotherhood, 1858–1924.* Dublin: Gill & Macmillan, 1976.
O'Connor, Frank. *The Big Fellow: Michael Collins and the Irish Revolution.* London: Corgi Books, 1969.
O'Connor, Ulick. *Oliver St. John Gogarty: A Poet and His Times.* London: Jonathan Cape, 1964.
O'Farrell, Fergus. *Cathal Brugha.* Dublin: University College Dublin Press, 2018.
O'Hegarty, P.S. *The Victory of Sinn Féin.* Dublin: University College Dublin Press, 2015.
O'Malley, Ernie. *The Singing Flame.* Dublin: Anvil Books, 1978.
Ó Muirthile, Seán. *History of the IRB.* Manuscript. Archives Department, University College Dublin.
Pakenham, Frank. *Peace by Ordeal: An Account, from First-Hand Sources, of the Negotiation and Signature of the Anglo-Irish Treaty, 1921.* London: Jonathan Cape, 1935.
Ring, Jim. *Erskine Childers.* London: John Murray, 1996.
Ryan, Desmond. *Michael Collins and the Invisible Army.* Dublin: Anvil Books, 1968.
Talbot, Hayden. *Michael Collins' Own Story.* London: Hutchinson, 1922.
Taylor, A.J.P., ed. *Lloyd George: A Diary by Frances Stevenson.* London: Hutchinson, 1971.
The Treaty Debates. Houses of the Oireachtas. https://www.oireachtas.ie/en/visit-and-learn/centenaries/treaty-debates/explore-the-treaty-debates/
Townshend, Charles. *The Partition: Ireland Divided, 1885–1925.* London: Allen Lane, 2021.
Walsh, Maurice. *Bitter Freedom: Ireland in a Revolutionary World, 1918–1923.* London: Faber & Faber, 2015.
Wilkinson, Burke. *The Zeal of the Convert: The Life of Erskine Childers.* Washington: Robert B. Luce, 1976.
Wilson, Trevor, ed. *The Political Diaries of C. P. Scott, 1911–1928.* London: Collins, 1970.
Younger, Calton. *Arthur Griffith.* Dublin: Gill & Macmillan, 1981.

Jonathan White as Prime Minister David Lloyd George delivering an ultimatum to the Irish delegation in *The Treaty*, in the Kevin Barry Rooms at the National Concert Hall, Dublin.
(R to L, Karen Ardiff, Ian Toner, Patrick Moy, Shadaan Felfeli, Simon O'Gorman, Jonathan White, Ali White and Camille Lucy Ross.) ©Photo by Ste Murray

Haughey|Gregory

Haughey|Gregory was first presented by Fishamble: The New Play Company on 8 February 2018 on the Abbey Theatre's Peacock Stage, and subsequently toured nationally, including to Mountjoy Prison, Croke Park and Leinster House, with the following cast:

Barry	Peter Coonan / Michael Glenn Murphy
Tony Gregory	Ruairí Heading
Charles Haughey	Morgan C. Jones
Eileen	Janet Moran
Liam	Jonathan White
DJ (voice recorded)	Larry Gogan

Directed by	Conall Morrison
Costumes designed by	Joan O'Clery
Sound designed by	Ivan Birthistle and Vincent Doherty
Dramaturgy by	Gavin Kostick
Hair & make-up designed by	Val Sherlock
Produced by	Eva Scanlan

Haughey|Gregory was commissioned by Fishamble: The New Play Company and developed with support from NIC 2020, Maureen O'Sullivan TD, ASTI, and the Croke Park Community Fund.

Characters

In Summerhill Parade:
Tony Gregory
Barry
Liam
Eileen

In Fianna Fáil:
Charles Haughey
P.J. Mara
Bertie Ahern
Des Traynor
Martin Mansergh
Desmond O'Malley
George Colley
Martin O'Donoghue

Others:
Garret FitzGerald
Worker Jane
Worker Bob
Worker Joe
Mrs O'Donoghue
Newsreader
City Manager
Corporation Official
The Consultant
Returning Officer
Ceann Comhairle (Speaker)
Reporters
Bartender
Photographer
Haughey's Secretary
Government Official
Dáil Chorus
DJ

The cast play multiple roles. In the original production, roles were allocated amongst a cast of five as follows:

Tony Gregory; Desmond O'Malley

Barry; Bertie Ahern; Des Traynor; George Colley; Worker Joe; Reporter One; Photographer; Dáil Chorus

Liam; Corporation Official; P.J. Mara; Martin O'Donoghue; Worker Bob; Martin Mansergh; Garret FitzGerald; Ceann Comhairle; Reporter Two

Eileen; City Manager; Newsreader; Reporter; Bartender; Worker Jane; Mrs O'Donoghue; Haughey's Secretary; Government Official; Dáil Chorus

Charles Haughey; Returning Officer; The Consultant

The Dáil is the Irish parliament.

A TD (Teachta Dála) is a member of the Irish parliament.

The taoiseach is the Irish prime minister.

Fianna Fáil and Fine Gael are the leading parties in Irish politics, dating back to the civil war split in the republican movement.

The 'Stickies' are Sinn Féin The Workers' Party, previously known as Official Sinn Féin.

As a loose guide to the play's historical accuracy, characters with surnames are real people, though their actions and words are imagined; the other characters are fictionalised, based on a wider group of real people. Where dates are signalled, the chronology is accurate.

The stage consists of three desk areas: stage right, a cheap, old table and chairs, with a bare lightbulb overhead; stage left, a plush desk and chair; upstage centre, the secretary's desk with a typewriter and radio. Telephones on each desk. On or beside the secretary's desk, an overhead projector. A mic stand stage front. All are 1970s or 1980s vintage. Projected on the back wall (from the overhead projector), the titles:

BASED ON A TRUE STORY

On the radio as the audience enters: the **DJ** *counts down the charts of July 30, 1978, culminating in* You're the One That I Want, *by John Travolta and Olivia Newton-John.*

The radio is used throughout, with bursts of music between scenes and songs fading up again during a scene where there is dumb-show action. Songs may be introduced by the DJ where useful.

As the audience settles, Eileen handwrites on the acetate the word 'loosely', so that the projected titles now read:

LOOSELY BASED ON A TRUE STORY

She places a new acetate on the projector. She writes on it (or has already done so) the location and date of the first scene. This device continues throughout.

Dublin Corporation – August 1, 1978

The **Corporation Official** *steps up to the microphone.*

Corporation Official (*to audience*)   Em, thank you all for coming. I'll just, eh, hand you over now to, eh, the City Manager.

City Manager   Thank you, Seán. I'm very pleased to be announcing today that the Inner City Committee of Dublin Corporation has decided to proceed with the Development Plan for Dublin. This will allow us to take immediate steps to regenerate the urban fabric of the North Inner City – a place which, as you all know, has for decades been *blighted* by urban decay. The housing stock has long been falling into disrepair. It is neither viable nor desirable to refurbish it further.

Accordingly, we will be starting immediately on de-tenanting these buildings. As soon as the de-tenanting is done, we will be able to proceed with revitalising the streetscape and environment: there will be parkland, pitches, playgrounds . . . wider streets . . . car parking . . . and, of course, the Inner City relief route motorway, so we can all get into the city centre more comfortably . . .

The first stage in this process will be to demolish the existing nineteenth century housing – (*As if ridiculous.*) you know, some of it even dates from the eighteenth century . . .

A little laugh.

We'll be doing this at Foley Street, Gardiner Street, Corporation Street and Summerhill. All told, we will be knocking approximately 700 flats, to be replaced with high- quality, modern town houses . . . Sixty of them.

(*Aside.*) Those tenants not rehoused will get priority on the housing list, of course.

(*Wrapping up.*) I expect trees to be growing on Summerhill in five years . . . Thank you. I'll take your questions.

On the radio: Heart of Glass, *by Blondie.*

Lourdes Hall, Sean MacDermott Street – March 1, 1979

Barry *steps up to the microphone.*

Barry (*to audience*)   Eh, tanks for coming. I'll, eh – The, eh, the chairman of the North Centre City Community Action Project –

Liam   The N treble-C A P.

Barry   Eh, Kneecap – Tony Gregory.

Gregory *takes a last, nervous look at his notes as he approaches the microphone.*

Gregory   Go raibh míle maith agaibh, a chairde, as a bheith linn / don crinniú seo inniú.

Barry   Tony! In *English*!

Gregory *glares at him.*

Gregory   We're here today to talk about housing . . . There are 5,815 families on the housing list of Dublin Corporation at present.

He grows in confidence as he continues. He is unpolished, but has a natural charisma.

2,407 families are currently sharing with other families – many of them young married couples, starting families – marriages that don't last, sometimes, because of the strain of bringing up kids when there's no room for them . . .

Another two and a half thousand families have no private bathroom . . . Some of them don't even have a *toilet* in the flat – they have to use a bucket at night so as not to have to send the kids out into the corridor . . .

I know many of you know what this is like first hand. I know you don't want to be given a house somewhere miles away. You want to live *here*, where your families have lived for generations, in this community . . .

The Corporation talks about 'revitalising' the 'urban fabric' – with its motorway and multi-storey car park. But who's going to use them? *You*'re not. You're going to be 'de- tenanted'.

We in the North Centre City Community Action / Project –

Barry (*reflexively*) Kneecap.

Liam (*insistent*)   The N treble-C A P.

Gregory   We are here today to launch our Alternative Housing Plan – a plan that will house 2,250 people *here*, in the centre city.

But the Plan is not enough. Because, on its own, the Corporation won't pay it any attention. We have to force them to listen to us . . . We're going to have a sit-down protest . . . On Gardiner Street . . . At rush hour. This Friday, 5pm – when they're all trying to get back to their nice homes in the suburbs. I hope you'll all join us.

On the radio: Oliver's Army, *by Elvis Costello and The Attractions.*

The NCCCAP, Summerhill Parade – April, 1979

For the news reports, **Eileen** *becomes the* **Newsreader** *and her desk the news desk.*

Barry *and* **Liam** *are boisterous, celebrating;* **Gregory** *is working at the table, pensive.*

Newsreader   Dublin Corporation has today announced significant changes to the Development Plan for Dublin, following local opposition to the plan which saw an activist jailed after a sit-down protest on Gardiner Street.

Barry (*singing* The Internationale)
  Arise, ye workers from your slumber,
  Arise, ye prisoners of want.

Liam *joins in.*

Barry *and* **Liam**   For reason in revolt now thunders,
  And at last ends the age of cant!

Barry   Free the Dublin 1!

Liam (*laughing*)   The Dublin 1!

Barry (*laughing*)   'Dublin 1' – geddit, Tony?

(*Gesturing to the place.*) Dublin 1.

(*Pointing to* **Liam**.) The Dublin 1.

Liam (*singing*)   So comrades, come rally,
  And the last fight let us face . . .

Barry *and* **Liam**   The Internationale
  Unites the human race.

Gregory   What's next?

Liam *launches into the song* Part of the Union, *by The Strawbs.*

Barry *joins him.*

Gregory (*turning back to his work*)   Jesus.

Liam   Jesus would ye enjoy the fuckin' win.

Gregory (*contemptuous*)   The 'win'. We've had *one win*, Liam. But we have to beat them *every time*. They only have to beat us once, and everything we've fought for is undone. They'll be back with this development plan – or more like it. More motorways running through our community . . . More housing being bulldozed . . . More families being de-tenanted . . .

Barry   And we'll *fight* them!

Liam   Mobilise people.

Barry   On the streets.

Liam   In the community.

Gregory   It's not enough.

Barry   Enough for *what*?

Gregory   To make a difference.

Liam   It *has* / made a difference –

Gregory   A *sustainable* difference. A difference in how things are run. Not just *campaigns*, not just *blocking* things – but getting our hands on the levers of power.

Barry   Listen to him! You'd think he wanted to run for the Corpo!

They laugh. Until **Liam** *realises* –

Liam   He does want to run.

Barry (*horrified*)   You're / joking –

Gregory (*dead straight*)   The local elections are a couple of months away. We have a platform, now. A profile. We've had a win. We can build on it.

Barry   Build what – an *empire*?

Gregory   Spare me the claptrap, Barry.

Liam (*to* **Barry**)   Hang on – hear him out.

(*Probing.*) Build what?

Gregory   A movement.

Barry   This *is* a movement. A *community* movement.

Gregory   A *political* movement. One that can win seats.

Barry (*suspicious*)   Seats –

Liam (*testing*)   In the Corpo?

Gregory   Or the Dáil, maybe.

Barry Well you'd better go out and get yourself a silk fucking scarf then, if you want to be a TD. And a posh car for your / free fucking parking.

Liam Hear him out!

(*To* **Gregory**.) What use are seats? The system is stacked against us.

Gregory Maybe it's not that black and white. Maybe there are people on the *in*side of politics who want to do things. Good things. But they don't have the political support. Maybe if we had someone on the inside, we could help catalyse that.

Barry Ah this is fucking revisionism.

Gregory Think about it! You, on the outside, in the Project – protesting and lobbying. And me on the inside – your voice in the Corporation chamber – your voice in the back rooms where the decisions are made.

Barry And you supposedly a socialist! Where did you get this reformist rubbish?

Gregory Could you leave off the orthodoxy for even a moment?

Beat.

Barry (*a concession*) Look, if what you want is to *use* the electoral system to make a point about politics, there's something we could do . . .

Gregory Yeh?

Barry We could run a joke candidate.

Gregory Ah if you're not even going to / make an effort –

Barry Like whatshisface – Kermit –

Gregory Kermit?

Liam The frog?

Barry The Muppet . . . If we got people to vote for a muppet, it would show how alientated people are / from the system.

Liam You can't just run a muppet for election.

Barry They're *all* muppets running for election. The Dáil? It's the fucking Muppet Show.

Liam You have to be a real person / to run for election –

Barry We'll get someone to change their name –

Gregory (*disbelieving*) To 'Kermit'.

Barry By deed poll.

Liam To 'Kermit' or 'Kermit the Frog'?

Barry Kermit-the-Frog Gregory – like Dublin-Bay Loftus.

Gregory Ah this is bullshit.

Barry No *this* is bullshit. Look at the people you're talking about working with – Fianna Fáil – Fine Gael – one more reactionary than the other! Emigration gets rid of the dissidents, they use the Church to shut up those who remain and they co-opt anybody who's left by convincing them the country depends on international capital to survive.

Gregory What use is it theorising ourselves out of power? The levers of power are held by politicians – the decisions about money, legislation, services, housing. Why would you remove yourself from that?

Barry Because it's *corrupt*.

Gregory *Party* politics is corrupt. But I could run as an Independent – a community candidate.

Liam We have a platform already – as community *activists*. Politics is a very different route. It's elitist. People don't feel the same about politicians as about activists . . . We're growing participation here, building capacity. It's *slow* – but we're making headway. Turn ourselves into a political movement, we jeopardise all of that.

Gregory One stroke of a bureaucrat's pen through a budget line and this Project – all our work – is gone. Having someone elected will help protect it.

Barry What happened to the fucking revolution, Tony?

Gregory I don't want to spend my life waiting for it.

Beat.

I can't do it without you.

No response. **Gregory** *leaves.* **Liam** *looks after him.* **Barry** *looks at* **Liam**.

Barry You're not going to support him on this fuckin' ego trip.

Liam *shrugs.*

Barry He'll just be one voice like all the rest – drowned out in the mud-slinging – scrabbling for crumbs of media time so his voters remember he's alive.

Liam Maybe he'll be different.

He leaves. **Eileen** *has entered, ignored or unseen by* **Barry**. *She is chewing gum.*

Eileen (*impatient*) Excuse me?

Barry (*intemperate*)   What?

Eileen The job.

Barry (*dismissive, forgetting*)   What job?

Eileen The job in the fuckin' window. Jesus.

Barry Was that how they taught you to apply for jobs in school?

Eileen You miss careers guidance if you leave after your Inter. Do you need a secretary or don't you?

He appraises her.

Barry Why do you want to work here?

Eileen 'Cause me ma said 'Go out and get yourself a fuckin' job'.

Barry With that attitude, I'm surprised you haven't had any luck.

Eileen I thought I *had* a job. In the presbytery. But Father O'Sullivan kept saying, 'You're so good, Eileen', and there was no sign of him paying me. And eventually I copped on he thought I was just helping him out of the goodness of me fuckin' heart.

Barry And did you talk like this with Father O'Sullivan?

Eileen Do you think I'm fuckin' stupid?

I thought yiz were all *activists* in here – why are *you* so square?

Barry (*spotting something*) Are you interested in activism?

Eileen I'm interested in anything that'll pay me a fair wage at the end of the week . . . But if it helps change this kip, that's a bonus.

Barry Can you type?

Eileen I done a typing course.

Barry That's not the same thing.

Eileen I can type better than your current secretary.

Barry We don't have a secretary.

Eileen There you go.

He gives her the nod. She moves to the desk, turns on the radio, and starts to sort papers, etc.

On the radio: Tainted Love *by Soft Cell.*

Eileen (*to audience*) So I got the job. And Tony was elected to the Corporation . . . I was secretary to the *Project* – the North Centre City Community Action Project, Kneecap.

Liam The N treble-C A P!

Eileen but Tony used to come in and get me to do his typing for him. Which was grand, as long as that didn't clash with my duties / here at the Project.

Barry What's that?

Eileen (*caught*) It's Tony's typing.

Barry And have you done the typing I gave you?

Eileen Tony said this was urgent.

Barry (*shouting*)   Tony!

Gregory (*entering*)   Ah what are you moaning about now.

Barry   I'm trying to run a fuckin' project here –

Gregory   And I'm trying to build a political movement –

Barry   And your 'movement' does not take precedence over this Project.

Gregory   It's just a letter –

Barry   It's *always* a fucking letter – when I need to get letters out.

Gregory   I'm trying to get a bathroom for Mrs Lillis –

Barry (*escalating*)   Don't get self-righteous with me! / We got you elected.

Gregory   Don't be so high-handed! / Do you want me to –

Eileen (*intervening*)   I'll do it in me *lunch break*. Jesus. I'll get it all done.

They back down.

Eileen (*to audience*)   The only other thing was . . . Tony was a bit tight with the headed notepaper – he only ever left enough for the exact amount of letters . . . so I went through a lot of Tippex . . .

Gregory *collects his letter. He examines it closely, rubbing his hand over a bit of Tippex and then spotting an error.*

Gregory   That should be a *semi*-colon.

Eileen   Wha'?

Gregory (*pointing it out*)   See.

Eileen (*'whatever'*)   Yeh.

Gregory   If we don't write clearly, we can't think clearly. And if we can't think clearly, we can't change anything.

Eileen (*a routine*)   Yes, Tony.

(*To audience.*) In December that year, 1979, Jack Lynch resigned as taoiseach. George Colley was the favourite to replace him, but he was beaten in the leadership race by . . . Charles Haughey So Charlie became taoiseach The media *hated* him . . .

Chorus of Reporters   Taoiseach! Mr Haughey!

Reporter One   Mr Haughey, you have considerable wealth, the source of which has never been disclosed. / Would you like to disclose that now?

Haughey   I would not necessarily assume that I am a wealthy man, if I were you. Ask my accountant.

Reporter Two   Mr Haughey, do you feel you have now been fully rehabilitated since your reported involvement in the smuggling of arms to the IRA in 1970?

Haughey That is very much now a matter for history. I am leaving it to the historians.

Reporter Two Will you *help* the historians write the history?

Haughey I will write my own.

Eileen And Fine Gael – they *really* hated Charlie.

FitzGerald Deputy Haughey's motives have been widely impugned . . .

Eileen Garret FitzGerald.

FitzGerald even by people within his own party. They have attributed to him an overweening ambition which they see as a wish to dominate, even to *own* the State. Deputy Haughey comes with a flawed pedigree.

Eileen No sooner had Charlie taken over, but he came on the telly – to talk to us directly . . .

Haughey I wish to talk to you this evening about the state of the nation's affairs . . . The picture is not, unfortunately, a very cheerful one . . . As a community we are living a way beyond our means. This cannot possibly continue.

Eileen In May 1981, Charlie called a general election. He lost narrowly to Garret, who put together a minority government relying on support from Independents . . .

Then Garret found a big hole in the public finances, and he and John Bruton, the finance minister, decided we needed an austerity budget. They put VAT on children's shoes –

FitzGerald (*defensive*) Not charging VAT on children's shoes was unfair. Some women have smaller feet, and therefore they were able to buy children's shoes for themselves – VAT-free! It had to be stopped.

Eileen The Independents pulled their support and, in January 1982 – just seven months after it was formed – Garret's government collapsed . . . all because of / the VAT on children's shoes.

FitzGerald (*insistent*) But the idea that my government collapsed *because* of the VAT on children's shoes is erroneous. The actual reason was because of a change to food subsidies / which antagonised the Independent TD Jim Kemmy –

Eileen Whatever. There was another general election. And Tony ran.

Dublin Central Count Centre, Bolton St – February 19, 1982

Gregory *is closely watching the count. His right wrist is in plaster. He holds a clipboard.* **Liam** *joins him.*

Newsreader And now the latest from the election count . . . Fianna Fáil appear to be ahead on first preferences, but it's not yet clear if they will have enough of a lead to form a government . . . In Dublin Central, Bertie Ahern appears to have topped the poll; his transfers will be crucial in deciding the rest of the seats there. One of those watching those transfers most anxiously will be the Independent candidate, Tony Gregory.

Gregory (*pointing to the figures*)   Is that *all* we got in Summerhill?

Liam   According to the tally.

Gregory (*disbelieving*)   And in Gardiner Street?

Liam (*reassuring*)   There's still plenty of boxes to open. (*Checking his figures.*) Drumcondra . . . Glasnevin . . . Clontarf . . .

Gregory (*contemptuous*)   You think they like me in the leafy suburbs?

Liam   Maybe this is a longer-term project.

Barry *arrives, carrying a letter.*

Gregory   We saved these people's houses! What do we have to do to get their votes?

Barry   I just got a letter at the Project . . . From the Department of Social Welfare.

Liam *takes the letter.*

Barry   They're closing us down. Withdrawing our funding. As of the end of March.

Liam   They can't do that!

Barry   They're doing it. The cunts.

(*To* **Gregory**.) They're targeting us – I told you this was a mistake.

Gregory (*to* **Liam**)   Show me those numbers again.

He immerses himself in the clipboard data, amidst glances at the ongoing count.

On the radio: Arise and Follow Charlie, *by The Morrisseys.*

Home of Charles J. Haughey, Abbeville, Kinsealy

Haughey *is following the news.* **P.J. Mara** *and* **Bertie Ahern** *arrive.* **Ahern** *scribbles figures on a notepad.*

Newsreader   As the count progresses, Fianna Fáil's lead in the general election appears to be tightening. It's now too close to call between the possible alternative governments of Charles Haughey's Fianna Fáil and a Fine Gael-Labour coalition led by Garret FitzGerald.

Haughey (*contemptuous*)   'Garret the Good' . . .

Mara   We're up on last year. Two per cent, maybe three.

Haughey   They tried to tax children's shoes for fuck's sake, Mara! We should be up *more*.

Ahern (*sniping*)   It was the campaign – we weren't prepared. We should have / been anticipating it.

Mara (*sniping back*)   *Nobody* was prepared, Bertie – it was a freak election.

Haughey   O'Malley and his fucking hyenas – they'll come for me.

Ahern   It's early days yet, Boss.

Newsreader   With a number of constituencies still to declare, it's looking increasingly likely that this election will produce a hung Dáil . . .

(*Taking a feed from her ear-piece.*) Oh, I think we have a result now in Dublin Central, where there are two seats still to be decided . . . We'll go live now to the count . . .

Count Centre – February 20

Returning Officer   The results of the tenth count in Dublin Central, following the distribution of Luke Belton's vote.

Newsreader   There are three contenders now for the last two seats . . .

Returning Officer   Michael O'Leary . . .

Newsreader   The leader of the Labour Party.

Returning Officer   499 votes, giving him 6,511.

Newsreader   That should put O'Leary over the line.

Returning Officer   Alice Glenn . . .

Newsreader   Fine Gael.

Returning Officer   351 votes, giving her 5,412.

Newsreader   That may not be enough. All eyes now are on the young Tony Gregory.

Returning Officer   Tony Gregory . . .

Newsreader   The Independent community candidate.

Returning Officer   1,182 votes, giving him 7,737.

Cheering from **Barry** *and* **Liam**.

Returning Officer   Alice Glenn is thereby eliminated. I declare Michael O'Leary and Tony Gregory elected.

Liam   Where's your muppet now, eh?

Barry   Fuck Kermit – we have a fuckin' TD!

They burst into song, picking **Gregory** *up as they do so and hoisting him onto their shoulders.*

Barry/Liam *Arise, ye workers from your slumber . . .*

Gregory Put me down!

Barry/Liam *Arise, ye prisoners of want . . .*

Gregory I'll see you later.

He heads for the exit.

Barry (*disbelieving*) Where are you going?

Gregory (*as he leaves*) Offaly.

Barry (*going after him*) Tony!

Liam *holds him back.*

Liam Leave him.

Barry But what the fuck's in *Offaly*?

Liam His mother's grave.

Kinsealy

Haughey *is working at his desk – making lists, doing sums.*

Newsreader It has been a difficult election for Charles Haughey. Not only has he apparently failed to win a majority, but a number of anti-Haughey members of Fianna Fáil have taken seats formerly held by Haughey supporters . . . In Dublin West, Haughey critic Liam Lawlor has taken the Fianna Fáil seat from Haughey's sister in law, Eileen Lemass . . .

Haughey (*growling*) Lawlor!

Newsreader In Kildare, Charlie McCreevy, who was expelled from Fianna Fáil after calling Haughey 'unfit to lead', has topped the poll.

Haughey McCreevy!

Newsreader And in Carlow-Kilkenny, the Fianna Fáil seat has been taken by Jim Gibbons . . .

Haughey At least Gibbons has the guts to stab me in the front.

Newsreader In Dublin Central, George Colley, Haughey's opponent in the leadership race, has been comfortably elected . . . Martin O'Donoghue, who was dropped from the front bench by Mr Haughey, has been returned in Dun Laoghaire . . .

Haughey The barbarians are at the gate . . .

He starts dialling.

Newsreader And in Limerick East, George Colley's close associate, Desmond O'Malley, topped the poll.

Haughey (*on phone*) Bertie! This is going to mean a heave . . . Start phoning around. Take the temperature . . . Tell Mara to move the parliamentary party meeting forward – to Thursday. Let's lance this boil.

On the radio: The Lion Sleeps Tonight, *by Tight Fit.*

Office of Desmond O'Malley TD

Desmond O'Malley *dials a number.* **Mrs O'Donoghue** *answers one of the other phones.*

Mrs O'Donoghue O'Donoghue's, hello?

O'Malley Desmond O'Malley here, Mrs O'Donoghue – is Martin there?

Mrs O'Donoghue He's just gone out, Desmond . . .

O'Malley *curses silently.*

Mrs O'Donoghue He said he'd be back shortly. I'll ask him to call.

O'Malley Please do, Mrs O'Donoghue, thank you.

He goes to hang up.

Mrs O'Donoghue I hope the family are all well, Desmond.

At some point during the following, **George Colley** *picks up another phone and dials, but get an engaged tone and hangs up in frustration. He thinks, and then rings another number, with the same result.*

O'Malley Very well, thank you Mrs O'Donoghue. Good / night now.

Mrs O'Donoghue And your mother.

O'Malley Yes, indeed, thank God. I'll say good / night now.

Mrs O'Donoghue I always say it's the family elections are hardest on.

O'Malley Yes, of course. Absolutely. I'll / say good night now.

Mrs O'Donoghue The nerves. It is agonising.

O'Malley It must be. I / should be going now.

Mrs O'Donoghue Oh it is. I mean, Martin gets nervous, of course, but me, I can barely / stand it.

O'Malley Indeed, Mrs O'Donoghue. Well, please ask him to call me. / Goodbye.

Mrs O'Donoghue I will of course, Desmond.

O'Malley (*trying to hang up*) Good bye now.

Mrs O'Donoghue Good bye, Desmond.

O'Malley Bye.

Mrs O'Donoghue Bye now, Desmond . . . Bye. Bye.

O'Malley Bye.

O'Malley *finally gets the phone down and immediately dials again.*

Colley *answers instantly.*

Colley Colley.

O'Malley George.

Colley Desmond!

O'Malley Yes.

Colley I've been trying to get you.

O'Malley I was talking to Mrs O'Donoghue.

Colley Jesus, this is no time for chatting. We should be organising.

Martin O'Donoghue *arrives home. His conversation with his wife overlaps with that of* **O'Malley** *and* **Colley** *on the phone.*

Mrs O'Donoghue Martin – Desmond O'Malley was looking for you.

Colley What does Martin think?

O'Donoghue What did he say it was about?

O'Malley He wasn't in.

Mrs O'Donoghue He didn't say.

Colley What do you think?

O'Donoghue I'll call Colley first.

O'Malley This is two election failures in a row. We'll never win an overall majority with Haughey as leader.

During the following, **O'Donoghue** *calls* **Colley**, *but fails to get through. He hangs up and tries* **O'Malley** *– and fails.*

O'Malley The country doesn't trust him. He's a cancer.

Colley There's never been a leadership contest at a time like this.

O'Malley There may never be a time like this again! If he puts together a deal that makes him taoiseach, he'll be unmovable.

Colley Who's going to stand against him.

O'Malley Me . . .? You . . .? Martin . . .? *Any* of us.

Colley I need to talk to Martin. I'll call you back.

He hangs up and dials. **Martin** *answers.*

O'Donoghue O'Donoghue.

Colley Martin – George.

O'Donoghue Finally! Where have you been?

Colley On the phone!

O'Donoghue Jesus, George, this is no time for chatting. I've been trying to get you.

Colley You're the one who went out!

O'Donoghue (*on a tangent*) Here – imagine if, when you wanted to phone someone, you just phoned *them*, instead of their house or office – and they'd have their own phone *on them*.

Colley What?

O'Donoghue Never mind –

Colley Don't talk fucking nonsense. Now, which of us is going to move against Haughey?

Summerhill Parade – February 21

Newsreader We now have the final results of the 1982 general election.

During the news, **Gregory** *starts doing the sums on the overhead projector. He writes '83' at the top and circles it. Next: three empty columns, headed 'Charlie', 'Garret' and 'Others'.*

Newsreader Charles Haughey's Fianna Fáil have won 81 seats – just two short of an overall majority.

Gregory *writes '81' in the Charlie column.*

Newsreader Garret FitzGerald's Fine Gael have won 63 seats and the Labour Party 15, giving a Fine Gael-Labour coalition 78 seats – three short of Fianna Fáil.

He writes the sum in the Garret column.

Newsreader That means the next government will likely be decided by the smaller political groupings: the three TDs of Sinn Féin The Workers' Party

He writes 'Stickies x 3' in the Others column.

Newsreader and the four Independents. The Independents are the outgoing Ceann Comhairle, Dr John O'Connell;

He writes their surnames in the Others column.

Newsreader   the former Fianna Fáil TD, Neil Blaney; the former Labour TD, Jim Kemmy; and, in Dublin Central, the young community activist, Tony Gregory.

Gregory *steps back to ponder it.*

Eileen (*joining them, excited*)   What do we do now?

Gregory   A pot of tea would be great, Eileen.

Liam   O'Connell will likely be Ceann Comhairle again, so he won't vote.

Barry *steps up to the projector and strikes out* **O'Connell***'s name.*

Liam   Blaney's basically Fianna Fáil.

Barry *strikes out Blaney's name and adds '+1' to the Charlie total.*

Liam   Jim Kemmy's ex-Labour.

Barry   But he just brought down the last government.

Liam   He could never vote for Haughey.

Barry *strikes out Kemmy's name and adds '+1' to the Garret total.*

Barry   Three votes in it.

Liam   So if the Stickies go for Garret . . .

Barry *strikes out 'Stickies' and adds '+3' to the Garret total. He does the sums: each column totals 82. Just one name is left in the Others column: 'Gregory'.* **Barry** *circles it.*

Liam   Fuck.

Barry   Jesus.

Gregory   So, lads. Do you still think I shouldn't have run?

On the radio: Party Fears Two, *by The Associates.*

Kinsealy

Haughey (*on phone*)   First things first, Mara. If we don't crush this heave, I won't be here to do a deal with Gregory. (*He hangs up.*)

Haughey's Secretary   Mr Haughey? Mr Traynor is here for your weekly meeting.

She shows **Des Traynor** *in.*

Haughey   Ah.

(*Shaking hands.*) Good news or bad news, Traynor?

Traynor   Well, the election fundraising went well.

Haughey   Good –

Traynor   But . . . your own account is . . . a bit bare . . .

Haughey Overdraft?

Traynor About a hundred and twenty five. Thousand.

Haughey That's up.

Traynor Considerably.

Haughey Why?

Traynor Eh, well, eh, you're living beyond your means, Boss.

Haughey I thought that was my line, Traynor.

Traynor (*trying again*) There's too much going out . . . And not enough coming in.

Haughey Isn't that your job?

Traynor There's only so much I can do, Boss . . . I took in fifty-three grand last month. I'm expecting a similar . . . contribution . . . in the next few weeks. That should tide you over. But the bank are . . . anxious . . .

Haughey About what?

Traynor About your loans.

Haughey What's the urgency?

Traynor *hesitates.*

Haughey Spit it out, Traynor.

Traynor As long as you're leader, well . . . they wouldn't want to rock the boat . . . But . . .

Haughey Do you think I'm not going to be leader, Traynor?

Traynor (*backpedalling*) I didn't say that, Boss. / That's not what I meant.

Haughey You think these plotters are smarter than I am?

Traynor I / don't think that.

Haughey More *popular*?

Traynor I just said / the bank was anxious.

Haughey No party in its right mind would throw out a leader who's about to be elected taoiseach. And I'm about to be elected taoiseach again, Traynor.

Traynor But the numbers, Boss. O'Malley's people / are moving.

Haughey I'll *have* the numbers, Traynor.

Traynor Yes, Boss.

Suddenly emollient, offering his hand.

Haughey Thank you as always for your good – and important – work, Mr Traynor. You just keep things ticking over.

Traynor Yes, Boss.

Haughey And make sure your contacts are reassured – I'm going to be taoiseach again. Very soon.

On the radio: I Won't Let You Down Again, *by Matthew Perryman Jones.*

Summerhill Parade

Barry *is pacing, excitedly.* **Gregory** *is brooding.* **Liam** *is nervy.*

Newsreader With Sinn Féin The Workers' Party refusing to say who they will support for taoiseach, all eyes now are on the young Dublin Central Independent, Tony Gregory. Days ago, he was an unknown councillor. Today, he holds the balance of power. As yet, he has given no indication of who he intends to support – Garret FitzGerald or Charles Haughey.

Barry This is *it*. The fucking revolution.

The phone rings. **Eileen** *answers.*

Eileen The North Centre City Community Action –

(*Interrupted.*) Yes, Kneecap.

Liam N treble-C A P!

Eileen Yes, Tony Gregory works from here.

Barry (*ignoring the phone*) We can bring the whole thing down . . . Expose it for the sham that it is.

Eileen Ah hah.

Gregory So . . . Haughey or FitzGerald . . .

Eileen (*hanging up*) Thank you for calling.

Gregory What a choice . . .

Eileen (*making a note*) The Corpo's Works Department is letting people go. She wants us to try and save her son's job.

Liam A gangster capitalist . . .

The phone rings.

Barry Or a reactionary imperialist . . .

The phone calls continue in parallel to the dialogue between the three men, who barely notice **Eileen**'s *comments on the phone or to them.*

Eileen The North Centre City – (*Interrupted.*) Well, yes, Tony Gregory's office. What can I help you with?

Barry You're going to have to protect yourself.

Liam How does he do that?

Eileen Contraception?

Barry Don't get into bed with either of them.

Eileen I think you need to talk to your doctor about that, love.

Barry Why should we accept the choices that the establishment forces on us?

Eileen Oh. I see.

Barry We don't have to play their games.

Eileen (*hanging up*) Thank you, love. Bye.

(*Making a note.*) She thinks we should be able to get condoms without a prescription.

The phone rings.

Gregory What would that get us?

Barry A bit of dignity.

Eileen Tony Gregory's office, hello.

Gregory If I'm not supposed to vote for a taoiseach, what the hell am I supposed to do?

Barry Do what you were elected to do – represent people. Help fix their problems. Help them mobilise.

Eileen Uh huh.

Gregory And how am I supposed to do that if I'm entirely on my own?

Barry The way we've always done it.

Eileen (*hanging up*) Thank you.

Barry By making noise. Agitating. Speaking out.

Eileen (*making a note*) The Summerhill flats tenants' group wants us to get them bathrooms.

Gregory That's a crap idea.

Liam Why does it have to be one or the other – why can't we combine with others who share our values?

The phone rings.

Eileen (*posh*) Office of Tony Gregory, TD.

Barry Who shares our values?

Eileen The army?

Liam The Stickies.

Gregory The fucking Stickies.

Barry But the bang-bang stuff!

Eileen Sorry, who's beating up who?

Barry There's too much bad blood between Tony and the Stickies to work together.

Eileen Ah. I see.

Liam Maybe there's too much in common not to. Their policy platform is close to ours.

Eileen (*hanging up*) Thank you.

(*Making a note.*) Apparently prisoners are being abused at the military prison in the Curragh. He wants us to get it closed.

Barry Even if you could work with the Stickies – there's only three of them. What use is that?

The phone rings.

Liam If we agreed a common platform, we could bring it to FitzGerald and Haughey – we'd have more leverage.

Eileen Hello?

Gregory (*musing*) And cover.

Eileen No, I'm *not* Mr *Gregory*'s secretary – I'm the secretary to the N –

Gregory We'd be less exposed . . .

Eileen Yes . . . Alright!

(*Hanging up; making a note, bemused.*) He wants us to see if we can get the lead out of the petrol.

The phone rings.

Barry Christ!

Eileen (*answering*) Tony Gregory's office.

Liam Reach out to the Stickies.

Barry (*to* **Eileen**) What do they think this is – auction politics?

Liam Suggest a common front.

Eileen I will, yeh, missus.

Gregory A left bloc?

Eileen (*hanging up*) Thanks for taking the trouble.

Barry What does *she* want?

Eileen She's living in a one-room flat, with two kids, on Gloucester Place. No bathroom. They're on the housing list, but it's not going anywhere.

Beat.

She wants us to get her a home.

On the radio: Our House, *by Madness.*

Office of Sinn Féin The Workers' Party, Leinster House

Worker Bob *takes out Easter lily badges and sticks them to his and* **Worker Joe**'s *lapels.*

Worker Jane Right, let's get started. / I think we should –

Worker Bob Em, *before* we start / shouldn't we –

Worker Jane Can I just / say that –

Worker Bob We don't have a chairman.

Worker Jane Exactly. / I was just –

Worker Bob So how can we start?

Worker Jane Well, we should / probably elect one.

Worker Bob Are you the chairman?

Worker Jane No. / I was just

Worker Bob So how can you start the meeting?

Worker Joe She's *acting* / as chairman.

Worker Bob What?

Worker Joe Let's say she's acting chairman.

Worker Bob Did you vote for her? Was there a vote? Did I / miss a vote.

Worker Joe We don't *need* a vote / for acting chairman.

Worker Bob Is that in the standing orders?

Worker Jane Comrades, I think it's important that we make some progress / on our agenda.

Worker Bob That's why we need a chairman.

Worker Jane I propose myself as acting chairman.

Worker Joe Seconded.

Worker Jane Thank you. Are there any other nominations?

Silence.

Worker Jane Thank you comrades. I call this inaugural meeting of the Sinn Féin The Workers' Party Parliamentary Party to order. I think the first item on our agenda is / correspondence.

Worker Bob The election of a chairman.

Worker Jane We've just agreed that I'll be / the chairman.

Worker Bob The *acting* chairman. Now we have an acting chairman, we can procede to a proper election for chairman.

Worker Jane Right. Well then . . . I'd like to propose myself for chairman . . . Are there any other nominations?

Worker Bob I'd like to propose myself.

Beat.

Worker Jane Right. Well, I suppose we should have a show of hands.

Worker Bob We should have a secret ballot.

Worker Joe There's only three of us.

Worker Bob Exactly.

Worker Joe Why do we need a secret ballot?

Worker Bob The dangers of groupthink.

Worker Jane Right.

Tearing a sheet of paper into strips and handing them out.

Worker Jane Comrades, write the name of the candidate you support for the position of chairman.

(*To* **Worker Joe**.) As you're the only member not contesting, would you be Returning Officer?

Worker Joe *collects, opens and smooths the ballots and puts them in piles.*

Worker Joe I would like to declare that our acting chairman has duly been elected chairman.

Worker Bob Congratulations, Comrade.

You don't have your sticky-backed Easter lily on.

He pins one on her.

Worker Bob There now.

Worker Jane Thank you, Comrade. Comrades, as the new chairman of the Sinn Féin The Workers' Party Parliamentary Party, I would like to move on to correspondence. The first item is a letter from . . . Tony Gregory.

Beat.

Worker Joe The former comrade, Tony Gregory?

Worker Jane He wants to meet to discuss the possibility of a 'left alliance' in the new Dáil . . .

Worker Bob He's a fucking splitter.

Worker Joe He's a *dangerous* splitter – he left with Costello.

Worker Bob That didn't work out too well for Costello.

Worker Jane He didn't *join* Costello.

Worker Bob Even worse – he's a *loner*.

Worker Jane He's a *socialist*. And we find ourselves sharing the balance of power with him.

Beat.

We should meet him.

Worker Bob He's an egotist. He left us. He left the Socialist Labour Party. He left the Irish Republican Socialist Party . . . You can't advance the interests of the working class if you're not prepared to work with others.

Worker Jane If we agreed a platform with him, we could put it to FitzGerald and Haughey. Secure some real gains for the working class.

Worker Bob That's the Labour strategy – and it's destroyed them. This is the long game. We're building a working class movement. We've just made a small breakthrough getting the three of us elected. Do a deal with one of the reactionary parties now and we jeopardise that.

Worker Jane *looks to* **Worker Joe** *– he agrees with* **Worker Bob**.

Worker Jane I'll write to him declining his invitation.

Worker Bob Don't decline it!

Worker Jane But / you agreed.

Worker Bob *Accept* it!

Worker Jane You just said / this is the long game

Worker Bob We're not going to do a deal with him. But we'll *talk* to him. Keep people guessing. And keep ourselves in the news.

Kinsealy

Haughey (*on phone*) They'll use a stalking horse. He who wields the knife never wears the crown.

Ahern *enters.* **Haughey** *hangs up.* **Mara** *enters during the following.*

Haughey Right, Bertie. (*Cuing him.*) This Gregory fellow.

Ahern He's thirty-five, Boss. Scholarship boy – O'Connell's. Now a schoolteacher. Mother from a small farm in Offaly – then a waitress in Dublin. Father was a docker. They lived in a one-roomed flat in Ballybough. Moved to a house on the Canal in Sackville Gardens. Still lives there, with his brother.

Haughey Not married?

Ahern Bit of a lady's man.

Haughey *looks at him as if this is a barbed comment.*

Haughey Politics?

Ahern Republican socialist. He was in the Officials –

Haughey The fucking Stickies.

Ahern That had him kicked out of one of his first teaching jobs . . . Then Seamus Costello split from the Officials and formed the INLA, and Gregory followed him out.

Haughey He was close to Costello?

Ahern Very.

Haughey And it was the Official IRA shot Costello?

Ahern On the North Strand. A stone's throw from Gregory's house.

Haughey So there isn't a chance in hell that Gregory will do a deal with the Stickies.

Ahern You never know, Boss. He's a dark horse, Gregory.

Haughey Mara?

Mara He's an individualist. You need to split him from his group . . . Bring him out here, to Kinsealy . . . Seduce him . . .

Haughey *ponders.*

Haughey Set it up, Mara.

On the radio: Poison Arrow, *by ABC.*

Summerhill Parade – February 22

Newsreader As negotiations towards the formation of the next government continue, the Independent TD Tony Gregory today met with the Sinn Féin The Workers' Party. They have released a joint statement saying they are continuing to explore the possibility of a left alliance.

They arrive back in to the office, exhausted and frustrated.

Gregory　Reminds me of why I left the Stickies in the first place.

Barry　Well at least nobody shot anyone.

Gregory　What's next?

Eileen　Mr Haughey's coming in tonight. We're still waiting to hear back from the other one –

Liam　FitzGerald.

Barry　I'll leave you to it. I don't want to meet fucking either of them.

Gregory　We meet them together.

Barry　What's the point in me being there? I don't think we should be talking to them.

Liam　Well in fairness to FitzGerald, at least he has some kind of vision for social justice.

Barry　It's a sham! At least Haughey doesn't dress himself in self-righteousness.

Liam　Haughey just says what people want to hear. He's a populist.

Barry　That's just what people say when they disapprove of what's being said.

Liam　He nearly started a war in the North just to prove his green credentials.

Gregory　There *is* a war in the North! Or hadn't you noticed.

Liam (*escalating*)　That's not a war! It's a mindless sectarian conflict –

Barry　Fomented by your former comrades in the republican movement, Tony.

Gregory　They're fighting to free themselves from British imperialism, a / plight to which we abandoned them.

Barry　Ah that's fuckin' / nonsense.

Liam　What a load of hackneyed / claptrap.

Barry　If this is about the North, Tony / then I'm out altogether.

Gregory　It's only a hundred miles up the road!

The phone rings. **Eileen** *answers, quietly.*

Liam　It's this square mile *here* I'm worried about.

Eileen (*covering the phone*)　What's 'Kinsealy'?

Sudden silence.

Gregory　I'll take it.

Eileen (*faking it*)　I'll transfer you to Mr Gregory now.

She holds the phone out for **Gregory**. *He takes it.*

Gregory (*guarded*)　Gregory here.

Mara (*into phone*) Ah, Mr Gregory. P.J. Mara here. Mr Haughey is very much looking forward to meeting you and your team this evening . . .

Gregory (*aware of his colleagues*) Yes.

Mara I just thought – Mr *Haughey* just thought – Well, sometimes it's useful to establish a . . . rapport . . . between the principles in a negotiation . . . A certain . . . trust . . . or affinity . . . Man to man, as it were . . . We thought perhaps you might like – you might find it *useful* to meet with Mr Haughey, informally, *socially*, here at Kinsealy, this afternoon . . .

Gregory (*watching the others*) This afternoon . . .

Mara Yes . . . Just yourself . . .

Gregory Just myself . . .

Barry Are you out of your mind?

Liam No fucking *way* are you meeting him on your own.

Barry We meet them *together*.

Gregory *eyes them.*

Gregory Tell Mr Haughey we're looking forward to welcoming him to Summerhill this evening.

He hangs up. He looks at the two of them. Uneasy.

Gregory We'd better get prepared.

Barry If this becomes about you and Haughey and a United Ireland – I'm out.

Gregory It's not about a United Ireland.

Liam If we make this about the North . . . it'll split us.

Beat.

Gregory We'll park the North.

They each check to see do they trust each other.

Gregory Eileen, have you the list of the calls we've been getting? The issues?

Barry What is this, an auction?

Liam No! We can make it more than that! Not just local issues. A programme of *reform*. A *national* programme.

Office of Desmond O'Malley TD

Newsreader RTÉ News has learned that there is likely to be an attempt to remove Charles Haughey as leader of Fianna Fáil. No challenger has yet declared but the leading candidates are thought to be the former Minister for Economic Planning,

Mr Martin O'Donoghue, Haughey's former rival for the leadership, Mr George Colley and the former Minister for Industry and Commerce, Mr Desmond O'Malley.

O'Malley   A motion of no confidence will force him out.

O'Donoghue   It's too risky. It's sordid.

Colley   What if it fails?

O'Malley   It won't fail if we work together.

O'Donoghue   It'd be very damaging to the party.

O'Malley   There's no nice way of doing this.

O'Donoghue   If we know we have the numbers, why not just go to him and tell him?

O'Malley   He'll think we're bluffing.

O'Donoghue   We could bring some Haughey people with us to confront him.

O'Malley   Why would they help us?

O'Donoghue   If they see the writing on the wall.

Colley   And then?

O'Malley   A leadership contest.

Colley   Between *who*?

O'Malley   Whoever wants to.

O'Donoghue   I'd like to.

O'Malley   It might be the three of us.

Colley   It won't work.

O'Donoghue   We'll cross that hurdle when we come to it.

Colley   Why are we kicking him out, if we don't know who's going to replace him?

O'Malley   It hardly *matters* who.

Colley   It'll matter to the party. 'The devil you know . . .' We need to put a clear proposition to them. A head to head.

O'Donoghue   At the parliamentary party?

Colley   A straight vote to decide the party's nominee for taoiseach.

O'Donoghue   That's audacious.

O'Malley   It's risky.

Colley   It's clean.

Beat. They agree.

O'Donoghue So we'll need to choose a challenger.

They look at each other, warily.

Colley We can ring around. Take soundings.

O'Donoghue See who the parliamentary party prefers?

O'Malley Whoever emerges as the favourite, we all back him. No wavering.

Beat. He fixes them.

We get one shot at this. We have to take Haughey out before he does a deal that makes him taoiseach.

On the radio: Eye of the Tiger, *by Survivor.*

Summerhill Parade – February 23

Newsreader There have been further reports today that senior members of Fianna Fáil are planning to call a motion of no confidence in Charles Haughey at the parliamentary party meeting this week. The uncertainty over his leadership is believed to be jeopardising the talks on government formation.

Liam (*looking out the window*) It's him.

Barry Who's he with?

Liam (*puzzled*) No one.

Barry He drove himself?

Liam (*peering out*) No, that looks like yer man Bertie driving the car . . . But he's not coming in.

(*To the room.*) Charlie's on his own.

Haughey *enters, regally, and looks around him, taking in the poor surroundings. He spots* **Gregory**'s *wrist in plaster.*

Haughey What's wrong with your wrist?

Barry (*a dig*) He fell off a horse.

Haughey *glares.*

Gregory I fell off a ladder putting up posters.

Haughey I try to avoid putting up posters myself.

They're not sure if this is a joke. He eyes them. Long beat.

Haughey I know what I want, gentlemen. What do you want?

Eileen *hands* **Gregory** *a page; he hands it to* **Haughey**. **Haughey** *sits. He starts to read. He winces up at the bare light bulb.*

Haughey Would you not get a shade for that?

Barry We've no money.

He reads to the end. He looks at each of them.

Haughey Well, gentlemen. I think we can do business. Let me get back to you with some further proposals.

(*Afterthought.*) In the meantime – I'll send you round a lampshade.

Office of Desmond O'Malley TD – February 24

The plotters are reviewing the newspapers. **Colley** *and* **O'Donoghue** *are ecstatic.* **O'Malley** *is brooding.*

Newsreader The Irish Independent this morning has the inside story on what's being called the 'Dump Haughey Campaign'. They claim that 46 of 81 Fianna Fáil TDs are backing Desmond O'Malley against Charles Haughey – and they name most of them. Later in the programme, we'll be asking, could this spell the end of Charles Haughey's controversial leadership? And what would this mean for the formation of a government?

O'Donoghue 46!

Colley We're finally taking back the party!

O'Donoghue From the men in mohair suits.

Colley How does it feel to be the next Minister for Finance, Martin?

O'Donoghue (*mock serious*) Sobering.

O'Donoghue And you, George – Foreign Affairs?

Colley (*bowing towards* **O'Malley**) I serve at the pleasure of the party leader.

O'Donoghue Congratulations, Desmond.

O'Malley *looks up, bemused.*

Colley Our next leader.

O'Donoghue And taoiseach.

O'Malley We're fucked.

Colley We're way out in front.

O'Donoghue We have the momentum.

Colley Charlie's supporters will abandon him in droves.

O'Donoghue There's no way back for him.

O'Malley It's meant to be a *secret* ballot.

Colley   That doesn't matter any more.

O'Donoghue   You're too far ahead.

Colley   He can't reach you.

O'Malley (*waving the newspaper*)   It's not *me* he's trying to reach – it's my supporters! The fucking Indo has just given Haughey their names!

Fianna Fáil Offices, Leinster House

Ahern *and* **Mara** *are working their way through phone-call lists;* **Haughey** *is working at his desk.*

Ahern (*on the phone*)   Yes, I see you're on this list in the Indo . . .

Mara (*on the phone*)   The 'Dump Haughey Campaign' . . .

Ahern   I'm glad *you* were surprised. Because the Boss was *very* surprised.

Mara   Yes, it's a vulgar name – and it's a vulgar project.

Ahern   Not that he's one to bear a grudge. No! But he has one hell of a long memory.

Mara   Whatever happened to loyalty, eh? Of course, the Boss is very loyal.

Ahern   He remembers his friends, too, of course. He rewards . . . loyalty.

Mara   He expects to be doing a deal in days . . . And then he'll move very quickly to appointing a government.

Ahern   Loyalty's very important when you're forming a government . . . and have a lot of positions to fill.

Mara   It would be a great shame if we were to lose the chance to form a government because some of our own people were disloyal . . . That would be a difficult thing to forget . . .

Ahern (*suddenly angry*)   Well just don't forget who got you started.

He slams down the phone. **Mara** *hangs up. They look at each other and nod. Each scratches out a name on his list and makes the next call.*

Haughey   Calm, Bertie.

Ahern   Duck off a water's back, Boss.

A **Reporter** *enters the office, nervously.*

Haughey   Who the fuck are you?

Reporter   They told me just to come on in –

Ahern   Sorry, Boss. / I forgot to mention –

Reporter   The Irish Press, Mr Haughey – My editor – Em –

Haughey   Yes?

Reporter   I was asked to ask you, well –

Haughey   Well?

Reporter   Given that the numbers are stacked against you in the leadership contest . . . are you going to resign?

Haughey   Would you fuck off.

He goes back to his papers.

Reporter (*taken aback*)   Pardon –

Haughey (*exploding*)   That's *fuck off*! Do you want me to spell it for you? F U C K *off*.

Ahern   Ah Boss, she's only doing her job.

Haughey *looks at* **Ahern** *for a beat, and instantly calms down.*

Haughey   What was your question again?

Reporter (*bewildered*)   Eh – Are you going to resign?

Haughey (*smooth*)   That's complete nonsense. I have no intention of resigning. In fact, I doubt there'll even be contest. The party is totally united behind me.

Reporter (*leaving, bemused*)   Thank you, Mr Haughey.

Ahern *nods to* **Mara**, *who leaves.*

Ahern   Time to go, Boss.

Haughey   All in hand, Bertie?

Ahern   All in hand, Boss.

Fianna Fáil Meeting Room, Leinster House – February 25

Mara (*to audience*)   A dhaoine usail, a chairde . . . I know you're all looking forward to this demonstration of the great traditions of independence, debate and democracy in our great party, Fianna Fáil . . .

Ahern *arrives with* **Haughey**, *signalling to* **Mara**.

Mara   Please welcome . . . our party leader and the next taoiseach . . . Charles J. Haughey!

Rapturous applause.

Mara   Now, on the agenda for this evening's parliamentary party meeting is / the leadership challenge –

O'Malley (*standing*)   If I may –

Mara (*faux surprise*)   Mr Desmond O'Malley.

O'Malley (*through gritted teeth*)   Eh, in the interests, eh, of the unity of the party, I would like to withdraw my challenge to Mr Haughey's leadership . . . I look forward to working closely with Mr Haughey in government as we go forward.

Applause. Cheers. **Haughey** *basks in it.*

Haughey (*to audience*)   We are a totally united party. And we are going to give this country stable government for the next five years.

He returns to his desk.

Haughey (*shouts*)   Mansergh!

(*Muttering.*) Probably in some dusty library somewhere. MANSERGH!

Martin Mansergh *enters, carrying a messy folder of documents.*

Mansergh   You were looking for me, Mr Haughey?

Haughey   Gregory, Mansergh.

Mansergh   Eh, *Martin* Mansergh, Mr Haughey.

Haughey   I know who you are! The Gregory thing! There's no time to lose.

Mansergh (*fumbling with his files*)   Oh yes, I've been going through their proposals . . . They have some . . . interesting ideas on taxation . . .

Haughey   It's all about the *local*, Mansergh. Have you talked to my brother in the Corporation?

Mansergh (*fumbling the papers*)   Yes . . . he recommends a refurbishment scheme for the Corporation flats – to put showers in them.

Haughey   Why can't they just wash in the bath?

Martin Mansergh   They don't have baths.

Haughey *reflects.*

Haughey   Mansergh – if we're to prise Gregory away from his lefty friends, we're going to have to give him more than showers . . . Think bigger, Mansergh. Much bigger.

On the radio: Mickey, *by Toni Basil.*

Summerhill Parade

Barry *is stopped by the* **Reporter** *outside the office.*

Reporter   Excuse me – is this Tony Gregory's office?

Barry (*annoyed*) No.

Reporter Oh. Do you know where I can find him?

Barry You can usually find him here.

Reporter (*confused*) Oh.

Barry What do you want?

Reporter I'm with the Irish Press. I'm writing a piece on the Inner City. / I was hoping to –

Barry The what?

Reporter The Inner City. / I was hoping to –

Barry What's that?

Reporter Well, around here –

Barry Summerhill Parade?

The **Reporter** *looks around, confused.*

Reporter Well, yes, / but –

Barry Or are you looking for Sean MacDermott Street?

Reporter Well / that's not quite –

Barry Or Sherriff Street?

Reporter Not exact / ly.

Barry Or Ballybough? Or Gardiner Street? Or Foley Street?

Reporter I don't know / where that is –

Barry These streets have *names*, love. *Histories.* Where the fuck is the 'Inner City'? *What* city? It's just a thing made up by sociologists. 'Inner City' isn't a *place* – it's a *problem.*

C'mere . . .

He leads her to the top of a flight of steps.

Barry See them steps. Count them.

Reporter What?

Barry Go on. Count them.

The **Reporter** *counts.*

Reporter Thirty-two.

Barry Twenty-seven.

Reporter What / do you mean?

Barry (*impatient*)   How many steps are there?

Reporter (*tentatively*)   Thirty-two.

Barry   But this is the Twenty-Seven Steps. Everyone knows that.

Reporter   I don't / understand.

Barry (*conceding*)   There used be twenty-nine. But then they added a few.

Reporter (*exasperated*)   But why is it called the Twenty-*Seven*?

Barry   *Originally*, there were twenty-seven. So people called it the Twenty-Seven Steps. Then some steps were added for some reason, so the number of steps changed. But the place hasn't. It has a *name*. That name has a *history*.

Beat.

'Inner City' is a concept. A label. An abstraction.

(*Gesturing.*) This isn't an abstraction. This is where we live.

Beat.

You're our guest. Learn the names.

Summerhill Parade – March 2

Eileen (*to audience*)   Garret FitzGerald had been slower to get in touch – but when he eventually came to Summerhill Parade, he came prepared . . .

(*To* **FitzGerald**.) This way, Dr FitzGerald.

FitzGerald   Thank you . . . I've taken the liberty of preparing a document as a basis for our discussions.

He hands out ring binders with a bulky document inside. They each take one and look through it.

FitzGerald (*opening the document*)   I think the most pressing issue, clearly, is / education.

Gregory   Housing.

Beat.

FitzGerald (*conceding*)   Housing.

Gregory   You've seen the state of the housing here.

Barry   Summerhill.

FitzGerald   Yes . . .

Gregory   Gardiner Street.

FitzGerald   Yes . . .

Barry   Sean MacDermott Street.

FitzGerald   Henrietta Street.

Gregory   Yes . . .

FitzGerald   It's extraordinary, isn't it? Some of the finest examples of Georgian architecture in these islands . . . Did you know Henrietta Street was built by Luke Gardiner – who gave his name to Gardiner Street? In the 1720s . . . He was a member of parliament as well – an MP – though for Tralee, I think, curiously . . . I must –

He makes a note to himself.

Gregory   Social housing. We want to see a major scheme on the Dublin Port site.

FitzGerald   Ah yes, the Port site. Of course . . .

(*Flicking through his document.*) I think we could put together a consortium to buy it.

Barry (*skeptical*)   A consortium?

FitzGerald   Yes – it's all in here. But – (*Checking his watch.*) I'm afraid I'm under time pressure.

I think the most efficient thing would be to proceed through this in sequence. As you know, I have a long-standing interest in education. / There's an extensive proposal here –

Barry (*impatient*)   The kids here leave school at fourteen.

FitzGerald   Exactly. But *why*?

Barry   Because their parents and their grandparents left school at fourteen . . . They left to go and work in the docks . . . But when the containers came in, the work all went.

FitzGerald   Which is why we have to equip this new generation for the new economy.

Barry   *What* new economy?

FitzGerald (*as if obvious*)   Technology.

Barry (*disbelieving*)   Technology?

FitzGerald   I've been talking to a company in the multinational sector about setting up a pilot scheme. We'd put computer terminals in schools, with training courses on them. The whole thing would be run from the multinational's mainframe in London . . . It would be practically cost-neutral. And if you factor in the long-term productivity gains . . . (*He checks his document.*) which I estimate to be / in the region of –

Gregory   I think a more immediate concern for local kids might be basic materials.

Barry   Like school books.

Gregory   *Copy* books.

FitzGerald   Of course, of course. I have a whole *plan* here. This whole area will be led by an Educational Task Force.

(*Impatient at their interruptions.*) Let's look at the detail. If you see, on page four, I suggest . . .

On the radio: Computer Love, *by Kraftwerk.*

They fall into detailed discussion; time passes. Suddenly, **FitzGerald** *glances at his watch.*

FitzGerald   Oh good lord, I'm late.

(*Getting up, fussing.*) My apologies.

Gregory   But we haven't talked about the Dublin Port site –

FitzGerald   Yes, well, it's all in there.

Barry   And housing.

FitzGerald (*leaving*)   Go over the document and let me know what you think.

Gregory   But do you agree there could be social housing on the Port site?

FitzGerald (*fussing*)   Yes, yes – in principle, of course.

(*As he leaves.*) Oh – have you thought about where the money would come from?

On the radio: Town Called Malice, *by The Jam.*

Summerhill Parade – March 3

Eileen *enters with a large envelope containing spiral-bound documents each with a shiny cover.*

Eileen   This just arrived.

Gregory   What's this?

Barry   From who?

Eileen   Someone in a fancy car.

Barry   Haughey.

She hands them out. They each examine them.

Gregory (*reading*)   'The Inner City Problem.'

Barry   For fuck's sake.

Gregory   *tosses his copy.*

Liam   Typical Haughey – put a shiny cover on it and think that'll impress us . . . How'd it go with FitzGerald?

Eileen He'd done his homework.

Gregory But it was the wrong homework.

Barry (*reading*) Wait . . . This is good. On the local stuff – it's good.

Gregory *takes his copy up again and starts flicking through it.*

Liam It's clientelism.

Gregory We can broaden it out. Give it a national focus. Let's get a response together.

In dumb-show, with music: they pore over the document and debate while **Eileen** *types.*

Haughey *arrives. He takes a seat at the end of the table, automatically assuming the Chair. He carries copies of his Inner City Problem document and other papers.*

Haughey (*grandiloquent*) Well, gentlemen. The Inner City Problem –

They wince; he doesn't notice.

Haughey I intend to solve it.

Eileen Coffee, Mr Haughey.

Haughey Thank you.

He sips and grimaces.

Haughey (*appalled*) What is that?

Eileen (*puzzled*) Nescafé.

Haughey I'll get you a coffee machine.

Gregory We have prepared some further thoughts, in response to your proposals.

He slides over a copy of their own document. **Haughey** *picks it up and starts to read it. He suddenly throws it down.*

Haughey (*alarmed*) I can't nationalise the fucking banks! What do you think this is, North Korea?

Barry The control of capital by the private sector reinforces the oppression / of the working class.

Haughey We're reliant on international borrowing to fund the State. That requires market confidence. No Fianna Fáil taoiseach would *ever* nationalise the banks.

He scratches a line through the previous paragraph and reads on.

Haughey (*disbelieving*) You want to put an oil refinery in Dublin Bay?

Barry The Russians would pay for it.

He puts a line through it and reads on.

Haughey (*eyebrows raised*)   The Kenny Report – that old canard?

Liam   It's the key to achieving a sustainable housing policy.

Haughey   It's the key to destroying wealth and undermining the constitutional right to private property.

Liam   Land has become a commodity. Speculators are hoarding it, driving up prices. Making it unaffordable for the Corporation to acquire for social housing. The Kenny Report addresses that.

Haughey   I'll consider putting a tax on derelict sites.

Liam   That's just tokenistic!

Haughey   I can't just abolish property rights!

(*To them all.*) Gentlemen – these are *national* issues.

Liam   This is a national programme.

Haughey   Your expertise is local. That's what I need. The Inner City Problem.

They look at each other. Beat.

Gregory   We want to see Dublin Corporation return to building large-scale social housing.

Haughey   Excellent.

Gregory   This year, we think they could build 1,600 houses . . .

Haughey (*noting it*)   Very good.

Gregory   Rising to 2,000 by 1984.

Haughey   Good.

Liam   But that's beyond their current capacity.

Haughey   We'll ringfence funding for it.

Gregory (*pushing it on*)   We believe there's potential for a large-scale public housing scheme on the Dublin Port site.

Haughey   I'll nationalise it.

Liam   Where are you going to get the money?

Haughey   I'm a Keynesian. I believe in borrowing for investment.

Gregory (*moving on*)   We have proposals for creating 3,000 new jobs in this area . . . at a cost of 20 million pounds.

Haughey   Over how long?

Gregory   Three years.

Haughey   Have you factored in inflation?

Barry   They're just initial / calculations.

Haughey   It's currently running at almost 19 per cent.

(*Making a note.*) That will need to be *30* million then.

He goes back to the document, making notes, initialling things as he approves them. They watch carefully, warily.

Haughey   You're pushing an open door, gentlemen.

He picks up his papers, to leave.

Haughey   I'll send you my official response later.

(*To* **Gregory**, *an afterthought.*) My wife . . . and children . . . If I'm to be elected taoiseach on Tuesday, I want them to be there. She'll need to make arrangements – it would help if I could give her some notice.

Beat.

Gregory   We'll be back to you before.

On the radio: What?, *by Soft Cell.*

Summerhill Parade – March 8 – Monday – 10am

Gregory, **Liam** *and* **Barry** *are sitting/standing/striding around, pensive, each turning things over in his own mind.* **Eileen** *is going through papers.*

Newsreader   With the Dáil due to resume tomorrow there is still no confirmation of whether there is likely to be a deal to secure the election of a taoiseach. Neither Sinn Féin The Workers' Party nor the Independent, Tony Gregory, have stated who they will support.

Liam   We should talk to FitzGerald again.

Barry   What for?

Liam   Show him what Haughey is offering. See if he can match it.

Barry   He won't.

Gregory   Even if he was willing to match it, he wouldn't be able to get it over the line. He has 63 seats. Labour are barely interested; but even with 15 Labour *and* Jim Kemmy *and* me, he's still one short of Haughey. He needs the Stickies as well. The Stickies strung us along last time. FitzGerald is all over the place. There isn't a hope in hell of him pulling together a deal.

Liam   We can go back to the Stickies.

Gregory   They just wanted a bit of the media attention. They've no interest / in a deal.

Liam   But their *agenda* / is a left-wing one.

Barry   Their agenda is building the fucking Stickies. It's the long game.

Liam   If we got FitzGerald on board, we'd have something concrete to bring to them.

Gregory   It's too late!

Liam   There's twenty-four hours.

Gregory   We have to prepare a document. Get it printed. Signed. Witnessed. It's Haughey – or no one.

Liam   What's *our* long game?

Gregory   The long game is, in ten, or twenty, or *thirty* years from now, *this* will be the moment that the rot stopped – that this community was shown a bit of respect – that it started to / recover.

Liam   The long game is we make Charles J. Haughey taoiseach. So whatever comes next – this is on us.

Barry   Don't be so fucking melodramatic.

Liam   You've changed your tune.

Barry   Haughey surprised me. He gets it. He's a Northsider.

Liam   Who cares about the fucking *river*?

He stands for everything we're against! With his horses. And his mansion. His island. His property speculation. His dubious money . . .

He'll run the State like a fiefdom. I don't think he even *believes* in the State . . . He ran guns to the fucking Provos, for Christ's sake.

Gregory   Well, at least somebody was willing to stand up for / the nationalists.

Barry   We agreed to park the North!

Liam   I'm not talking about the North! I'm talking about the character of the man he wants to make taoiseach.

Gregory   I have *one* of 166 votes. Because of a freak of politics we have the chance to make that vote count for our people – the people ringing that phone. The people who want to save their son's job from cutbacks in the Corpo, or . . . or who just want a fucking bathroom. This is the most influence they've ever had.

Liam   This is a *stroke*!

Gregory   It's not a stroke if it's out in the open. We're going to shout it from the rooftops.

Liam   If anyone else did this, we'd call it a stroke – it's exactly how we believe politics *shouldn't* work.

Eileen   Why?

This silences them.

Eileen   Why shouldn't it work like this?

Liam   Because it's clientelism.

Eileen   You mean . . . he's doing something for us cause we're doing something for him?

Liam   Eh, yeh.

Eileen   So what's wrong with that?

Liam   Politics should be about doing what's right *because* it's right. Because it's in the national interest – for the greater good.

Eileen   But isn't 'clientelism' just what happens in politics all the time? Except we're never the client.

Beat.

Liam   He's just promising us whatever we want – he doesn't even know where he's going to get the money . . . At least FitzGerald *believes* some of this stuff about social justice . . . We may never have this influence again. Let's keep trying . . . One last effort to create an alternative.

Ante-room to the office of the Taoiseach – March 8 – 4pm

The **Gregory** *team are waiting for* **FitzGerald***. Impatient.*

Barry   This is fucking offensive.

Gregory   Relax.

Barry   How long have we been we here?

Liam   Just fifteen minutes. He's the Taoiseach!

Barry   What are we doing here anyway? He doesn't get it.

Liam   We said we'd give it one more try. He agreed to meet us.

Barry   *Exactly. We* requested it. We're pursuing *him*. He's not pursuing us.

Gregory   *Haughey*'s pursuing us.

Barry   We're pushing an open door.

Liam   It's *too* open.

Gregory (*worried*)   There's a catch.

Liam   There *is* a catch: he's C.J. Haughey. We do this, and there's no going back. You'll have made him taoiseach. You'll be *forever* associated with him.

Beat.

Can you live with that?

A long beat. **Gregory** *looks hard at* **Barry**, *then at* **Liam**. **Barry** *looks at* **Liam**.

Gregory Anyone see a phone?

Liam Why?

Gregory To call Haughey.

Liam Fuck this.

He leaves.

Barry There's one out in the corridor.

Gregory Come on.

They leave. A **Government Official** *enters.*

Government Official They were here a moment ago, Taoiseach.

FitzGerald *enters.*

FitzGerald They appear to be here no longer.

Government Official I'll go and look for them.

FitzGerald Leave them go.

He looks at his watch.

FitzGerald It seems I have a speech to write.

Government Official (*puzzled*) Speech, Taoiseach?

FitzGerald The delicate art of congratulating Charles J. Haughey on becoming taoiseach. It didn't go so well the last time.

On the radio: the DJ introduces the week's number one, Come On Eileen, *by Dexys Midnight Runners. The song fades up and down throughout the following scene.*

Summerhill Parade – March 8 – 5pm

Barry, **Liam** *and* **Gregory** *are frantically collecting together pieces of paper from the various documents they've used during the process – it is panicked throughout.*

Gregory (*shouting*) Eileen!

(*To* **Barry**.) I thought you said she was on standby? EILEEN!

Eileen (*arriving*) I'm here.

Gregory Where were you?

Eileen You know, for a socialist, you're not very big on workers' rights.

Gregory We've to type up a document for Haughey.

Eileen (*tongue in cheek*)   Will that be headed notepaper?

Gregory   Ordinary paper'll be fine.

Eileen *lines up the paper in the typewriter.*

Eileen   Ready. Is this a deal?

Liam (*arriving*)   It's a *programme*.

Gregory (*dictating*)   Title page: 'Agreements reached by Charles J. Haughey TD and Tony Gregory TD'.

She types.

Gregory   Jesus, can you not type any faster?

Eileen   The more you hassle me, the slower I get.

Gregory   Where did you learn?

Eileen   Some crappy course run by a local project.

The typewriter pings.

Eileen   Page!

She tears out the page and one of the others takes it and she loads the next page.

Gregory (*dictating*)   Page one. Section one.

(*Checking his notes.*) Employment.

Music. They work on the document in dumb-show: **Gregory** *dictates,* **Eileen** *types and the others organise their papers.*

The typewriter pings.

Eileen   Page!

She tears out the page and one of the others takes it.

Gregory   What's next?

Barry   Housing.

Gregory   Where's the proposal?

Liam (*finding a page amidst the chaos*)   Here it is!

Gregory (*scanning it*)   Just include that page as it is.

He gives it to **Eileen** *who gives it to whoever is collating the typed pages.*

Gregory   Next?

Barry   The Development Authority.

Music. The dumb-show resumes.

The typewriter pings.

Eileen Page!

Gregory Next!

Liam *is staring at a page he's found.*

Liam The Kenny Report.

Barry He threw that out.

Liam We could put it back in.

Gregory What if he walks away?

Barry He *can't* walk away. Throw it *all* in.

Liam *gives the page to* **Gregory** *who gives it to* **Eileen** *who gives it to whoever is collating the document.*

Music and dumb-show.

The typewriter pings.

Eileen Page!

Gregory Next!

Liam What about the motorway?

Barry We forgot the fuckin' motorway!

Gregory Where is it?

Liam *(finding a piece of paper)* I've got it!

He passes it to **Gregory**.

Gregory *(dictating)* Section six. Transport . . .

Music and dumb-show.

The typewriter pings.

Eileen Page!

Gregory What else?

Eileen *(remembering)* Condoms!

Liam What?

Eileen That lady who phoned – she wanted us to get the law changed on condoms – so you could buy them without prescription.

Gregory Ah now –

Liam I don't think –

Barry We're pushing the boundaries out with this already.

Music and dumb-show.

The typewriter breaks.

Eileen   Fuck!

Gregory   What's wrong?

Eileen (*to* **Barry**, *aghast*)   I told you I needed a new typewriter.

Gregory   What are we going to do?

Eileen   Mrs Manley down the road – she has one.

Gregory (*to* **Eileen**)   Take these and finish them down there.

Liam (*after her*)   Don't forget the carbon paper!

Music and dumb-show. They tidy up the office. The music continues into the next scene.

8.30pm

Barry *looks out the window.*

Barry   He's here!

Liam   Where's Eileen?

Gregory   Come on, Eileen!

Haughey *enters.* **Eileen** *rushes in just after him carrying two copies of the document, bumps in to someone and drops them. Everybody bends down to pick them up and rearrange them, except* **Haughey** *and* **Gregory**, *who watch each other.*

Haughey   So I can tell my wife and children to be there tomorrow?

Gregory   I think you've probably told them already.

The others produce the two documents for signing. **Haughey** *takes one, sits down, and starts to scan it. He comes to a page and stops.*

Haughey   The Kenny Report.

He takes out a pen.

Liam   It's how we truly solve the housing crisis. For the long term. We change the whole incentive structure around land.

Haughey   You want to tell some farmer that the State is going to take his field, build fifty houses on it, and only pay him what he'd have got if he sold it to his neighbour for grazing? There'd be another land war.

Beat. A face off.

Haughey   I can increase capital gains tax on land that's being sold for development. So there's some clawback to the State, at least.

Gregory *and* **Barry** *look at* **Liam**. *He looks at them and at* **Haughey**. *He gives in.* **Haughey** *puts a line through the para.*

Gregory   Eileen – will your typewriter manage one last line?

As **Haughey** *continues reading,* **Gregory** *scribbles a line on a scrap of paper. She bashes it out on the typewriter and they add the extra page to the documents.*

Haughey *comes to the end and signs with a flourish. He passes it to* **Gregory**, *who signs, and they sign the second copy.*

Haughey   Well, gentlemen. As Al Capone once said, it was good doing business with you.

He bows and turns to leave.

Liam (*aside, to* **Eileen**)   They got Al Capone in the end, didn't they? I think it was / his taxes.

Barry   Eh, Mr Haughey?

Haughey   Yes.

Barry   Would you fancy – Would you join us for a drink?

Beat.

Haughey   I'd like that, yes.

They grab their coats.

Barry   We're going for a pint with Mr Haughey, Eileen –

Eileen (*hopeful*)   Yes?

Barry   Will you lock up when you're done?

Eileen   Yeh. Sure, yeh.

They emerge from the office.

Gregory   Oh, I thought it would be good to capture the occasion for posterity. I called a photographer.

Haughey   Ah, the Press? The Independent?

Gregory   The Northside News.

Photographer (*from off*)   Mr Haughey! This way!

Haughey *gives a regal wave to a non-existent crowd. FLASH!*

Gregory (*bemused*)   But there was nobody there. Who were you waving to?

Haughey   You write your own history, Tony.

On the radio: My Camera Never Lies, *by Bucks Fizz.*

Belton's Bar & Lounge

The **Bartender** *brings their drinks.*

Bartender   Gin and tonic. Red wine. Two Guinness . . . That'll be four pound ninety-one.

Beat.

Haughey (*unperturbed*)   Ah. I never carry cash.

Gregory *pats his trousers.*

Gregory   I seem to be out, myself.

Barry *and* **Liam** *look at each other – they've been stung.*

Bartender   When you manage to dig it up between youse, you can drop it up to me.

Barry *and* **Liam** *dig in their pockets.*

Barry   Jesus, almost a fiver for a round of drinks.

Liam (*finding a crumpled note*)   I've got it.

Barry   Good man. I'm going to the jacks.

Haughey *and* **Gregory** *are left on their own.*

Haughey   You're from around here, Tony?

Gregory   Down the road.

Haughey   Ballybough?

Gregory   Charleville Avenue, originally.

Haughey   A house?

Gregory   A flat.

Haughey   How many rooms?

Gregory   One.

Haughey   A tenement.

Gregory   If you like.

Haughey   How many of you?

Gregory   Four. I've an older brother.

Haughey   How long were you there?

Gregory (*shrugs*)   Ten, twelve years. Then we moved to a house on the canal, Sackville Gardens.

Haughey   A Corporation house?

Gregory We couldn't get one.

Haughey Why not?

Gregory There was just two kids. They told my mam, 'Come back when you've six'. But she'd married late – she was too old for more children . . . They didn't care.

Haughey A State that can't provide homes for its people is unworthy of the name.

Gregory That's what we're trying to change.

Haughey What happens when this deal falls?

Gregory Why would it fall?

Haughey Events, dear boy, events . . . Even with your vote, this government will be hanging on a thread. When it falls, this deal is over.

Gregory It is what it is.

Haughey But you can do so much more.

Gregory It's a long game.

Haughey Not so long if you have people around you.

Gregory I *have* people around me.

Haughey Good people – but they're not *political*. You need a political machine.

Gregory We're building our machine.

Haughey Not just a local one.

Beat.

A national one.

Gregory *looks at him.*

Gregory Fianna Fáil?

Haughey It could be a good fit.

Gregory My father had a photo of Michael Collins over his bed till the day he died.

Haughey (*shrugs*) My father was in the Free State army . . . This isn't tribal, Tony. We believe in the same things. Community. Decency. Getting things done. A fair Ireland. A United Ireland.

Beat. **Gregory** *is inscrutable.*

Haughey How do we make it so that no mother in Ireland is ever refused a home again?

Long beat.

Gregory Maybe we do it one community at a time.

Haughey *assesses him.*

Haughey If you change your mind – you'll be pushing an open door.

On the radio: Promised You a Miracle, *by Simple Minds.*

The Dáil – March 9

Newsreader With the Dáil meeting today for the first time since the general election, it is still unclear whether either of Dr Garret FitzGerald or Charles Haughey will command the support necessary to be elected taoiseach.

General Dáil hubbub.

Ceann Comhairle I call on Deputy Gregory to make his maiden speech.

Heckling.

Ceann Comhairle Deputies are reminded to treat the speaker with respect.

It quiets as they wait to see what **Gregory** *will do.*

Gregory Go raibh maith agat, a Cheann Comhairle . . .

Dáil Chorus Where's your tie?

Jeering on this, and then it quickly quiets again as he speaks.

Gregory Dublin Corporation's housing programme has been a scandal for years.

Audible suspense – will it be **FitzGerald** *or* **Haughey**?

Gregory Mr Haughey has committed himself –

Uproar.

Gregory to the allocation of 91 million pounds for housing in 1982.

The hubbub and heckling continues throughout.

Four hundred new houses in the north-central-city area will be started immediately. A total of 1,600 houses will be built this year in the Dublin Corporation area, rising to 2,000 houses a year by 1984.

Dáil Chorus What about the rest of the country?

Gregory Deputy Haughey has committed to allocating a further 20 million pounds to Dublin Corporation's budget.

Dáil Chorus Gregory, you've been bought.

Ceann Comhairle Deputies are reminded of the custom that maiden speeches should not be interrupted.

Gregory Deputy Haughey has committed himself to funding an immediate work force of 500 men for a Dublin Corporation environmental works scheme, at a cost of 4 million pounds.

Dáil Chorus   How much is he up to now?

Dáil Chorus   115 million!

Gregory   He has committed to hiring 150 additional craftsmen for the Corporation's repairs and maintenance service, at a cost of one million, five hundred thousand pounds.

Dáil Chorus   It's a disgrace.

Dáil Chorus   The most expensive vote in history.

Dáil Chorus   A new low in Irish politics.

Ceann Comhairle   We should have some silence to hear the Deputy in possession, without interruptions.

Gregory   Deputy Haughey has committed that the controversial and destructive motorway plan into the centre city will not now proceed.

Dáil Chorus   'Not in my back yard' politics.

Gregory   Deputy Haughey has given a commitment to nationalise the vital twenty-seven acres of the Dublin Port and Docks site, and to develop it to serve the needs of centre-city communities.

Dáil Chorus   How much will *that* cost?

Dáil Chorus   The country is *broke*!

Gregory   He committed to provide a community school for the neglected centre-city area, at a cost of three million pounds.

Dáil Chorus   What about Cork?

Gregory   Deputy Haughey has committed himself to the establishment of a *national* community development agency, with a budget of two million pounds.

Dáil Chorus   Who's going to *pay* for this?

Dáil Chorus   Where's the money coming from?

Gregory   He has made a major commitment to pre-school education . . . He has committed himself to advances in the taxation of derelict sites, of office developments, of financial institutions and of development land . . .

Dáil Chorus   'Tax the rich' – same old, same old.

Gregory   Once a Government have been elected they will receive my support only / in so far as –

General abuse.

Gregory   *Only* in so far as they pursue the programme of agreed commitments.

Dáil Chorus   The tail wagging the dog!

Gregory   Beidh mé ag votáil mar sin ar san an Teachta Ó hEochaidh sa toghachán le haghaidh an Taoisigh.

Ruckus.

Ceann Comhairle   I am putting the question: 'That Deputy Charles J. Haughey be nominated Taoiseach'.

On the radio: Arise and Follow Charlie, *by The Morrisseys.*

Office of the Taoiseach – July 1982

Ahern *has a clipboard.* **Eileen** *has a notebook.* **Gregory** *and* **Haughey** *stand off, observing.*

Eileen (*next item in her list*)   Mountjoy Street.

Ahern   Thirty-one units. Underway.

She ticks it off.

Eileen   Seville Place and Oriel Street.

Ahern   That's thirty-three / units.

Eileen   It should be a *hundred* units!

Ahern   Over *two* years. Thirty-three this year and . . . we have sixty-four planned for next year. The CPO order on Oriel Street might slow that down, but it's underway.

She glances to **Gregory***; he nods.*

Eileen   Rutland Street.

Ahern   Sixty units this year – in train – and thirty-three expected early next year.

Eileen   The showers scheme.

Ahern   Currently being installed in the 183 flats at Liberty House.

Eileen (*impatient*)   There's 3,000 flats to be done.

Ahern   The Corpo says they can do 500 a year. We've put up a million pound for it.

Eileen (*nodding to* **Gregory**)   OK. That's my list.

Ahern   Thanks for coming in, folks.

Gregory   There's something else.

He exchanges glances with **Eileen**.

Haughey   A problem?

Gregory   Yes.

Haughey   With the deal?

Gregory   Not with the deal. At least, it's not *in* the deal.

Haughey   Go on.

Gregory Drugs.

Haughey (*bemused*) Drugs?

Gregory *nods to* **Eileen**.

Eileen Heroin.

Beat.

These last few months . . . since we did the deal . . . it's got some kind of hold amongst the young ones . . . The pushers started by bringing in cheap hash to lure the kids in, and then pushed the heroin at them . . . You can see them injecting – in the stairwells of the flats, in doorways . . . It's going from brother to sister – it's like some kind of plague . . . A habit costs a hundred pound a day. They're robbin' to pay for it.

Haughey Bertie.

Ahern Yes, Boss.

Haughey Will you get the Garda Commissioner on the phone?

Ahern *dials.*

Ahern Get the Garda Commissioner.

Haughey (*suddenly intimate*) I'm bollixed . . . I'm going out to the island for a few weeks. When I'm back, we'll fix this.

Ahern (*into phone*) I'll put him on now.

(*Handing him the phone.*) Boss.

Haughey Commissioner! . . . Yes, thank you . . . Commissioner, I believe there's a problem with heroin in the Inner City . . . Yes . . . Put whatever resources you can into it, will you? Let's discuss it in September . . . That's all.

Thank you.

He hangs up.

Eileen But it's not a crime issue.

Haughey You said they're thieving to pay for it.

Eileen That's the *effect* of it. But the cause is the same as the other things – their lives are empty. My da never recovered after he lost his job on the docks. The community never recovered. The only difference now is that the drugs is giving them something to do.

He faces up to her.

Haughey Your community will never be abandoned again.

He breaks off.

Now, if you'll excuse me – the weather could turn at any time. I have a helicopter to catch. Are you going anywhere nice for your holidays?

Eileen   Donabate.

Haughey   Why don't you come out to Inishvickillaun for a visit?

Beat.

Gregory   Maybe next year.

They shake hands and part.

On the radio: Nebraska, *by Bruce Springsteen.*

She turns to the audience.

Eileen   He didn't get his few weeks on his island . . . In the middle of August, the guards caught Malcolm MacArthur – the murderer – in the apartment of the Attorney General . . . That was the end of Charlie's holidays . . .

A blizzard of 'Taoiseach! Taoiseach!' and questions:

Reporter One   Taoiseach, where was the Attorney General?

Reporter Two   Taoiseach, will this bring down the Government?

Reporter One   Taoiseach, what's going on?

Haughey (*to the media, tired*)   It was a grotesque situation, an unprecedented situation, a bizarre happening, an almost unbelievable mischance.

Eileen   'GUBU', we called it, after that. In the meantime, the national finances were a disaster, and Charlie launched a new austerity drive. But then Fianna Fáil lost two TDs – Jim Gibbons had a heart attack; Bill Loughnane died. Suddenly, Charlie didn't have the numbers to push through his cuts . . . Tony's vote wasn't enough any more – Charlie needed the three Workers' Party TDs as well – the Stickies – but they were determined to vote against the cuts . . . It looked like it was all over . . . but Tony thought there was one more roll of the dice . . .

Office of Sinn Féin The Workers' Party, Leinster House

Gregory *joins the three Sinn Féin The Workers' Party TDs.*

Worker Jane   I call this meeting of the Sinn Féin The Workers' Party Parliamentary Party / to order.

Gregory (*intemperate*)   Can we forget about the formalities?

Beat. They assess each other with hostility.

Gregory   We don't have to like each other. God knows, I've enough reason to dislike you. But I do believe you're in this for the same reasons I am. / That you're in it for –

Worker Joe *We're* here for the working class.

Gregory And so am *I*.

Worker Bob Your 'deal' isn't in the interests of the working class – it's in the interests of your constituency.

Gregory Have you read it? At least *half* of it is progressive *national* issues / from taxation to education.

Worker Bob And how much progress have you made with those 'national' issues?

Gregory That's the *point*. We haven't had *time*. If you sign up to this deal, now – if you support Haughey – there's at least half a chance the stuff in the deal will happen. If you vote against Haughey, there's *no* chance. You'll be shooting yourselves and the working class in the foot.

Worker Joe Don't come in here all high and mighty / lecturing us about the working class.

Gregory Don't treat me as if I'm just some parish-pump / cretin.

Worker Bob You sold out.

Worker Jane These new cuts are savage – we can't support them.

Gregory So *help* me. I'm *inside* the room. I have influence. *We* could have influence. Haughey is . . . committed.

Worker Joe Haughey's a bourgeois reactionary.

Gregory He's a *pragmatist*. You can do business with him. If you vote against him now, everything we've achieved collapses –

Worker Joe What have you achieved?

Gregory Just the *start*. Housing. Jobs. It's all to play for – land taxes . . . banking regulation . . .

Worker Bob It's all just helping capitalism insulate itself against upheaveal.

Gregory I'm living in *this* world. The world where families are *still* living in one-room flats. Without fucking bathrooms. Where working class communities are being ravaged by a heroin epidemic because there's no jobs and there's no policing and there's no services and there's no way out. And I have a chance to help bring some money and . . . attention and . . . light. And Haughey is *backing* it – it's not just bullshit – he's not stringing me along. He *gets* it . . . And you're going to sacrifice all that because it doesn't fit with your 'dialectical praxis' . . .

Worker Jane We're building a *movement*, Tony.

Worker Joe You had a chance to be a part of it, but you thought better.

Worker Bob It's the long game. There's more at stake here than flats for a few families . . . and bathrooms.

Beat.

Gregory No. No there isn't. How could there be anything more at stake than that.

The Dáil – November 9, 1982

Ceann Comhairle Deputy Gregory.

Ruckus and heckling.

Gregory My position supporting Deputy Haughey's government has become increasingly untenable. But in his short time as taoiseach, and despite the many difficulties he had to contend with, Deputy Haughey's involvement was genuine and honourable . . . So, in this vote of confidence in the Government today, it is my intention . . . to abstain.

Dáil Chorus Have the courage of your convictions!

Dáil Chorus You're a hypocrite!

Gregory The Irish left's failure to unite . . . Their failure to *use* their combined strength to win badly-needed concessions from a minority government . . . is a terrible mistake . . . It's a mistake for which history and the working class people of this country will not forgive us . . . It will be the left's downfall.

Jeering.

Eileen (*to audience*) So Charlie's government collapsed, and that was the end of the deal . . . Some of the houses were built . . . We got the community school, Larkin College – though it took seventeen years . . . The motorway was killed off for good, thank God . . . And the Docks was transformed – though an 'international financial services centre' wasn't quite what we'd had in mind for a community facility . . .

We never got the lampshade. Or the coffee machine. Or the trip to the island . . .

And – well, you all lived through what happened after. The 80s. The 90s. The Celtic Tiger. The Boom . . . The Bust.

In the meantime, Charlie's money caught up with him . . . By the time he died, in 2006, he had been pretty well humiliated . . .

And then cancer caught up with Tony, in 2008 . . .

That was the year of the bank guarantee, and the budget, it was ferocious. Tony came into the Dáil – to speak against the education cuts that were coming in.

Beat.

He was terrible thin.

Beat.

Labour had a motion down, against the cuts, and he went to them looking for speaking time. That was how the system worked: as an Independent, he had to beg for his time from the parties. And they didn't give it to him.

Beat.

That was his last time in the Dáil. He died two months later, in January 2009. He was sixty-one.

And then, in 2015, a drugs war exploded on our doorsteps – a 'feud', the papers called it – and suddenly everybody was interested in us again. The taoiseach, Enda Kenny, he brought half his cabinet across the river to a meeting – it was like they were going into the jungle.

And and in all the papers, and on the radio, and in the Dáil, it was all talk about 'the Inner City Problem', again . . . And so they sent another problem-solver in, to do another report. This time, they say, it's going to be different.

Inner City Regeneration Briefing – February 2017

The Consultant *brings the mic stand down-stage.*

The Consultant   Em, thank you all for coming. Over the past four months I have walked through the North East Inner City, visiting projects, groups, residents.

This is a prime location with huge development and economic potential . . . But there are pockets here of extraordinary deprivation and dereliction . . .

This indicates that the previous approaches to solving problems here have not succeeded. Something needs to change . . . The *narrative* needs to change. We need to change the narrative of the North East Inner City . . .

Accordingly, I recommend we rebrand the name of the area without losing its identity – to be decided by the Community, of course. Something like 'Dublin's North Central City Quarter', perhaps . . .

Thank you. If we have time, I'll take some questions.

He waits, then leaves, turning off the overhead projector as he does so.

On the radio: Old Town, *by Thin Lizzy.*

Selected Bibliography

Gilligan, Robbie. *Tony Gregory*. Dublin: O'Brien Press, 2011.

Gregory, Noel. 'Reminiscences and Musings of a Forgotten Age' in *Detecting a Break In*, edited by Martin Byrne. Dublin: Scribbles from the Margins Press, undated.

Sheehan, Ronan, and Brendan Walsh. *Dublin: The Heart of the City*. Dublin: The Lilliput Press, 2016.

Tóibín, Colm. *The Trial of the Generals: Selected Journalism 1980–1990*. Dublin: Raven Arts Press, 1990.

Joyce, Joe, and Peter Murtagh. *The Boss: Charles J. Haughey in Government*. Dublin: Poolbeg Press, 1983.

Collins, Stephen. *The Power Game: Fianna Fáil since Lemass*. Dublin: O'Brien Press, 2000.

Smyth, Sam. *Thanks a Million Big Fella*. Dublin: Blackwater Press, 1997.

Whelan, Noel. *Fianna Fáil: A Biography of the Party*. Dublin: Gill & Macmillan, 2011.

Ahern, Bertie. *The Autobiography*. London: Hutchinson, 2009

FitzGerald, Garret. *All in a Life: Garret FitzGerald — an Autobiography*. London: Macmillan, 1992

McDonald, Frank. *The Destruction of Dublin*. Dublin: Gill & Macmillan, 1985.

Hanley, Brian and Scott Millar. *The Lost Revolution: The Story of the Official IRA and the Workers' Party*. Dublin: Penguin Ireland, 2009.

The archives of *Hot Press, In Dublin, The Irish Times, Magill, North Inner City News*, Oireachtas.ie.

In particular: journalism by Gene Kerrigan, Seán Kilfeather, Fintan O'Toole, Jason O'Toole, Mary Raftery.

Photojournalism by Derek Speirs

Peter Coonan as Barry, Ruairí Heading as Tony Gregory and Janet Moran as Eileen in *Haughey|Gregory*.
©Photo by Anthony Woods.

Guaranteed!

Guaranteed! was commissioned and first produced by Fishamble: The New Play Company in June 2013. It toured throughout Ireland during the second half of the year, and to the Abbey Theatre in 2014, with the following cast and crew:

Governor	Peter Daly
Minister for Finance	Peter Hanly
Taoiseach	Darragh Kelly
Attorney General	Mark Lambert
Senior Official	Caitríona Ní Mhurchú / Ali White
Directed by	Conall Morrison
AV designed by	Kilian Waters
Costumes designed by	Paula O'Reilly
Produced by	Marketa Dowling

Characters

Sean FitzPatrick, *chairman of Anglo Irish Bank*
David Drumm, *chief executive of Anglo*
AIB Boss *and* **Board members**
Bank of Ireland Boss

Bertie Ahern, *Taoiseach and leader of Fianna Fáil*
Brian Cowen, **Tánaiste** *and* **Minister for Finance** *when we first meet him, later* **Taoiseach** *and leader of Fianna Fáil*
Brian Lenihan, **Minister for Finance** *(also Fianna Fáil)*
Enda Kenny, *leader of Fine Gael*
Pat Rabbitte, *leader of the Labour Party*
Michael McDowell, *leader of the Progressive Democrats*

Department of Finance Officials *and* **Press Officers**
Central Bank Governor *and* **Official**
Financial Regulator, Inspectors *and* **Official**
NTMA Boss *and* **Official**
Attorney General
Secretary General

Narrator
Newsreaders
Master of Ceremonies
Professor Tobias Just
Hedge Fund Director *and* **Analyst**
Developer
Waitress

The taoiseach is the Irish prime minister. The tánaiste is the deputy prime minister. The Dáil is the lower house of parliament. The Seanad is the senate, or upper house.

As far as possible, I have avoided using real names in the text. This facilitates combining different roles into one character, and also facilitates the attribution of actions to an institution where it may not be clear precisely who in that institution was responsible.

The cast all play multiple parts. Most of the roles are not gender-specific, though the contemporary Irish audience could identify many of the real people behind the unnamed roles, and most of those were men.

Prologue

On stage: stacks of file boxes, documents on top or spilling out of them; a large office table (on castors); a set of swivel office chairs, on castors. There may also be: a water cooler; a filter coffee station; landline phones; desk lamps; a PC; a flipchart on easel; copies of the books and reports that provided source material for the play.

The cast enters, in suits worn casually – a jacket over a shoulder here, a tie loose there. They carry their scripts, spiral bound with black covers. They are relaxed: they are not in character.

Newsreaders and officials are not consistent characters – they may be played by different people in different scenes.

Scene titles (date and location) are projected above the stage, ideally with the classic typewriter sound effect.

The scene titles and the introductory scene description may be spoken, and characters may be introduced, by the **Narrator**, *whenever useful.*

The **Narrator**'s *lines may be distributed amongst the ensemble.*

Narrator   This play is based on a true story.

Some of it is literally true. When you see us speaking at public events, our words are based closely on verbatim records, though sometimes different speeches and events have been combined.

And some of it is invented. When you see us speaking in private – behind closed doors, as it were – those conversations are imagined, but based on some documentary record: internal documents, media reports, the official inquiries, or conversations with people involved in these events.

We know the decisions that were made. The question the play tries to answer is: how did they arrive at them? Sometimes, we've had to guess.

The first titles are projected as the cast populate the first scene.

January 28, 2005
The Four Seasons Hotel, Dublin

Sean FitzPatrick *is addressing the guests at his retirement dinner.*

Sean FitzPatrick   You know, I didn't see myself as a *banker*. I was the entrepreneur. I was the businessman …

I wouldn't have been seen as a great lender … I wasn't technically good … I didn't have respect for hugely intelligent people …

I was more into people that could relate to other people; people that could talk in the ordinary way. People that could go out and have a pint …

I was brought up to believe that to have a passion was what it was all about …

Anglo has been my life … As it happens, my predecessors as CEO left at 56. Now I'm leaving at 56. It's time for me to do other things … I'll be chairman, of course. But I'll be a hands-off chairman. David's in charge now.

A final reflection before he leaves.

You know, the real thing in life is not to be bright, but to be lucky. I have been lucky …

Deals could be done here – deals *can* be done here. Done well, and done efficiently.

That is our magic. The magic of Anglo.

Applause.

July 14, 2005
The Boardroom, AIB Boss Bankcentre, Dublin

A meeting of the board of **AIB Boss**.

AIB Boss   Gentlemen, let's get started, shall we?

Dissenting Voice   Could I—

AIB Boss   As you all know, of course, we are proposing selling our headquarters—

Dissenting Voice   Before—

AIB Boss   Bankcentre – this building – our home … It will be a—

Dissenting Voice   Sorry—

AIB Boss   sale-and-leaseback deal—

Dissenting Voice   Do you mind if I—

There are dismissive mutterings from the other board members: 'And he's off', 'Here we go again', etc.

AIB Boss   Of course … not. Go ahead.

Dissenting Voice People are watching for a sign that the property market has peaked. And now they're going to see the bank selling *its own property* …

Aren't they going to read that as the bank trying to get out at the top? 'So long, suckers.' Doesn't it look like a vote of no confidence in the market?

AIB Boss But the whole *point* is that we're *selling* the property in order to *have* more money to *lend* to people who want to *buy* property.

Mutterings of agreement from the other board members.

This sale will give us a significant capital injection which we can then lever up ten, twelve times. That will be over a *billion* in new lending. That's hardly a vote of 'no confidence' in the property market.

Board Member 1 We're playing catch-up here with Anglo.

Dissenting Voice But we're already growing our lending at 25 per cent per year. Why do we need to—

Board Member 2 Anglo is growing at 40 per cent.

Board Member 3 Anglo can give loan approval *overnight*. We can't match that.

Board Member 1 They're eating our lunch.

Board Member 2 It leaves us vulnerable.

AIB Boss Shareholders demand growth. If we don't deliver growth, then—

Board Member 3 A takeover could be on the cards.

Dissenting Voice By Anglo?

Board Member 2 It's not inconceivable.

Dissenting Voice I just think the property market could be overvalued—

Board Member 1 Have you *seen* the statistics? We're heading for a population of *eight million*. There's a *shortfall* in houses in Dublin at the moment.

Board Member 2 The fundamentals are sound.

Board Member 3 Do you remember the '80s? You couldn't *get* a mortgage.

Board Member 1 People are *entitled* to mortgages. That's the great revolution – we have democratised money.

Dissenting Voice Yes but there's still *risk* involved—

Board Member 2 We have *reinvented* the risk architecture!

Board Member 1 Provisions haven't exceeded one per cent since 1991.

Board Member 3 You know what that *means*, don't you?—

Dissenting Voice Yes—

Board Member 3 We. Don't. Lose. Money. On. Loans. We haven't lost money in fifteen years.

The **Dissenting Voice** *is chastened (or frustrated) into silence. The Chairman intervenes, placatory, smoothing over the cracks on his board.*

AIB Boss Gentlemen, gentlemen, we need to move on.

We expect to sell Bankcentre for just over €350 million and to lease it back again for an annual rent of around €16 million.

Pause.

Are there any objections? No?

A side glance at least to the **Dissenting Voice**, *who is defeated.*

AIB Boss Excellent. Now, I think we've a report from the remuneration committee?

October 11, 2006
Deutsche Bank Research, Frankfurt

A research briefing.

Prof Dr Tobias Just I am interested in risk. Risk and house prices …

In the 1990s, Germany had a construction boom. Berlin, in particular.

The country was reunited. The Berlin Wall had been torn down. The city had to be rebuilt.

It was the new capital! The East had to be brought up to the standard of the West!

The Government moved to Berlin. Thousands of workers moved to Berlin. People from all over the world moved to Berlin …

In Ireland, for some years now, the rate of construction has been greater than in Berlin at the peak of the post-reunification boom …

He lets this settle in.

So, what is happening in little Ireland? What wall has been torn down? Has the country been reunified? Are you building a new capital?

January 24, 2007
The World Economic Forum, Davos

Master of Ceremonies (*with rising excitement*) Ladies and gentlemen … The moment you've all been waiting for … The Mercer Oliver Wyman Best Bank in the World …

In the $10 billion valuation category, this bank has given the best return to shareholders *in the world* since the turn of the millennium …

Drum roll.

The 2006 Best Bank in the World is … Anglo Irish Bank.

Applause. **David Drumm** *stands to accept the award and poses for a photo.*

March, 2007
Ard Fheis season

The party leaders address their members (i.e. the audience) during ard fheis (*party conference) season.*

Bertie Ahern   Good evening members of Fianna Fáil …

Enda Kenny   Members of Fine Gael …

Bertie Ahern   As you know, the economics of stop-start, boom-bust hold no attractions for us.

Enda Kenny   Fianna Fáil's policy is driven by the developer and the speculator.

Bertie Ahern   So we will make commitments that are affordable today *and* tomorrow …

Enda Kenny Government should be in the business of helping people *buy* their home, not standing in *their way.*

Bertie Ahern   Since 1997, we have reduced income tax rates by thirteen percentage points.

Enda Kenny   So, we promise an end to Stamp Duty as we know it.

Bertie Ahern   Now, we will reduce the standard rate from 20 per cent to 18, and the higher rate from 41 per cent to 40 per cent …

Enda Kenny (*desperately trying to keep up*)   And we promise lower income taxes for every taxpayer.

Pat Rabbitte, *stands and elbows* **Enda Kenny** *aside.*

Bertie Ahern   We will raise pensions by €100.

Pat Rabbitte   A Labour government will favour the *working* family …

Bertie Ahern   We will provide two thousand new gardaí.

Pat Rabbitte   So we will introduce a 2 per cent cut in the standard rate of income tax …

Michael McDowell, *stands and elbows* **Pat Rabbitte** *aside.*

Bertie Ahern   Four thousand more primary school teachers …

Michael McDowell   The Progressive Democrats will cut the standard rate of income tax to *seventeen* per cent …

Bertie Ahern   We will join the LUAS Green and Red lines.

Michael McDowell   and the higher rate to 38 per cent—

Bertie Ahern (*drowning him out*)   We will open Metro-North and Metro-West … We will reopen the Western Rail Corridor. We will complete the five inter-urban motorways. And the Atlantic Road Corridor. And the Border Road Corridors as well.

Bertie Ahern *finishes in triumph.*

May 1, 2007
Investor Relations Magazine Awards, Conrad Hotel, Dublin

Master of Ceremonies   And, no surprises this time … For the fourth year in a row … The Investor Relations Magazine Grand Prix award 2007 for best overall investor relations goes to … Anglo Irish Bank!

Cheers.

July 2, 2007
The Seanad

A statement to the Irish senate by the **Tánaiste**, *Brian Cowen* (*who will later become Taoiseach*).

Tánaiste   We should encourage positive sentiment about the housing market. It is important not only for house purchasers but also for jobs …

The fundamentals are right. The demographics are strong. Our supply of housing has not yet reached European levels.

Beat.

We shouldn't send an overly pessimistic message to the market by suggesting an imminent collapse or something which would make people step back from the market again.

There is clear evidence that our policy has been working and that a soft landing is in prospect.

September 14, 2007
A hedge fund, London

The **Director** *of a hedge fund addresses one of the fund's analysts, reviewing his work; his/her tone is neutral.*

Director   Two years ago, you said Northern Rock was overrated. You said we should bet against it: take a short position. And we did.

And then they announced record profits. The market liked them. A lot. But you said the market was wrong. We increased our bet.

Last January, they announced record profits again. That *cost* us. Other hedge funds closed out. You said they were wrong. I trusted you.

Then, this summer, the credit crunch hit. I thought we might be finally in for a payday. But Northern Rock rode it out. Their loan book was solid. They increased their dividend.

Others funds closed out. But you said – stay.

Analyst I did.

Director At 9.30 last night, the Bank of England authorised an emergency loan to Northern Rock. This morning their share price is down—

Analyst Twenty-two per cent. Last I looked.

Director The BBC is reporting queues outside their branches. It looks like there's a run. The first bank run in 150 years …

The **Director** *marvels for a moment.*

They'll have to be guaranteed. Probably nationalised.

Beat.

That was a good bet.

Analyst It's your money.

Director It's our *investors'* money. And this is why they give it to us.

Now, here's what I want to know. People think Northern Rock is fucked because it sold sub-prime mortgages. But that's only half the problem.

Northern Rock is fucked because it gave out those loans with money it got cheap, wholesale. And because of the credit crunch, there isn't any of that money any more. And there isn't going to be for a long time.

So here's my question. Who else is like Northern Rock?

Beat.

Analyst There's an Irish bank –

Director *Irish*?

Analyst Anglo Irish Bank.

Director AIB Boss?

Analyst Not *Allied*. *Anglo*. They're the third Irish bank.

Director So they must be tiny.

Analyst They were, but—

Director But?

Analyst   —they've been growing their loan book at 40 per cent a year.

Director   For how long?

Analyst   Ten years.

Director   *Ten years*? But no bank can sustain that kind of growth –

Analyst   They boast about it. I can show you their presentations …

Director   How?

Analyst   Lower costs. Wholesale money. And aggressive lending.

Director   Mortgages?

Analyst   Commercial property. Development. But they hide it.

Director   They *hide* it?

Analyst   They say they're 'diversified'. 'Business banking', not property. But it's all secured on property.

Pause. The **Director** *thinks.*

Director   I take it you've already taken a short position on them?

Analyst   A small one. Just ten million.

Director   Increase it. Now. Let's go to a hundred. And then I want you to do some fieldwork …

If they're rotten, what about the other Irish banks? Go over there. Talk to people.

Builders. Brokers. People who know what's … happening.

There's going to be more Northern Rocks.

And if we are going to make some serious money, we need to see them coming.

September 17, 2007
Fianna Fáil Parliamentary Party meeting, Druid's Glen, Wicklow

Bertie Ahern   I want to take this opportunity to state loud and clear that the Irish economy is strong and growing.

It is a cliché to talk about the fundamentals being sound, but the fact is: they are!

There is no place for negativity. No need for any pessimism.

Above all, there is no place for politically motivated attempts to talk down the economy.

October, 2007
Office of the Financial Regulator, The Central Bank, Dublin

The **Financial Regulator** *chairs a meeting of his inspectorate.*

Financial Regulator Thank you all for coming in. I wanted to do a quick debrief on the 'five by five' exercise. You've each been in one of the five main banks looking at their exposure to their five biggest developers. I have your reports. Could you just rattle through your concerns?

Inspector 1 In the case of—

Financial Regulator Anonymised, please. I need hardly say how sensitive this is.

Inspector 1 —Bank ... X? ... One of their biggest clients. They couldn't get a 'net worth' statement from him.

Financial Regulator Why not?

Inspector 1 He wasn't willing to give them one.

Financial Regulator Ah hah. Anything else?

Inspector 1 Em, yes, actually. I encountered some confusion around the overall indebtedness of their clients.

Financial Regulator What kind of confusion?

Inspector 1 Their figures didn't add up.

Financial Regulator Ah hah.

Inspector 1 They gave me a figure for one client's total exposure, which included his debts to another bank as well.

Financial Regulator And?

Inspector 1 I checked with the other bank. The figure was out by a bit.

Financial Regulator How much?

Inspector 1 A billion.

Financial Regulator Ah hah. (*Turns to the others.*) Anything else?

Inspector 2 Get this. One of the largest clients of—

Financial Regulator Bank Y.

Inspector 2 Bank Y – one of their largest clients. When they calculated his net *worth*, they included €100 million *that they had loaned him.*

Financial Regulator What kind of stress tests are they all doing?

Inspector 4 Bank ... Z does 'ad hoc' stress tests.

Financial Regulator What's an 'ad hoc' stress test?

Inspector 4 Well, they looked at the impact of the smoking ban on the pub trade, for example.

Financial Regulator Well, that could stress some loans, I suppose – loans to pubs ... But are they testing for the risk to loans if GDP fell – or interest rates rose – or there was a fall in the property market?

Inspector 4   No. But how would they? They've no economist on staff …

Financial Regulator (*reflecting on all the problems*)   This is not good … (*Decides.*) I'm going to have to write to the banks.

November, 2007
A new shopping centre, West Dublin

The hedge fund **Analyst** *from before meets a property* **Developer**.

Waitress (*delivering a coffee*)   Your latté.

Analyst   The cream-cheese bagel?

Waitress   It's on its way.

Developer (*with mild derision*)   I'm not a 'bagel' man myself.

Analyst (*looking around and gesturing to the surrounds*)   You built the place.

Developer   Hah. Fair point. So what is it you want?

Analyst   Just your sense of things.

Developer   You flew to Dublin and then got a taxi out here to get my 'sense of things'?

Analyst   I'm meeting other people. I'm doing … some research on the Irish property market.

Developer   *What* property market?

Analyst   That bad?

Developer   Sure nothing's moving. Nothing's moved since last year.

Analyst   Building, or selling?

Developer   Both. The problem is: an empty site's worth nothing; and an unfinished building's worth *less* than nothing … but, even in a crash, a finished building's not worth *nothing* … There has to be *something* in it …

So they've got to keep building. Once they've started. If they can.

Analyst   But if they've no cash flow, how can they keep things on site?

Developer   The banks. The banks are as fucked as the builders. They've got to keep them building. So they're keeping the money coming, just to get the things built.

Analyst   But the outstanding loans?

Developer   They're just rolling up the interest.

Analyst   So they're giving out more money … and none's coming in?

Developer   That's the height of it.

Analyst   If nothing's selling, why haven't prices come down?

Developer Because nobody can afford to sell at the prices people might pay. The banks won't let them. They'd rather sweat it out. They think it'll come good.

Analyst Will it?

Developer Here's the thing. Ten years ago ... '97, '98 ... a house in Dublin cost you roughly a hundred grand. A few years later, it was two hundred grand. By last year, it was four hundred grand.

Analyst And now?

Developer There's no market now. There's no average price.

Analyst And when the market gets going again?

Developer They'll fall ... maybe 40 per cent.

Analyst And the banks ...?

December, 2007
Office of the Governor, The Central Bank

Central Bank Official I have the draft of the Financial Stability Report, Governor.

Governor Thank you.

He takes the report and looks through it.

You know, I think we should cut that reference to a 'likely 15 per cent overvaluation in house prices'. We don't want to be accused of crying wolf, again.

(*With relief.*) Anyway, things are finally slowing down of their own accord. You have the paragraph on that?

Central Bank Official (*pointing to it in the document*) It's there.

(*Reads.*) 'The *underlying* fundamentals of the residential market continue to appear strong and the current trend in monthly price developments does not imply a *sharp* correction ... The central scenario is, therefore, for—

Governor (*approvingly*) A soft landing.'

Central Bank Official Yes.

Governor Good. I think we're nearly there.

February 26, 2008
The Dáil

Leaders' Questions in the Irish parliament. Heckling and cheering threaten to drown it out throughout.

Enda Kenny Last Thursday, as the Tánaiste is aware, more dramatic facts emerged from the Mahon tribunal about Deputy Ahern's finances ...

Fact – more accounts with more lodgements were revealed.

Fact – the Taoiseach admitted to getting a gift of money when Minister for Finance and not declaring it to the Revenue.

Fact – £30,000 donated or collected by Fianna Fáil personnel for the Fianna Fáil Party was used for the purchase of a house …

This is paralysing the Government.

I want to know from the Tánaiste what action he proposes to remove that paralysis.

Tánaiste The Taoiseach is entitled to a fair hearing. I do not need lectures from the Opposition on my standards.

My standards relate to fair play and the hearing of the evidence.

They certainly do not relate to people being guilty before being proven innocent.

March 13, 2008
Office of the Financial Regulator

*The **Financial Regulator**, nervous, addresses a room of senior bankers.*

Financial Regulator It's time to circle the wagons, gentlemen … We're more than six months into the credit crunch and I know you've *all* been feeling its effects. You can't get funding as easily or cheaply as before. In some cases, it's difficult to get it at all …

I've asked you here today to give serious consideration to how you, our leading banks, can help each other in this time of liquidity crisis …

Mutual in-market support. To maintain the stability of the financial system. I'm asking you to pull on the green jersey.

March 16, 2008

Newsreader The global credit crunch today claimed its first major American casualty. The investment bank, Bear Stearns – Wall Street's fifth largest – was bought by JP Morgan Chase, backed by a government bailout. Bear Stearns had faced bankruptcy after a bank run provoked by fears over the bank's exposure to subprime losses.

March 17, 2008
Office of the Chief Executive, Anglo Irish Bank, St Stephen's Green, Dublin

Sean FitzPatrick, *chairman, and* **David Drumm**, *CEO, watch as the Anglo share price (projected above the stage) tumbles (It falls from €8.19 to €6.30 across the morning.)*

Sean FitzPatrick This is insane. It's a massacre.

David Drumm It's those fucking hedge funds.

Sean FitzPatrick You think it's coordinated?

David Drumm   It must be! It's fucking Paddy's Day. There's nobody working in Dublin. It's all coming from fucking London.

Sean FitzPatrick   They're spreading rumours again.

David Drumm   I'm calling the Regulator. He's got to stop it. And I'm not taking any bolloxology from him.

March 20
The Central Bank

The **Financial Regulator** *makes a statement to the media.*

Financial Regulator   Market participants who take unfair advantage by spreading false rumours while trading on the basis of those rumours are in breach of market abuse regulations and we will actively pursue those who may be engaged in this.

The **Governor** *of the Central Bank makes a statement to the media.*

Governor   The Irish banking sector remains robust and has no material exposures to the subprime market.

April 10
Investor Relations Magazine Awards, The Four Seasons Hotel, Dublin

Master of Ceremonies   Ladies and gentlemen … It's been a difficult time for all of us.

So, at this year's awards … we are rewarding the bank that has stayed out there, keeping up communications during the dark days …

Drum roll.

The Grand Prix award for Best Overall Investor Relations for 2008 goes to …Anglo Irish Bank.

Applause.

April 21
The National Treasury Management Agency
Dublin

An official from the Department of Finance visits the head of the **NTMA Boss**.

NTMA Boss   So … The Department of Finance wants us to place money on deposit in the Irish banks.

Senior Official   Yes.

NTMA Boss   To help ensure that they're liquid.

Senior Official   Yes.

NTMA Boss Because the market thinks they're bust.

Senior Official Well ...

NTMA Boss So they can't get any money from the market.

Senior Official (*uncertain*) Yes ...

NTMA Boss But they're *not* bust. They're just illiquid.

Senior Official Yes.

NTMA Boss So it's a confidence problem.

Senior Official Yes.

NTMA Boss And our putting money in them is a confidence trick.

Senior Official I don't think I'd put it—

NTMA Boss Of course not.

(*On a tangent.*) Do you remember the '90s?

When we could barely fund the country?

I wore out shoe leather in the City of London, trying to fund this State.

There was no confidence in Ireland. We couldn't raise any decent money. So we did it on the quiet ...

We built up a war chest in tiny amounts. We went to every possible bank. Sometimes to different desks in the same bank ...

So the markets wouldn't notice.

So we could keep the State open. And we succeeded ...

Managing the banks is your job. Or the Central Bank's. Whoever ...

Managing the State's money is my job ...

If you want me to put money somewhere, I need a direction from the Minister. In writing.

The **Senior Official** *exits. No niceties.*

NTMA Boss John!

The **NTMA Official** *enters.*

NTMA Official Boss.

NTMA Boss It looks like we're going to have to do something for AIB Boss and Bank of Ireland Boss—

NTMA Official You think they're sound?

NTMA Boss I hope so. But not Anglo.

NTMA Official Anglo?

NTMA Boss If we get a direction, we'll have to. But we'll make it just a token. Forty million or so …

It's an odd place. A bank with no branches. I don't get it.

NTMA Official Have you said anything – up the line?

NTMA Boss Sure there's no point. They don't listen to us.

May 8
Office of the Minister for Finance, Government Buildings, Dublin

An introductory briefing for the new **Minister for Finance** *(Brian Lenihan).*

Senior Official Minister, you're very welcome to the Department. To plunge you straight in, we've prepared a briefing on financial stability. As you know, there has been a shortening of maturity profiles in the money and capital markets characterised by an inability to roll over longer-term bonds—

Minister for Finance *Please!* I have read the brief. Just get to it.

Senior Official There's a liquidity crisis, Minister. The banks are constantly sailing close to the wind, so to speak. The slightest shock, and they might not be able to borrow more short-term money to repay their loans.

Minister for Finance But their own loans are good?

Senior Official Yes –

Minister for Finance But?

Senior Official But a prolonged liquidity crisis can lead to a solvency problem … which could leave a bank in need of rescue …

Minister for Finance And then?

Senior Official Till recently, we've thought that the State would only rescue a bank if it were considered 'too big to fail' – a pillar bank. But in the current volatility, there is a fear that the failure of any bank could have a domino effect.

Minister for Finance So *all* the banks are … too big to fail?

Senior Official Yes, Minister. That raises the question of giving a guarantee to a vulnerable bank, as the British Treasury ultimately provided for Northern Rock. The policy here is quite clear …

To *protect* the interest of taxpayers, the provision of an open-ended and legally binding State guarantee – which would expose the Exchequer to significant risk – is *not* part of our 'toolkit' for crisis management.

Minister for Finance So guarantees are ruled out?

Senior Official Well, under extreme circumstances they may be unavoidable. To *protect* the interest of taxpayers.

Minister for Finance   So guarantees are to be avoided to protect the interest of taxpayers … unless the interest of taxpayers requires a guarantee?

Senior Official   Yes, Minister … Further, nationalisation of a bank is regarded as a sub-optimal option—

Minister for Finance   A *bad* option.

Senior Official (*conceding*)   A bad option.

Minister for Finance (*impatient*)   But an option.

Senior Official (*implacable*)   In case it becomes such, we're currently drawing up draft legislation, Minister.

May 10
Clara, Co Offaly

An outdoor event to celebrate the election of the former tánaiste, Brian Cowen, as **Taoiseach.**

Cheers.

Taoiseach   There is one thing –

Cheers drown him out.

There is one thing we know more than any other, from our civic and religious heritage in this country, and that is that it is only by giving that we receive … It is only by stretching ourselves beyond our own self-interests that we'll find fulfilment in our lives … It is only by being part of a community, part of something bigger than ourselves, that we will have the sort of life that we hope for us and our children …

And that is what politics has to be about in this country. And that is what I hope to do, as leader of Fianna Fáil, as Taoiseach, and as a TD for Clara, and for all of Laois-Offaly.

He starts to sing – Paddy's Green Shamrock Shore.

Taoiseach (*singing*)   From Derry quay we sailed away on the twenty-third of May
   We were boarded by a pleasant crew, all bound for Amerikay

The date and the news bulletin come in over the song each time.

June 12

Newsreader   The people have decisively rejected the Lisbon Treaty referendum in a development that will be seen as an early blow to Brian Cowen as Taoiseach.

Taoiseach (*singing*)   We took on board fresh water fine, ten thousand gallons or more
   And we sailed far away for Amerikay, far from Paddy's green shamrock shore

June 28

Newsreader   The collapse in house construction has brought Ireland to the edge of recession, the Economic and Social Research Institute said today … This will be the first recession in a quarter of a century. The ESRI estimates that new house prices will fall by 24 per cent in real terms.

Taoiseach (*singing*) We were sailing three days, we were all seasick, not a man on board was free
We were all confined unto our bunks; with no-one to pity poor me
No mother dear nor father kind to hold up me head, which was sore

Which made me think more on the lassie I left on Paddy's green shamrock shore.

*The song continues under the **Minister**'s statement.*

July 8
The Department of Finance

Minister for Finance We are facing a shortfall of €3 billion in tax revenue this year.

All Departments, State Agencies and Local Authorities will be required to reduce their payroll bill by 3 per cent by the end of next year.

All expenditure on Consultancies and Public Relations will be cut by half.

This must be seen in context … Over the last eleven years, we have dramatically increased the state pension, child benefit, and the number of gardaí, teachers, doctors and nurses serving our people … We stand by our choices. Our careful stewardship of the economy has positioned us well to weather the current economic storm. Thank you.

Taoiseach (*singing*) Well we finally reached the other side in three and twenty days
We were taken on board by a man and led round in six different ways

We each took on a parting glass, in case we might never meet more

And we drank our health to old Ireland and Paddy's green shamrock shore.

As he reaches the final lines of the song, the date and location for the song appear.

August 23
Fleadh Cheoil, Tullamore, Co Offaly

Taoiseach (*singing*) So fare thee well, sweet Liza dear and likewise to Derry town
And twice farewell to my comrades kind who dwell in that same plot of ground

If fortune should ever favour me, or I too have money in store

I'll come back and I'll wed the wee lassie I left on Paddy's green shamrock shore.

September 3
The Cabinet Room, Government Buildings

*The **Minister for Finance** addresses the Cabinet.*

Minister for Finance This is the gravest challenge the country has faced since Ray MacSharry was Finance Minister.

VAT receipts, stamp duty, capital gains tax and consumer spending have collapsed.

The tax shortfall could now be over *five* billion.

We've had the biggest rise in unemployment in a decade …

We have to address this, decisively.

We need to move the budget forward. October 14th. That gives us six weeks. We'll have to cut across the board.

You have two weeks to come up with your proposals.

Newsreader Irish Nationwide Building Society has today been downgraded by the ratings agency, Moody's, citing falling property values and exposure to commercial property and development.

September 5
The Department of Finance

In the Department of Finance, three officials meet.

Senior Official Have you got the statement from Moody's?

Junior Official (*carrying a bundle of papers, awkwardly*) Here it is.

Senior Official (*rapidly reviewing it*) Christ … This has got to be bad news for Anglo too … Where are we at with the nationalisation bill?

Senior Official 2 I have the draft Heads here.

(*Handing over the papers.*) And this is from the Attorney General's office …

We need to include the phrase … 'for the purpose of maintaining the stability of the financial system' …

Senior Official (*scanning it*) Ok … Did you make those calls? The ex-bankers?

Junior Official They're on standby.

Senior Official 2 *Ex*-bankers?

Senior Official If we do nationalise, we're going to need someone to run it … People with experience, but not working in the sector at the moment.

Senior Official 2 Retirees?

Senior Official *Veterans*. We've started lining some people up … Quietly … The Taoiseach's on the Late Late tonight?

Senior Official 2 His Department are looking for briefing materials.

Senior Official Oh Christ. He's going to need a line on this.

September 5
The Late Late Show

*The **Taoiseach** is being interviewed on the RTÉ television talk show.*

Taoiseach When I look at the downturn that's coming, I have great faith in the tens of thousands of people who in their own businesses and their own lives, they're not wallowing, they're going to get up and fight and take on this battle that's ahead of us ... as we are, in Government ... There's a job to be done and it's our duty to do it.

September 6

Newsreader The American mortgage giants, Fannie Mae and Freddie Mac, have today been nationalised by the US Government because their debt levels posed a systemic risk to financial stability.

September 12
The Department of Finance

Senior Official Where is Nationwide at?

Senior Official 2 Well, it can lose a billion a day and make it to the weekend with Central Bank cash. Just about.

Senior Official Is that the worst case?

Senior Official 2 No ... Worst case, it loses two billion a day. On Wednesday, it runs out of cash ...

We've to get money somewhere to keep it open – probably the National Treasury Management Agency ...

We have to get the Dáil recalled and push through the nationalisation legislation.

Senior Official So let's say the NTMA Boss is called on for three billion. On top of the central bank cash of two billion. That's a possible exposure of five billion.

Senior Official 2 As long as the bondholders do nothing.

Senior Official What triggers a call by them?

Senior Official 2 A default. Or anything that's technically a default. They're another six billion.

September 13
The Press Office, The Department of Finance

The press officers are working on a statement.

Senior Official What have we got?

Senior Press Officer Here it is.

Senior Official Read it out.

Junior Press Officer (*reading*) 'The Government has taken a decision today to introduce legislation that will take ... "X. F. I."'?

Senior Official Ex-figh ...

Senior Press Officer 'Financial Institution X'.

Senior Official Nationwide.

Senior Press Officer It's a code.

Junior Press Officer Of course.

Senior Official We're not putting it on paper. Anywhere.

Junior Press Officer It's just – I find it difficult to *hear* it ... X F-

Senior Official (*fluently*) Ex-figh.

Junior Press Officer It's like something out of a sci-fi movie.

Senior Official Can we just DO it?

Junior Press Officer You don't mind if I just use 'Nationwide' in here? So I can really *hear* it ...

(*Reading.*) 'The Government has taken a decision today to introduce legislation that will take Irish Nationwide Building Society into public ownership ... It is important to stress that Irish Nationwide is solvent and—

Senior Press Officer Don't beg the question.

Junior Press Officer I don't— (know what you mean.)

Senior Press Officer Don't 'stress' it – just say it. Directly.

Junior Press Officer 'Irish Nationwide is solvent.'

Senior Press Officer That's it.

The **Junior Press Officer** *makes a note and continues.*

Junior Press Officer 'This pre-emptive action by Government will give certainty to customers and the market about the underlying strength of Irish Nationwide ...'

Senior Official Go on.

Junior Press Officer 'Customers of all financial institutions can have confidence that the wider financial system in Ireland remains strong, well-capitalised, liquid and profitable.'

Senior Press Officer It needs something more.

He thinks, then dictates, slowly, working it out as he goes.

'If any ... *depositor* ... has difficulty in contacting INBS –

Junior Press Officer 'Irish Nationwide.'

Senior Press Officer What?

Junior Press Officer Use the full name. INBS sounds ... corporate.

(*Relishing the words.*) 'Irish Nationwide.' It's more—

Senior Official Oh for Christ's sake! Don't use either fucking name ... It's *Xfi*. It hasn't even happened yet. Imagine if you repeated this outside, by accident – because you were saying it in here and it got stuck in your brain.

Junior Press Officer I just need to *hear* it ...

(*Precious.*) That's my skill.

Senior Official You DON'T need to fucking hear it. *You* need to *write* it. *I* need to hear it.

Junior Press Officer ' ... they can rest assured that this action is being taken to safeguard their position ... Their money is, therefore, safe.'

Senior Official That's good. Straight.

Senior Press Officer Oh – one more thing.

(*Dictating.*) 'Xfi is a going concern. Borrowers must, of course, continue to meet their own loan obligations.'

Senior Official Yes.

September 14

Newsreader The American bank Lehman Brothers is on the verge of bankruptcy today as federal authorities scramble to find a solution that will save Wall Street's fourth largest investment Bank.

September 14
Kilcrumper Cemetery, Fermoy, Co Cork

The **Taoiseach** *gives the oration at the annual Liam Lynch commemoration.*

Taoiseach Liam Lynch, the leader of the Army of the Republic, fought not for an abstract freedom, he fought for the freedom of the Irish people to chart their own destiny ...

He died for an Ireland which was to be no longer a colony promoting the interests of an imperial power, but a vibrant and sovereign country ...

In 1921, he wrote: 'we can scarcely realise what a fine country Ireland will be when freedom comes.'

This country's War of Independence was about empowering our people economically, socially and culturally.

In our time, it is our duty, too, to work for such an Ireland, and for the common good.

September 14
The Press Office, the Department of Finance

Senior Official We'll need a website.

Senior Press Officer Plenty of bandwidth.

Senior Official You can't have it crashing.

Senior Press Officer A helpline.

Senior Official It's all about confidence.

Junior Press Officer What if they get through?

Pause.

Senior Official Reassurance.

Senior Press Officer What if they come in?

Junior Press Officer Come in where?

Senior Press Officer Come in fucking here.

Junior Press Officer Why would they come in here?

Senior Press Officer Because they want their money. And this Department may have just taken over their bank.

Senior Official Queues! Can you imagine what would happen if—

Junior Press Officer They might queue outside the *Department of Finance*?

Senior Press Officer (*realising*) Northern fucking Rock!

Senior Official We can't let that happen.

Senior Press Officer The media'll have a field day.

Senior Official We'll have to allow people inside—

Senior Press Officer Discretely. Somehow.

Senior Official But if they come in, they have to be seen to. They'll need a place to wait. Not packed. And a few minutes with a – a calm civil servant.

Senior Press Officer Where?

Junior Press Officer The atrium in the new building – that could be a waiting area?

Senior Official Okay. Good. Good.

September 15
Fianna Fáil Parliamentary Party Meeting, Clayton Hotel, Galway

The **Minister for Finance** *is accosted by the press.*

Reporter Minister, you and the Taoiseach have consistently blamed international shocks for the downturn here. Are you not evading responsibility for Fianna Fáil's role in creating a property bubble?

Minister for Finance *Two* of the *four* principal investment banks in New York, Lehman Brothers and Merrill Lynch, *no longer exist* today. That is dramatic news in the banking world. I think that we're entitled to talk about international factors after that.

Reporter But are you confident our banks can withstand the turmoil?

Minister for Finance It is tremendous that our banking system has shown resilience in the face of such banking trends.

Our banks uniquely have weathered the storm to date despite many more venerable institutions being unable to do that. Thank you.

September 16

Newsreader The American government has today nationalised one of the world's largest insurance companies, AIG. AIG had insured many of the loans that banks gave to other banks and was believed to be systemic for the global economy.

September 18
The Department of Finance

David Drumm *of Anglo Irish Bank makes a presentation to officials of the Department of Finance.*

David Drumm Old-fashioned banking. That's what we do…

The Anglo culture is relationship based. It's driven by a highly experienced and well established management team – men you know well …

We are more profitable and better capitalised than either AIB Boss or Bank of Ireland Boss.

We have a strong culture of asset quality. We have €69 billion in loans. Less than half a billion of those are impaired …

The market focus on Anglo is irrational.

We have twenty-five years of steady performance through various economic cycles. These values will stand to us. We believe the market will recognise them … In time.

Pause.

But we may not have time. We need your help. We need liquidity support. It's getting urgent.

Drumm *finishes and leaves. His phone rings. He answers.*

David Drumm (*on phone*)   Sean.

Sean FitzPatrick (*on phone*)   Well? How'd it go? What did you tell them?

David Drumm (*on phone*)   I told them we needed the moolah.

Sean FitzPatrick (*on phone*)   And are they going to give it to us?

David Drumm (*on phone*)   We'll see, Sean. We'll see.

September 18

Newsreader The British and Irish financial regulators have today banned the short selling of financial stocks. The move is aimed at protecting the banking system from speculation by hedge funds, in the wake of the global credit crunch.

September 18
The Department of Finance

*A **Junior Official** bursts into the **Minister**'s office.*

Junior Official Minister – the radio.

Minister for Finance What radio?

Junior Official (*with urgency*) Can you turn on the radio?

Minister for Finance I don't think I have a radio.

Junior Official It's Liveline, Minister.

Minister for Finance Oh Christ. What is it?

Junior Official They're talking about the banks.

Minister for Finance What are they saying?

Junior Official Joe Duffy said we shouldn't believe them if they—

Minister for Finance Who? Believe who.

Junior Official Them. The banks. He said if the banks say they're okay, we shouldn't believe them.

Minister for Finance He said WHAT?

Junior Official We'll have a transcript of it shortly, Minister.

Minister for Finance We have to get him off.

Junior Official Off?

Minister for Finance Off the air.

Junior Official I don't think that's poss—

Minister for Finance Get me the director general of RTÉ.

Junior Official (*leaving*) Yes, Minister.

Minister for Finance (*to himself*) Christ.

(*To official.*) Wait, wait!

Junior Official Yes, Minister?

Minister for Finance I'm going to have to go on the news.

Junior Official Yes, Minister.

September 20
Office of the Financial Regulator

David Drumm *meets the* **Financial Regulator**.

Regulator   David, what can I do for you?

David Drumm   Thank you for seeing me at such short notice, Regulator.

He is nervous, and therefore brusque.

Anglo is losing … a billion euro in deposits per day … We need liquidity to be able to meet depositor demands. I need an emergency credit line.

Regulator   How much?

David Drumm   Seven billion.

Regulator   Is that a precise figure David……..where did you get it from?

Beat.

David Drumm   I had a team working on the numbers.

Regulator I'm afraid … I'm somewhat embarrassed about this, David … I can't authorise it … There are 'collateral' issues … You'll have to go straight to the Central Bank.

September 20
Crinkle Sports and Recreation Centre, Crinkle, Birr, Co Offaly

Taoiseach   Handball is synonymous with Crinkle – it's been played here since the army barracks was built at the turn of the nineteenth century … So I'm particularly delighted to now declare this Handball Alley officially open.

September 20
Office of the Governor of the Central Bank

David Drumm   We're losing a billion euro in deposits per day, Governor … We need €7 billion in liquidity … I need an emergency credit line.

Governor   I don't have it, David. You'll need to tap the big boys.

David Drumm   AIB Boss? Bank of Ireland Boss? They'd rather see us collapse …

Governor   There's nothing I can do.

David Drumm   The ECB then. Can you ask them? That's what they're for. They have endless liquidity.

Governor   Collateral. You don't have the collateral.

David Drumm   We do have the collateral.

Governor   Not up to their standards.

David Drumm (*disbelieving*)   You can't help us.

Governor I'm afraid there's just €4 billion in the system for back-up liquidity, David. And that's in various pots. It couldn't all be made available to Anglo.

David Drumm Governor – you're the lender of last resort.

Governor My hands are tied.

Saturday, September 20
Bright Beginnings Child Care Centre, Ferbane, Co Offaly

Taoiseach (*speaking in Irish*) Is mór agam gur iarradh orm an foirgneamh saintógtha seo do chúram leanaí oscailt go hoifigiúil …

It gives me great pleasure to declare Bright Beginnings Childcare officially open.

September 20
The Department of Finance

Minister for Finance Let's hear it.

Junior Press Officer 'The Government has decided to increase the limit for the deposit guarantee scheme from €20,000 to €100,000. The Central Bank and Financial Regulator have stressed repeatedly that Irish financial institutions are well capitalised and liquid with good quality assets.'

Senior Press Officer It's clear.

Minister for Finance It's not enough.

Senior Press Officer It does what it says on the tin.

Minister for Finance What's the *narrative*?

Junior Press Officer The what?

Minister for Finance What's the narrative? The *story*. What's our *message*?

Junior Press Officer 'Your money is safe, folks.'

Minister for Finance *Whose* money?

Junior Press Officer Their money. The people. Out there. We're increasing the protection for small depositors—

Minister for Finance No! That's just the *detail*. The *narrative* is we're telling the *markets* we're standing behind the banks. But we can't spell it out. We need a line that conveys that – to those who are listening.

Senior Press Officer 'The Government wants to … protect the … *whole* financial system … secure its stability … and …'

Minister for Finance 'Ensure that *all deposits* in Irish financial institutions are safe.' That's it. Get it out there.

September 22

Newsreader   The era of the great investment banks has come to an end today. The last two standing on Wall Street, Morgan Stanley and Goldman Sachs, are to become traditional bank holding companies, under the regulation of the Federal Reserve.

September 22
The Department of Finance

A meeting of the Domestic Standing Group, a crisis response group of officials from the Department of Finance, the Central Bank and the Financial Regulator.

Senior Official   Potential losses. What are we looking at?

Senior Official 2   Nationwide could be two billion.

Senior Official   Anglo?

Senior Official 2   As much as eight and a half?

Short beat.

Regulatory Official   Even in that scenario, their capital covers it. The problem is liquidity.

Senior Official   And the latest on liquidity?

Regulatory Official   Anglo's looking for seven billion. Goldman Sachs think Nationwide can last eleven days. Both could need ECB overnight money today.

Senior Official   Today.

Senior Official 2   Can we go into the bond market?

NTMA Official   There's no appetite for Irish bonds.

Senior Official   We need a war chest. Ballpark, what do we have? Cash. In the Exchequer ... ministerial funds?

Central Bank Official   Eight billion.

Senior Official   The Social Insurance Fund?

Central Bank Official   Three point three billion.

Senior Official   The Pension Reserve?

NTMA Official   One point five billion. But—

Senior Official   And in bonds – what do we have? The Central Bank?

Central Bank Official   Nine billion.

Senior Official   In the Pension Reserve?

NTMA Official   Two point five billion. But we're waiting on legal clarification as to whether we can—

Senior Official We'll leave it out – for now. And hold back say two billion for day-to-day needs … That's eighteen billion we can put our hands on at short notice.

Senior Official 2 That's a war chest.

Senior Official But is it enough of one?

September 25
The Department of Finance

A **Senior Official** *addresses a gathering of external consultants, introducing them to each other.*

Senior Official Good morning everybody. We've brought you all in together to ensure that we're all working off the same page, as it were. Just so everybody's clear: Merrill Lynch are advising on liquidity and the strategic options available to the Government … Goldman Sachs *were* advising Irish Nationwide and are *now* advising the Government on the situation *in* Nationwide …

An acknowledgement from one of the gathering: 'Oh, good idea.'

Price Waterhouse Coopers are investigating the liquidity position and asset quality of the loan books of Nationwide, Anglo and Irish Life & Permanent … Morgan Stanley are advising Irish Life and Permanent…And Arthur Cox, of course, are advising on legal aspects…

Has everybody got that? Good.

Now, let's start looking at options for our banks.

Newsreader The American savings bank Washington Mutual has become the latest casualty of the subprime crisis. It has been placed in receivership after a nine-day bank run during which it lost $16.7 billion in deposits.

The **Senior Official** *gets six polystyrene cups and places the cups upside down on the table to represent the six banks.*

Senior Official (*identifying the cups*) AIB Boss. Bank of Ireland Boss. Anglo. Nationwide. EBS. Irish Life & Permanent.

There are no bad ideas. Blue-skies thinking …

Pause.

Let's look at mergers.

Senior Official 2 (*moving the cups*) Merge the three smaller banks: Nationwide, EBS and Irish Life & Permanent.

NTMA Official It'd need a guarantee on the Nationwide loan book.

Regulatory Official And liquidity support.

Senior Official So what about Anglo then?

Regulatory Official   They'll need liquidity support also – but we leave them on their own.

Senior Official   And the big two – Allied and Bank of Ireland Boss?

Senior Official 2   Should be okay.

Senior Official   Okay. That's one scenario. Let me get that.

The **Official** *records this scenario – perhaps taking a photo of it.*

Central Bank Official   We could split Nationwide – retail and commercial.

Senior Official 2   Why?

Central Bank Official   The commercial side is worse – nationalise that, merge the retail with the others.

Senior Official 2   What about Anglo taking on Nationwide?

Regulatory Official   They know the loan book best.

NTMA Official   They'll need the guarantee on the Nationwide book. And liquidity support.

Regulatory Official   Could the EBS take Nationwide?

NTMA Official   With a guarantee? Possibly.

Senior Official   Could we get away without any mergers or nationalisations?

September 26
Office of the Chief Executive, Anglo Irish Bank

Sean FitzPatrick   Where are we at?

David Drumm   We lost five billion in corporate deposits this week.

Sean FitzPatrick   Retail?

David Drumm   We're down 440 million.

Sean FitzPatrick   What about the Central Bank – they'll help?

David Drumm   Unlikely. But let's say they come through with an asset swap. That nets two billion.

Sean FitzPatrick   That's not enough.

David Drumm   If we continue to lose money like this – and the markets remain closed to us – we're negative €12 billion in three weeks.

Sean FitzPatrick   Right then. We're on our five yard line. But this game's not over yet.

September 28
Office of the Governor of the Central Bank

The **Minister for Finance** *arrives for a meeting with the* **Governor**.

Governor Minister. The President of the European Central Bank, Jean-Claude Trichet, has asked me to—

Minister for Finance (*impatient*) What did he say?

Governor The crisis is spreading. Banks all over Europe are vulnerable ... *Holland* – Fortis is in trouble ... *France* – Dexia ... *Germany* – Depfa could bring down HypoRe.

Minister for Finance What does he want us to do?

Governor We can't have a Lehman's in Europe. We have to contain this. No bank goes down.

September 29

Newsreader After a traumatic weekend for the European banking system, a number of banks were rescued overnight ... amongst them Bradford & Bingley in the UK ... the northern European bank Fortis ... and the German bank Hypo Real Estate ... which was bailed out with €35 billion after liquidity problems arose in its Dublin-based subsidiary, Depfa.

September 29
8am
Anglo Irish Bank

Sean Fitz Patrick *and* **David Drumm** *watch the Anglo share price (projected above the stage) fall. (It falls from €4.15 to €2.30 across the day.)*

David Drumm (*on the phone*) What's the latest on liquidity?

(*Pause.*) Christ.

He hangs up.

Sean FitzPatrick What do we need?

David Drumm One point five billion.

Sean FitzPatrick For the week?

David Drumm For tomorrow.

Beat.

We have to go to the others. AIB Boss and Bank of Ireland Boss. We have to ask them to buy us.

September 29
9am

Newsreader All the major British banks have suffered sharp losses on the London Stock Exchange this morning ... as the rescue of Halifax Bank of Scotland by Lloyds TSB has been threatened by fears that Lloyds may suffer losses in the collapse of the northern European bank Fortis.

September 29
10am
AIB Boss Bankcentre

Sean FitzPatrick *and* **David Drumm** *meet with the head of AIB Boss.*

AIB Boss   Sean.

Sean FitzPatrick   Can we talk?

AIB Boss   Sean—

Sean FitzPatrick   Now.

AIB Boss   I don't think so, Sean.

Sean FitzPatrick   We need to discuss the … current situation. It's threatening us all.

AIB Boss   Sean, it's chaotic here.

Sean FitzPatrick   It's chaotic everywhere.

AIB Boss   We're under severe pressure.

Sean FitzPatrick   *You're* under pressure?!

AIB Boss   I don't think I can spare any time for discussions.

Sean FitzPatrick   We're in trouble. Serious trouble. It's in nobody's interest if this takes us down. I need to talk to you. Properly.

AIB Boss   We're all in difficulties, Sean. The whole market has dried up. We can't help you.

Sean FitzPatrick   I could get a meeting with the Taoiseach. We could go together. Set out our stall. A united banking front.

AIB Boss   I'm sorry Sean. You're on your own.

Sean FitzPatrick   Yes, well.

Beat.

Thank you for … taking the time.

11am

Newsreader   Franco-Belgian bank Dexia is down 20 per cent on the stock market so far today after fears over potential losses on a multi-billion loan to the troubled Irish- based bank Depfa.

12pm
Bank of Ireland Boss Head Office

Sean FitzPatrick *and* **David Drumm** *meet with the head of* **Bank of Ireland Boss**.

David Drumm   We need one point five billion to open tomorrow. The markets are completely closed to us.

Sean FitzPatrick It makes no sense at all. We're about to announce a profit for this year.

David Drumm We have a €69 billion loan book with just half a billion bad debts.

Bank of Ireland Boss What are you suggesting?

David Drumm We need collateral to raise new money from the ECB. If you were to lend us some of your residential mortgage loan book, that would cross that hurdle.

Pause. No answer.

Sean FitzPatrick Or you could put some money on deposit with us.

Beat.

David Drumm Or you could buy us.

Bank of Ireland Boss Buy Anglo?

David Drumm Or even part of it.

Sean FitzPatrick Why not? You'll never get better value.

Bank of Ireland Boss We are all having liquidity difficulties.

Sean FitzPatrick Will you think about it?

David Drumm We have some figures here.

(*Handing out a memo.*) Of course, we can put people on it, get you whatever numbers you need.

Sean FitzPatrick There's real value here.

Bank of Ireland Boss I don't think there's—

Sean FitzPatrick Just – have a look at the figures.

Pause.

Please.

Bank of Ireland Boss (*polite*) Of course. I'll have a look at the figures. But please don't expect—

Sean FitzPatrick We're not expecting anything. Except that you look at the opportunity.

Bank of Ireland Boss I'll look.

4pm

Newsreader The Icelandic government has taken control of the country's third-largest bank, Glitnir, after the bank faced short-term funding problems, provoking fears that Iceland could be facing financial ruin.

5.45pm
The Taoiseach's Meeting Room, Government Buildings

The **Minister for Finance** *is in conference with the* **Taoiseach**.

Taoiseach   AIB Boss and Bank of Ireland Boss are coming in.

Minister for Finance   They asked to?

Taoiseach   Yes.

Minister for Finance   What time?

Taoiseach   9.30.

Minister for Finance   That gives us some time to work through things. The Attorney General?

Taoiseach   On his way.

Minister for Finance   The Governor?

Taoiseach   And the Regulator.

A **Senior Official** *enters.*

Senior Official   I've been talking to the National Treasury Management Agency. They're sending over some people to run through the figures.

Minister for Finance   Are we bringing in the Cabinet?

Taoiseach   No, we'll do it on the phone—

Senior Official   Incorporeal?

Taoiseach   Yes. What's the latest with Anglo?

Senior Official   Fell by half on the stock exchange.

Taoiseach   We have to move. Tonight.

6pm

Newsreader   Shareholders in one of the largest American banks, Wachovia, have been almost wiped out today in a rescue deal with the bank Citigroup that sees Citigroup absorb up to $42 billion of Wachovia's losses on mortgages.

The **Taoiseach** *and* **Minister for Finance** *and* **Senior Official** *are joined by the* **Governor** *of the Central Bank and the* **Attorney General**.

Minister for Finance   Governor.

Governor   I have the liquidity update from PriceWaterhouseCoopers.

Taoiseach   Let's hear it.

Governor Anglo lost almost two billion today. They've no reserves left. They've borrowed 0.9 billion from the Central Bank already today. There's another … two billion due tomorrow.

Minister for Finance That's it. They can't open.

Senior Official They're bust.

Governor Anglo *isn't* bust.

Senior Official They can't meet their debts as they fall due. That's *bust*. They're insolvent.

Governor Not *necessarily*. They're *illiquid*. They've had a bank run. They can't get the money they need from other banks. The global banking system has seized up. It's a temporary market failure. It has nothing to do with their assets, their loans.

Minister for Finance So it *is* solvent?

Governor To the best of our knowledge *all* the Irish banks are solvent. Their loans are good.

Senior Official Anglo's loans *can't be* good. It's a *monoline* property bank. The property market is crashing.

Governor Its loans seem to be holding up. The management's estimate is three per cent impairments. And even if it does take a hit, it's well capitalised.

Minister for Finance *How* well?

Governor Well in excess of the required minimums.

Minister for Finance How *much*?

Governor Five billion in equity and five billion in junior debt? I don't have the accounts here.

Senior Official On a loan book of—

Governor Ninety billion.

Minister for Finance What was the stress case for losses?

Senior Official Seven point five billion.

Minister for Finance So that's within their capital.

Taoiseach If it's so well capitalised, what's the fucking problem?

Minister for Finance Its business model is broken.

Governor It relied on wholesale funding. That funding's dried up. Nobody trusts anyone. Nobody *can* trust anyone.

Senior Official If its business model is broken, we *should let it go*.

Governor We'd be a pariah in Europe! We *can't*—

Taoiseach *Okay*.

Beat.

Let's step back here. Anglo's in trouble. We get that. Now: let's just walk it through. Let's say … Let's say we do nothing. What happens?

Pause.

Attorney General Anglo doesn't open in the morning.

Taoiseach And?

Minister for Finance It's on the news.

Senior Official People arrive at their branches.

Governor (*horrified*) Just like Northern Rock.

Minister for Finance But Anglo is closed. There's nobody there to give out any money.

Governor So they panic. Maybe they come here—

Taoiseach But depositors are guaranteed. Up to 100k.

Minister for Finance They won't remember that. Not in the heat of the moment—

Governor Or they won't trust it.

Senior Official Anyway, the other banks will face bank runs.

Taoiseach Will they?

Senior Official Well what would you do if you heard an Irish bank had collapsed? You'd take out any money you had in any other Irish bank.

Governor None of the Irish banks can withstand a run at the moment.

Senior Official So the ATMs empty.

Attorney General The banks close their doors.

Taoiseach So what happens then?

Senior Official So say you're a young parent. And you need medicine for your child. But you can't get any money out to buy the medicine.

Minister for Finance Order breaks down pretty quickly.

Taoiseach Okay. So there's the risk of a run on the banks. Let's say we can avert that. Communications. We calm people. Assure them their money's safe.

Governor There'll be a corporate run anyway. Money is already flooding from the system.

Attorney General Nobody's going to lend an Irish bank anything.

Governor So the others will be next – tomorrow, it'll be AIB Boss who can't meet demands.

Senior Official Maybe there's a way of ringfencing Anglo – a way to separate them off, somehow, so we can let them go without the contagion.

Governor We can't let a bank go. Nobody, anywhere, is letting another bank go.

Minister for Finance We have to think of ourselves.

Governor Do you want to be responsible for Europe's Lehman's?

Senior Official Lehman Brothers was one of the world's largest investment banks. Anglo is a small bank on the western edge of Europe. We ringfence it – shield the others.

Governor We *can't* ringfence it. Where does Anglo reach to? *Every other* Irish bank.

How many other European banks?

What is the chain reaction if Anglo defaults? How many others default?

Look at the contagion from Lehman's. We cannot let a bank go down.

Have we not learned anything from the past two weeks?

Taoiseach So we're saying one bank is on the verge of bringing down our entire financial system?

Governor Not just ours.

Beat.

Taoiseach So we're looking for a rescue for Anglo. Let's look at the options.

Senior Official AIB Boss and Bank of Ireland Boss could support Anglo.

Governor They can't do that on their own.

Minister for Finance With our backing then. And the Central Bank. They could supply the funds Anglo needs, under guarantee.

Taoiseach Option two.

Minister for Finance Nationalise.

Taoiseach Anglo.

Minister for Finance And possibly Nationwide.

Governor In the middle of the night?

Attorney General The legislation is ready.

Governor But the practicalities … You'd need to have teams at the bank *before it opens—*

Taoiseach Can it be done overnight?

Senior Official Technically – perhaps. But we'd need to get started.

Governor   —And there are market dangers. Let's say you nationalise Anglo – the market will immediately expect Nationwide to be nationalised. So do them both – and then the market asks, who's next? The share price collapses, provoking further capital flight—

Taoiseach   Okay. Option three.

Senior Official (*teasing it out*)   Bid for time. Try and cobble together enough liquidity to get Anglo to the weekend and work something out at Europe …

Maybe something with asset swaps … Something that could allow Anglo to use non-ECB-eligible securities as collateral to swap for government bonds or cash—

Taoiseach   It has to be *simple*! We have to implement this tonight and signal it to the markets by the morning.

A child has got to be able to understand it.

(*Checking the time.*) We have twelve hours …

Pause.

What else?

Governor   A guarantee. It's the obvious solution.

Senior Official   For whom?

Governor   For them all. System-wide. The problem is confidence. It's the simplest statement of confidence there is.

Attorney General   What if that's not enough for Anglo?

Minister for Finance   We could nationalise Anglo *as well as* a blanket guarantee.

Taoiseach   So. On the table. We can … We can nationalise Anglo. We can give a blanket guarantee. We can give a blanket guarantee *and* nationalise. We can cobble something together, with liquidity support … What did Merrill Lynch say?

Senior Official   All of the above.

Taoiseach   Which did they recommend?

Minister for Finance   *Recommend*? You think they'd be that stupid?

Taoiseach   Where's the memo?

Senior Official   Which one?

Taoiseach   The most recent one.

Governor   I have the Friday one.

Minister for Finance   Wasn't there an update yesterday?

Taoiseach   Who's got it?

He waits for it, impatiently. Nobody has it.

WHAT DID WE PAY THEM FOR IF WE'RE NOT EVEN USING THEIR ADVICE?

Senior Official I'll get it.

6.30pm
Government Buildings

The National Treasury Management Agency team arrives at Government Buildings.

Junior Official The NTMA Boss?

NTMA Official That's us.

Junior Official How many of you?

NTMA Official We'll be five.

Junior Official We have a room for you.

NTMA Official Near the war room?

Junior Official Down the corridor.

NTMA Official Wifi?

Junior Official It's cabled. You have your own laptops?

NTMA Official We'll need a printer.

Junior Official I'll see what we can do. Here you are.

7pm
The Taoiseach's Meeting Room

The **Senior Official** *returns with the memo.*

Senior Official I've got the Merrill Lynch memo.

Taoiseach Read out what it says on the guarantee.

Senior Official (*reading, briskly*) 'This would be a complete State guarantee to all depositors and senior creditors of the six primary regulated financial institutions ... It should act immediately to stem outflows and encourage deposit inflows ... However, the scale of such a guarantee could be —

(*Pause.*) over €500 billion.'

Taoiseach Go on.

Senior Official 'This would almost certainly negatively impact the State's sovereign credit rating and raise issues as to its credibility ...

The wider market will be aware that Ireland could not afford to cover the full amount if required ...

It might also be poorly perceived by other European states if – as liquidity flows migrate – they come under pressure to do the same ...

Were there to be a co-ordinated response across Europe, that could make this option more viable …

Several European governments have already made comments in this regard.'

Taoiseach   That's *it*?

Senior Official   That's it.

Taoiseach   What did that cost?

8.15pm
A conference room

The team from the National Treasury Management Agency are crunching the numbers.

Senior NTMA Official   Okay, here's what we need. We want the total current exposure of the six main banks: AIB Boss, Bank of Ireland Boss, Anglo, Nationwide, Irish Life & Permanent, EBS.

We want that disaggregated: how much is deposits – retail, corporate, Irish, foreign.

How much is bonds – secured, senior, junior. How much is interbank. How much is Eurosystem.

Junior NTMA Official   But we don't have that kind of—

Senior NTMA Official   Just get me what you can, whatever we have … The total exposure.

And *liquidity*: What do we have. Where is it. When can we get it … Ministerial funds. Pension Reserve. Central Bank.

8.30pm
The Taoiseach's Meeting Room

Taoiseach   A blanket guarantee.

Governor   It's the simplest, most direct, most forceful action. The problem is liquidity – confidence. A guarantee puts the weight of the state behind the banks.

Senior Official   Five *hundred* billion euro! That's over *twice* the size of our economy. *Seven* times the size of the budget. How can we possibly honour that?

Governor   We have one of the lowest debt-to-GDP ratios in Europe. The markets won't second guess it.

Senior Official   Granted – it might stop the panic – briefly. And then they'll take a closer look, and think, 'what the *fuck?* – Ireland hasn't got 500 billion to bail out its banks!' And then – then they'll target the sovereign.

Governor   We're not talking about €500 billion. There are assets there to cover almost all of that. And if there are losses on the loan books, they're well capitalised to cover them.

Taoiseach And if the losses exceed their capital?

Beat.

Minister for Finance We have the Pension Reserve.

Senior Official It's too rushed. We don't have the data …

Let Anglo get funds from the Central Bank, and AIB Boss and Bank of Ireland Boss if it has to. We keep it open till the weekend …

Then we step in and nationalise if we have to. It gives us another five days to get a closer look at what's going on.

Taoiseach What if it moves too quickly? Another Lehman's goes down, somewhere.

The funding situation gets worse. Anglo will go and it might bring the others with it. We won't make it to the weekend …

Nothing we've done so far has stemmed this. The shorts ban; the deposit guarantee – we've tried the soft options.

If we try another half measure tonight and it doesn't work we'll be back in here later in the week trying something else. And we'll be weaker …

There are no good options. They're all bad. I'm looking for the least worst … the one that is least likely to explode in our faces.

9pm

Newsreader The Bush Administration's rescue package for its banking sector, the Troubled Asset Relief Programme, or TARP, was rejected by Congress this evening in a decision that has sent the markets back into panic.

A **Junior Official** *enters.*

Junior Official Taoiseach.

Taoiseach Yes.

Junior Official AIB Boss and Bank of Ireland Boss are here.

Taoiseach Where are they?

Junior Official In the Sycamore Room.

Taoiseach Did anyone see them?

Junior Official Anyone—

Taoiseach The press! Were they seen? Are there reporters at the gates?

Junior Official I don't think so.

Taoiseach They'll have to wait. Get them some coffee.

Beat.

Senior Official Merrill Lynch – the memo – they said senior creditors – bondholders – we guarantee them. Why? Why not just depositors?

Minister for Finance We tried depositors. With an implication that we'd stand behind the banks. It didn't work.

Governor The problem isn't small depositors. The problem is the markets …

There's nothing other than overnight money available.

And even that's closing to the Irish banks …

A deposit guarantee isn't enough – it won't assure the markets. We can't have second-guessing of this. It has to have maximum impact.

Attorney General Even if it could work, it wouldn't be legal. There's no distinction in law between depositors and other creditors. They're *pari passu*—

Senior Official They're what?

Minister for Finance Ranked equally.

Attorney General It's all just *debt* – if the bank goes bust, they get burned – bondholders *and* depositors.

Senior Official We can *change* the law.

Minister for Finance In the middle of the night?

Attorney General In one of the most open economies in the world?

Minister for Finance We don't suddenly change the law on contracts because we feel like it.

Attorney General We'd never return to the bond markets.

Taoiseach This is not a banana republic!

The **Junior Official** *enters again.*

Junior Official Taoiseach?

Taoiseach What is it?

Junior Official The Nine News, Taoiseach—

Taoiseach What do you—

Junior Official David Murphy's just said the government was in session with the banks and the regulators.

Taoiseach How the – How the fuck does David Murphy know the bankers are in my fucking office?

Minister for Finance It doesn't matter.

Taoiseach It does fucking matter. We have a few hours to work this out. On our own.

Once we announce that solution, people are going to be all over us.

If it gets out that we're in here now, they'll be all over us now.

No more talking to Murphy. Or George Lee. Or anyone. Not tonight!

11.15pm

Two hours later. They are going round in circles, exhausted, agitated.

Senior Official   And subordinated debt?

Minister for Finance   You don't guarantee subordinated debt. That's why it's called subordinated.

Governor   It may not be that simple.

Minister for Finance   The whole point is that it's risk-absorbing capital.

Governor   But who's bearing that risk?

Minister for Finance   It doesn't matter who's bearing the risk – whoever it is, if the risk goes bad, they get burned.

Governor   But they're the same people – the same institutions that hold subordinated bonds also hold senior bonds …

If the banks are going to get out of this, they're going to need to be able to issue new bonds.

If their bondholders get burned now, they won't be coming back for more in the future.

Attorney General   What precedent is there?

Governor   For what?

Attorney General   For such a guarantee.

Pause.

Governor   This whole situation is unprecedented.

Attorney General   Surely the guarantee isn't unprecedented. Isn't it a standard response to banking crises?

Taoiseach   So?

Attorney General   So what did they do with subordinated debt in other countries? And what happened afterwards?

Governor   I don't think it's realistic to be looking for that information in the middle of the night in the middle of a bank run.

Attorney General   But we've been working on this possibility for months!

Northern Rock was guaranteed a year ago!

For the past two weeks, since Lehman's, we've known we can't afford to let a bank fail.

Have we no more concrete information on what a guarantee is supposed to contain? Where is the *detail*?

Taoiseach   This isn't the time. We have to deal with this *now*.

Beat.

Let's hear what the banks have to say.

11.30pm
The Sycamore Room

The **Taoiseach** *and* **Minister for Finance** *join the bankers in the Sycamore Room.*

Taoiseach   Sorry to keep you waiting, gentlemen. Let's hear it.

AIB Boss   Our banks have been providing credit to the people and businesses of Ireland since the early 1800s ...

They survived the Famine. They survived wars. Recession. The currency crisis...

We did so because we were *prudent*. We ran branches. We took in deposits.

We didn't give mortgages to people who couldn't afford them.

Bank of Ireland Boss   Anglo has to pay out on a billion euro deposit in the morning. They can't meet it. They'll bring us down.

AIB Boss   Anglo is a cancer. It's spreading to the rest of us. You have to cut them off.

Minister for Finance   How bad is your own situation?

AIB Boss   Liquidity is ... drying up.

Bank of Ireland Boss   We have some excess but maturity dates are shortening all the time. It's getting dangerous.

Minister for Finance   How long do you have?

Bank of Ireland Boss   We can see the runway for sixty days. In the absence of a crisis.

Taoiseach   And if there's a crisis?

Bank of Ireland Boss   Less. Much less.

Minister for Finance   What if there's a bank run?

Beat.

AIB Boss   Days.

Bank of Ireland Boss   We are the nervous system of this economy. If people doubt us, the economy collapses.

Taoiseach   The immediate problem is Anglo. Can you solve that problem?

Bank of Ireland Boss   Can we fund it? We can do that. *If* we're guaranteed.

Minister for Finance   What kind of guarantee?

242   Colin Murphy's Political Plays

AIB Boss   System-wide.

Taoiseach   Work on the funds. We'll talk again later.

AIB Boss   You need to take Anglo out. Take it off the table. If you can't liquidate it, nationalise it.

Taoiseach   The media's mixed up Anglo and AIB Boss before.

AIB Boss   We're not in anything like the same danger as Anglo

Taoiseach   D'you think the world out there sees that? It's a similar bank in the same place. It's *systemic*.

Minister for Finance   I still think nationalisation makes a lot of sense.

Bank of Ireland Boss   They're cowboys.

Taoiseach   You all owe each other money … You all get your money from the same places. We can't prevent contagion … We nationalise Anglo, which of you is next?

They leave. Outside the room:

Minister for Finance   We know Anglo's the rogue agent.

Taoiseach   The *rogue agent*?! For the past ten years they've been our poster-boy! What about all the promises we've made that our banks are good?

Minister for Finance   If we nationalise it we can go in and sort it out, work out the losses. We can ringfence it.

Taoiseach   We don't have time.

Minister for Finance   We can push the button now.

Taoiseach   I am *not* fucking nationalising Anglo tonight!

Minister for Finance   So we do it at the weekend. That gives us time to prepare … We separate it off completely from the other banks. Stand behind them with a guarantee and take Anglo into care … That sends a clear signal to the market and lets us work out what's going on in Anglo.

Taoiseach   Stop looking for the perfect solution. It's too risky … The upside might be bigger but so is the downside … This *has* to work. I'm looking for the most impactful solution – the most effective. I'll park nationalisation till the weekend. But we have to *get to* the weekend.

September 30
12am
The Department of the Taoiseach

Two Department of Senior Officials enter, frantically searching through paperwork.

Junior Official   What are we looking for?

Senior Official 2   Anything from the Department of Finance.

Guaranteed! 243

Junior Official But *we're* from the Department of Finance.

Senior Official 2 (*impatient*) We're looking for a letter. From the Department of Finance.

Junior Official What letter?

Senior Official 2 Any letter!

Junior Official Any letter at all?

Senior Official 2 Just so long as it has the Finance logo – headed notepaper.

Junior Official Can't we use Taoiseach's headed notepaper?

Senior Official 2 No!

Junior Official Why don't we just go across the way and get some notepaper *from* Finance?

Senior Official 2 Because it's midnight and it's all locked up. So we're going to make some *new* notepaper out of an *old* letter.

Junior Official Of course. Who are we writing to?

Senior Official 2 The Governor of the Central Bank. We need him to make emergency liquidity available to Anglo in the morning. And he needs a letter of comfort from the Minister. And it needs to be on Department of Finance headed notepaper. There must be something here somewhere.

September 30.
12.30am
A corridor in Government Buildings

The bankers are talking separately on their phones.

AIB Boss Yeh, we're splitting it evenly with Bank of Ireland Boss. One billion.

Bank of Ireland Boss Just get me what you can … It's for Anglo – half from us and half from AIB Boss.

AIB Boss Hang on a sec.

(*To* **Bank of Ireland Boss**.) Did you get a sandwich?

Bank of Ireland Boss No.

AIB Boss I thought somebody mentioned some sandwiches.

Bank of Ireland Boss *shrugs, preoccupied with his phone call.*

AIB Boss For Christ's sake!

(*Returning to the call.*) Yes, short-term liquidity for Anglo …

(*Listens.*) Fully guaranteed …

(*Listens.*) Yes, one billion. By tomorrow morning.

(*Listens.*) Just make those calls and call me back.

(*Listens.*) No, we're not going anywhere.

1am
The Taoiseach's Meeting Room

Minister for Finance If we're going to give a guarantee … We have to legislate. Fast.

Taoiseach We could just do a statement. A verbal guarantee – 'your money's good.'

Minister for Finance We have to show we mean it. We have to nail it down.

Attorney General In the absence of legislation, people will challenge it.

Taoiseach Who's going to argue with a government guarantee?

Governor The banks that aren't guaranteed.

Minister for Finance If somebody credible questions it – before it's law – it could crumble. Let's say they pour doubt on our ability to get it past Europe—

Governor —And the markets believe them …

Minister for Finance —They'll go after us …

Governor They'll short Ireland.

Taoiseach *How* fast can we legislate?

Minister for Finance Three days?

Governor Has that ever been done before?

Minister for Finance If we go through the night. The Dáil tomorrow. Seanad Wednesday. Then Committee and back to the Dáil, Thursday. Maybe.

Taoiseach That's *if* we have the legislation.

Minister for Finance We'll have the legislation.

Taoiseach By tomorrow? From *scratch*?

Attorney General We can use the nationalisation bill we've been working on. That creates the same powers. We just strip out the nationalisation sections. I'll get working on it.

Governor But there's still three days. Three days when there's nothing behind this guarantee other than a press release. What if somebody challenges it?

Taoiseach What about Europe? Is it legal?

Senior Official Why wouldn't it be?

Taoiseach We're propping up *our* banks. At the expense of *their* banks.

Governor We've no choice.

Attorney General   It *is* legal – European Law – Article 87 – 'State aid' – it allows action to remedy a 'serious disturbance' in the economy.

Minister for Finance   But we have to make it clear that it is legal pretty quickly.

Attorney General   We have to be explicit. We can't pretend this is just a confidence measure – that there's no real problem. We have to be clear about the problem.

Senior Official   We need them on board – the Commission, the ECB, Ministers – all of them. At least tacit cooperation – nobody pouring doubt on it.

Minister for Finance   We need to work the phones. Head off any criticism.

Governor   I can call Trichet.

Senior Official   What time can we start calling?

Minister for Finance   First thing. We're an hour behind. We can start at six.

Senior Official   We'd need the Opposition on board?

Minister for Finance   I can call them in the morning.

Taoiseach   I'll call them.

Beat.

That's it, then. A blanket guarantee.

(*To* **Senior Official**.) Call the Cabinet. Start the phone calls.

(*To* **Minister for Finance**.) You'll work on the statement?

(*To* **Governor**.) Keep working on liquidity – check with the banks.

(*To* **Attorney General**.) You'll work through the legals?

(*To all.*) We'll meet back in an hour.

2.30am
The Press Office

Two press officers are working on a press release.

Senior Press Officer   Where's the latest draft of the press release?

Junior Press Officer   Here.

Senior Press Officer   Read it out.

Junior Press Officer   'The Government has decided to put in place a guarantee arrangement—

Senior Press Officer   '*Today*.' 'The Government has decided to put in place *today* a guarantee' – No.

Junior Press Officer   'Immediately.'

Senior Press Officer   Too panicked sounding.

Junior Press Officer   'With immediate effect.'

Senior Press Officer   Try it.

Junior Press Officer   'The Government has decided to put in place *with immediate effect* a guarantee arrangement to cover all deposits, covered bonds, senior debt and dated subordinated debt.'

Senior Press Officer   Okay. Okay. Check that with the AG and run it by the Minister.

3am
Office of the Taoiseach

Attorney General   Taoiseach.

Taoiseach   What's wrong?

Attorney General   The new wording.

Taoiseach   What new wording?

Attorney General (*handing over a sheet*)   The one the banks are pushing.

Taoiseach   What's wrong with it?

Attorney General   It's looser.

Taoiseach   Looser?

Attorney General We've got to keep it *tight*. We have to be careful with this wording … If there's any looseness in it, we might find ourselves guaranteeing more than we'd intended …

Taoiseach   Such as?

Attorney General Such as new bonds for *the lifetime* of the bond. Not just the guarantee period …

We can't give *any* implication that we're guaranteeing anything more than is *specified* …A loose word or two could make a big difference…

We're guaranteeing them for *two years*. At the end of the two years – the guarantee *expires*. Unambiguous. No room for doubt.

Taoiseach   Okay. Rein it in. Go back to the last draft.

3.30am
The Taoiseach's Meeting Room

Senior Official   Here is the latest draft.

He places a sheet in front of the **Minister**, *who scans it expertly.*

Minister for Finance (*intemperate*)   'Serious disturbance to the economy.'

Official   Minister?

Minister for Finance (*impatient*)   Where is it?

Official   We took it out – I thought—

Minister for Finance   It's a quote from the EU state aid regulations—

Official   I'll reinsert it.

Minister for Finance   We *need* it to get this over the line in Brussels!

Taoiseach   You should go home.

Minister for Finance (*looking at watch*)   It's hardly worth it.

Taoiseach   Even if you get two hours. You've to lead on this tomorrow.

Minister for Finance (*conceding*)   Okay … We should all go. We could be back in here tomorrow night …

(*A black joke.*) nationalising Anglo.

6am
Office of the Secretary General to the Government

Secretary General (*on the phone*)   Good morning Minister. This is the Secretary General. I'm sorry to disturb you.

(*Pause.*) Just after six, Minister.

(*Formal.*) Minister, the Taoiseach has asked me to call you and your Cabinet colleagues …A government decision needs to be taken on an incorporeal basis. The nature—

(*Listens.*) The nature of the decision is to put in place with immediate effect a guarantee arrangement to safeguard all deposits, covered bonds, senior debt and dated subordinated debt—

(*Listens.*) with the following banks: Allied Irish Bank, Bank of Ireland Boss, Anglo Irish Bank, Irish Life & Permanent, Irish Nationwide Building Society and the Educational Building Society.

(*Listens.*) Minister, do you agree or disagree with the decision?

(*Listens.*) Thank you Minister.

7.30am
Office of the Minister for Finance

The **Minister** *is mid-interview with a RTÉ* **Reporter**.

Minister for Finance   Don't forget, the State will actually make money from the guarantee – there will be a significant charge to the banks for the facility.

Reporter   Em. (*Awkward pause.*) What if it doesn't work?

Minister for Finance WHAT? You can't say that.

(*Breaking the interview.*) You cannot ask that question!

(*Over his protests.*) No— No— I'm sorry— Our economy is hanging by a thread. That thread is confidence.

Reporter (*confused*) But—

Minister for Finance *You* have a responsibility here too.

Reporter But—

Minister for Finance You have to consider the impact of your questions.

Reporter But … you have the question on your FAQ about the guarantee.

Minister for Finance What? Let me see that.

He takes the document offered by the **Reporter**.

Minister for Finance Who gave you this?

Reporter The press office.

(*Pause.*) Minister, it's the obvious question. If I don't ask it, it just leaves it hanging in everyone's mouths.

Minister for Finance Yes. Well. I suppose so. Give me a moment.

He collects himself.

Okay.

Reporter Minister, you said the guarantee was intended to restore confidence in the Irish banking system. But what if it doesn't work?

Minister for Finance There's no question of it not working. We are putting the weight of a sovereign state with the lowest debt-to-GDP ratio in Europe behind our banking system. We're sending a clear message: Ireland is open for business.

8am

Junior Official Minister. The Chancellor of the Exchequer is on the line.

Minister for Finance (*on phone*) Alistair.

Alistair Darling (*on phone*) We said—

Minister for Finance Alistair—

Alistair Darling No *surprises*.

Minister for Finance Alistair—

Alistair Darling You assured me – we assured each other – that there would be no surprises. I thought we had an understanding.

Minister for Finance I know Alistair—

Alistair Darling And then I turn on my radio at six am this morning and John fucking Humphrys is telling me that the Irish government has guaranteed 500 *billion euro* of its banks' debts!

Minister for Finance We had no choice, Alistair.

Alistair Darling That can't be, I think, I was just talking to the Irish Minister for Finance the other day and he assured me there would be no surprises. That's quite a fucking surprise—

Minister for Finance We had no choice.

Alistair Darling What do you mean, you had—

Minister for Finance It was two am. We had to do something before the markets opened. You saw what happened yesterday. They couldn't have taken another day of that.

Alistair Darling But surely there were other options.

Minister for Finance There may have been. But this is the one we went for.

Alistair Darling Have you considered the position this puts me in? Our banks are screaming at me – and it's only eight am. They are furious. You'll have to make sure there's no leakage of funds from our banks to yours.

Minister for Finance That will be explicitly provided for in the legislation. But we had no choice but to act in the interests of the Irish financial system. We had to put the weight of the sovereign behind our banks.

8.15am
Home of Sean FitzPatrick, Greystones, Co Wicklow

David Drumm (*on phone*) Sean, it's David.

Sean FitzPatrick (*on phone*) David.

Pause.

What is it?

David Drumm We're open for fucking business, Sean.

Sean FitzPatrick You—

David Drumm They've guaranteed the banks. Overnight.

FitzPatrick *takes a moment to take it in, then exhales deeply.*

Sean FitzPatrick Oh thank Christ.

David Drumm We sailed pretty close.

Sean FitzPatrick Too close … But this takes the pressure off.

David Drumm   Yes it does. Yes.

Sean FitzPatrick   It's a new day.

8.30am
Press conference room, Government Buildings

The **Minister** *is taking questions from reporters.*

Reporter   Minister, how can the State afford to take on such enormous liabilities?

Pause.

Minister for Finance   We have to have faith in ourselves as a nation and as a people that we are capable of having a viable banking system.

A pause while the press digest that, or try to.

Reporter   What does that mean, Minister?

Minister for Finance   I'm afraid you'll have to excuse me—

An eruption of questions drowns him out.

Reporters (*overlapping*)   Were the Cabinet unanimous in backing it?

Were the Cabinet phoned individually or was it a conference call?

Was the guarantee your idea?

Whose idea was it?

Did you consider nationalising Anglo?

Minister for Finance (*breaking in, insistent*)   I'm due at Cabinet.

He is gone.

11am A hedge fund, London

Director   We're being badly squeezed.

Analyst   It's a speed bump.

Director   Anglo is up almost 50 per cent.

Analyst   It's nonsense.

Director   So are the others … AIB Boss, Bank of Ireland Boss. All soaring.

Analyst   It's a house of cards.

Director   They're backed by the Irish state … You did great work. But it's time to close out.

Analyst   But it's just a speed bump. It's happened before. It always happens. Temporary reversals. Others panic. We hold our nerve … There is no value in that bank. In any of them. The guarantee is a placebo.

Director You have ice in your veins.

Analyst I met David Drumm on a flight to Dublin recently … He asked me if I was proud of what we were doing, shorting them, 'destroying good jobs' …

Director What did you say?

Analyst I told him I was just doing my job. 'Finding value.'

Director The canary in the coal mine.

Analyst You taught me.

Director We'll hold out. How long?

Analyst Not long.

October 23
Leinster Society of Chartered Accountants lunch, Dublin

The **Minister for Finance** *is making an informal speech. He is persuasive and assured.*

Minister for Finance The bank guarantee scheme was a necessary first step. It has been the cheapest bailout in the world so far … Our Government has a duty to give leadership on this issue and to ensure that we retain that viability in this country.

Thank you.

Blackout.

Selected Bibliography

Boyle, Dan. *Without Power or Glory: The Greens in Government*. Dublin: New Island, 2012.
Carey, Brian and Tom Lyons. *The FitzPatrick Tapes: The Rise and Fall of One Man, One Bank, and One Country*, Dublin: Penguin Ireland, 2012.
Carswell, Simon. *Anglo Republic: Inside the Bank that Broke Ireland*, Dublin: Penguin Ireland, 2012.
Cooper, Matt. *How Ireland Really Went Bust*, Dublin: Penguin Ireland, 2012.
Cooper, Matt. *Who Really Runs Ireland?: The Story of the Elite Who Led Ireland from Bust to Boom . . . and Back Again*, Dublin: Penguin Ireland, 2009.
Darling, Alistair. *Back from the Brink: 1,000 Days at Number 11*, London: Atlantic Books, 2011.
Honohan, Patrick. *The Irish Banking Crisis: Regulatory and Financial Stability Policy 2003–2008*, Dublin: Central Bank of Ireland, 2010.
Independent Review Panel. *Strengthening the Capacity of the Department of Finance* ('The Wright Report'), Dublin: Department of Finance, 2011.
Kelly, Simon. *Breakfast with Anglo*, London: Penguin Books, 2011.
Kenny, Ivor. *Leaders: Conversations with Irish Chief Executives*, Cork: Oak Tree Press, 2001.
Leahy, Pat. *Showtime: The Inside Story of Fianna Fáil in Power*, Dublin: Penguin Ireland, 2009.
Lewis, Michael, 'When Irish Eyes Are Crying', *Vanity Fair*, March 2011.
Lewis, Michael. *Boomerang: Travels in the New Third World*, New York: W. W. Norton & Company, 2011.
Lucey, Brian, Charles Larkin and Constantin Gurdgiev, eds. *What If Ireland Defaults?*, Dublin: Orpen Press, 2012.
McWilliams, David. *Follow the Money*, Dublin: Gill & Macmillan, 2010.
Marsh, David. *The Euro: The Battle for the New Global Currency*, New Haven: Yale University Press, 2011.
Murphy, David and Martina Devlin. *Banksters*, Dublin: Hachette Books Ireland, 2009.
Nyberg, Peter. *Misjudging Risk: Causes of the Systemic Banking Crisis in Ireland*. Dublin: Government Publications, 2011.
Regling, Klaus, and Max Watson. *A Preliminary Report on the Sources of Ireland's Banking Crisis*, Dublin: Government Publications, 2010.
Ross, Shane. *The Bankers: How the Banks Brought Ireland to its Knees*, Dublin: Penguin Ireland, 2009.
Soden, Mike. *Open Dissent: An Uncompromising View of the Financial Crisis*, Dublin: Blackhall Publishing, 2010.
Sorkin, Andrew Ross. *Too Big to Fail: Inside the Battle to Save Wall Street*, London: Penguin Books, 2010.
The archives of Finfacts.ie, *FT Alphaville*, IrishEconomy.ie, KildareStreet.com, NamaWineLake.com, oireachtas.ie, RTE.ie, the *Financial Times*, the *Irish Daily Mail*, the *Irish Examiner*, the *Irish Independent*, the *Irish Mail on Sunday*, the *Irish Times*, TheJournal.ie, ThePropertyPin.com, TheStory.ie, the *Sunday Independent*.

(L to R) Darragh Kelly as the Taoiseach, Peter Hanly as the Minister for Finance and Peter Daly as the Governor in *Guaranteed!*.
©Photo by Pat Redmond

Bailed Out!

Bailed Out! was co-commissioned by Fishamble: The New Play Company and Pavilion Theatre. It was presented by Fishamble at Pavilion Theatre from September 26, 2015, as part of Dublin Theatre Festival, with the following cast:

Brian Cowen	Denis Conway
Michael Noonan	Peter Daly
Brian Lenihan	Peter Hanly
Patrick Honohan	Mark Lambert
Chorus	Ali White

Directed by	Conall Morrison
Dramaturgy by	Gavin Kostick
Costume design by	Barbara McCarthy
AV design by	Kilian Waters
Produced by	Marketa Dowling

Characters

Chorus
Senior Official
Brian Lenihan, *Minister for Finance*
Brian Cowen, *Taoiseach (prime minister)*
Peter Bacon, *economist*
Michael Noonan, *Fine Gael TD (Teachta Dála – member of parliament), appointed finance spokesman in July 2010 and Minister for Finance in March 2011*
Patrick Honohan, *Governor of the Central Bank*
Jean-Claude Trichet, *President of the European Central Bank*
Dermot Ahern, *Minister for Justice*
John McGuinness, *Fianna Fáil backbench TD*
Olli Rehn, *European Commissioner*
Timothy Geithner, *United States Secretary of the Treasury*
Ashoka Mody, *International Monetary Fund mission chief to Ireland*
Assorted newsreaders, bankers, officials, backbench TDs, government ministers, reporters, presenters, international politicians and others.

In the original production, a cast of four men and one woman played all the parts. The **Senior Official** *also played the* **Chorus**.

Notes

The set may have: a mobile conference table. Some office chairs. A podium for speeches. A Bloomberg terminal. A whiteboard or acetate projector. A bank of shelves stacked with paper. A Tricolour. An EU flag.

Lenihan may have his own desk, separate from the conference table.

There should be a sense of constant work in the background – papers being passed around – memos drafted, distributed, corrected, redrafted.

Act titles, dates and bond prices should be projected.

Radio interviews, Dáil debates and speeches are based on transcripts.

Where characters are named, the actions attributed to them are based on the historical record, though the dialogue is imagined.

The Angelus chime is broadcast daily before the 6pm news on the national broadcaster, RTÉ, and so serves as a sound effect to introduce the news bulletins.

Prologue

The **Chorus** *addresses the audience. She holds a book: Stress Test by* **Timothy Geithner**. *She reads from it.*

Chorus   'Financial systems are built on *belief*...'

She holds up the book for the audience.

Chorus   Timothy Geithner – Treasury Secretary of the United States.

She returns to reading.

Chorus   'That's why the word credit is derived from the Latin for 'believe' – *credere*... That's why we say we can 'bank' on things we believe true...'

She looks up.

Chorus   The belief he's talking about is the belief that debts are going to be repaid. That the people who are owed money are going to get it back – no matter who pays it ... That's called 'confidence' – *market* confidence ... This is a story about debt, and markets, and countries – this country – and confidence ... It is a true story ... Some of it based on (*indicating the book*) first-hand testimony, and transcripts ... Some of it is based on secondary sources ... And some of it – well, we had to imagine it ... It starts on September the 30th, 2008.

She returns to the book.

Chorus   'Confidence is a fragile thing. When it evaporates, it usually evaporates quickly. And it's hard to get back once it's lost.'

She puts the book away.

Act I: The Bank Guarantee
September 2008 to February 2009

September 30, 2008

The sting for RTÉ's Morning Ireland *plays.*

Newsreader   In a bid to shore up confidence in the banking system, the Irish government has announced a guarantee on all 440 billion euro of the debts of the country's six principal banks.

Bankers at Irish Nationwide and Anglo Irish Bank immediately make phone calls.

Nationwide Banker   Email all your fucking contacts – We are now the safest place to deposit money in Europe!

David Drumm   We won't do anything blatant . . . But get the fuckin moola in, get it in!

John Bowe   Go on the Drummer!

David Drumm   Ah, I just should be recording these calls for the fucking crack.

He laughs.

Early October 2008

Senior Official   Minister – I have the latest estimates of Anglo's loan losses . . . They're not too bad.

Minister *for Finance* **Brian Lenihan** *takes the memo and reads.*

Senior Official   In the worst-case scenario, Anglo still makes a profit.

Lenihan   Better get a second opinion. Just in case. Have Peter Bacon take a look – at all the banks.

October 14, 2008

Chorus   In the meantime, a collapse in the construction sector has led the country into recession, and an early budget . . .

Angelus chime.

Newsreader   In a bid to tackle the crisis in the public finances, the Minister for Finance, Brian Lenihan, has announced two billion euro in tax increases and one billion euro in spending cuts – including cuts to medical card entitlements for pensioners.

Chorus   The Dáil.

There is ruckus in the Dáil chamber. As always in the chamber, **Taoiseach Brian Cowen** *and* **Lenihan** *sit together.*

Lenihan   This Budget provides an opportunity for us all to pull together so that we can secure the gains that have been made in this country . . .

The ruckus rises.

Lenihan   This budget is no less than a call to patriotic action.

Cheers from Government TDs and jeers from Opposition.

October 22 2008

Angelus chime.

Chorus   A week later.

Newsreader   Fifteen thousand pensioners protested outside Leinster House today –

Cowen   We're going to have to reverse the medical cards cut.

Lenihan   I've staked my authority on it Taoiseach!

Cowen   We're not taking on the fucking pensioners.

Angelus chime.

Newsreader   The Government today announced a u-turn on its changes to the medical card regime.

Cowen   The early budget was a mistake.

Lenihan   The early budget wasn't *enough*.

February, 2009

Chorus   Meanwhile, the economist Peter Bacon has been looking at the banks.

Bacon   When you guaranteed the banks, you tied them to the sovereign. The banks' debts became the State's debts. You've tasked me with finding out whether the banks have the assets to meet those debts. A bank's assets are mostly the loans it gives out. So the question is: how good are those loans?

Now, we know the property market is experiencing a severe downturn –

Lenihan (*mutters*)   So much for the 'soft landing'.

Bacon   So another way of asking that might be: how much of the banks' lending was on property?

Central Banker   Well Anglo was basically a property bank, but –

Bacon   It wasn't just Anglo. AIB Boss was nearly as bad. Bank of Ireland Boss was chasing them down the rabbit hole –

Lenihan   How much?

Bacon   Across the six guaranteed banks, approximately one hundred and sixty billion euro on –

Senior Official They lent a hundred and sixty billion euro just on *property*?

Bacon Eh, no. A hundred and sixty billion euro on *commercial* property . . . They lent a further hundred billion or so on residential property. So they lent *two* hundred and sixty billion euro on property.

They recoil.

Bacon But it's commercial where the worst of the losses lie.

Lenihan How *much* losses?

Bacon The market is still falling. It's impossible to be precise –

Lenihan Imprecisely, then.

Bacon Perhaps . . . thirty four billion euro.

Stunned silence.

Lenihan Thirty four billion, which we guaranteed.

Bacon Yes.

Lenihan How much is in the pension reserve?

Central Banker Twenty billion.

Lenihan So we don't have it.

Bacon It would appear you don't.

Lenihan So that would bankrupt us.

Bacon That *could* bankrupt you . . . if those losses fall all at once . . . But if you can spread them out over time, they could be manageable – over twenty years, say – long-term debt.

Cowen Can we do that?

Bacon That depends on confidence – market confidence . . . The markets are already betting that the banks are worse than you've said . . . That – in a worst-case scenario – the banks might bankrupt you . . . That means lending to the State is riskier – so they're charging the State a higher risk premium to lend it money . . .

But the more they charge, the more you have to save money elsewhere to pay those charges. The economy is already in recession – the extra cost risks damaging it further. If the economy gets worse, the property market falls further, and the banks' losses grow.

Central Banker It's a vicious circle.

Lenihan A vice grip.

Bacon I've heard it called a 'doom loop' . . . Eventually, you can't borrow any more. You default on the banks' debts. And you have to slash services and hike taxes to eliminate the budget deficit – overnight. That destroys any potential in the economy . . . It sends you back to the 1980s . . . Unless–

Cowen   Unless?

Bacon   You find another source of loans, to replace the market . . .

Senior Official   Like the IMF?

Bacon   It could be the only option.

Senior Official   A 'bailout'?

Cowen   That was our nightmare right through the 80s. The prospect of having to hand over the keys to the IMF . . . Like some banana republic. Not fit to run ourselves . . .

Beat.

Lenihan   This vicious circle . . . How do we break it?

Bacon   You have to convince the markets that you're *committed* to paying for the guaranteed banks' losses. And that you're *able* to pay them . . . You show them you're committed by recognising the losses up front, and making a plan to pay them off over time. And you show you're able to pay them by dealing with the crisis in the public finances so that you can carry the extra debt.

Senior Official   But they're not *our* losses! We should rescind the guarantee. Let the losses lie where they fall – on those who lent money to the banks.

Lenihan   We put the guarantee in *law*.

Senior Official   The bankers *lied* –

Central Banker   There's no evidence that –

Senior Official   They lent a hundred and sixty billion euro on commercial property during a property bubble . . . and then they came to us and claimed they just had a *liquidity* problem!

Cowen   We're not reneging on a sovereign guarantee! . . . If the banks don't pay their debts, they'll collapse.

Senior Official   The Central Bank – we could print the money –

Central Banker   That would force us out of the euro –

Lenihan   I'm not going to be the Finance Minister that takes us out of the euro.

Cowen (*to* **Bacon**)   What's your plan?

Bacon   Clean the banks of the bad loans. Warehouse them in a new agency – a national asset management agency. Sell them off over time, as the market recovers . . . And recapitalise the banks with long-term bonds, to make up for the losses.

Senior Official   A national asset management agency . . . 'NAMA' . . .

They study the memo.

Cowen Will it work?

Bacon It's a confidence play . . . It will work if the markets *believe* it can work, and keep lending to you . . . If they don't, then it won't.

Beat.

Cowen (*to* **Lenihan**) Can we handle the deficit?

Lenihan We'll have to.

Cowen The banks. This 'NAMA' . . .

Senior Official The legislation will be complex.

Cowen Get working on it.

Bacon You'll need to get the European Central Bank on side. You'll need the ECB to lend the money to the agency so it can buy the loans from the banks.

Central Banker I'll talk to Trichet.

Cowen This country is not defaulting. And we're not being bailed out. We'll pay our way.

Act II: A Thousand Cuts
February 2009 to October 2010

February 28, 2009

Chorus The Fianna Fáil ard fheis.

Lenihan *watches* **Cowen**'s *speech.*

Cowen It is the greatest honour of my life to lead this Republic, but like you, I wish these were better days . . . Now more than ever, we need a 'meitheal' spirit.

Lenihan *reacts skeptically.*

Cowen Daoine ag obair le chéile ar son a chéile. People working together for each other . . . There is a future to be fought for. I will lead that fight. Tagaigí liom a chairde.

April 7, 2009

Angelus chime

Newsreader In the emergency budget today, his second budget in just six months, the Minister for Finance, Brian Lenihan, will attempt to tackle the eighteen billion euro deficit that has emerged in the public finances.

Dáil *ruckus.*

Lenihan The consensus view of the Irish economy suggested a 'soft landing' . . . That prediction proved wrong.

Heckles. **Cowen** *shifts uncomfortably.*

Lenihan But in our short history as a nation, we have faced adversity and we have prevailed. This budget is rooted in a determination to control our own destiny.

Heckles.

August, 2009

Angelus chime.

Newsreader The Governor of the Central Bank, John Hurley, is the latest senior figure to announce his retirement in the wake of the financial crisis. He retires with an annual pension of €175,000 and a lump sum of €575,000.

Lenihan What do you think of Patrick Honohan for the governorship of the Central Bank?

Official Patrick Honohan? But he's an economist!

September, 2009

Chorus   By September, the NAMA legislation is ready, and the Minister brings it to the Dáil.

She hands **Lenihan** *a memo.*

Angelus chime

Newsreader   The National Asset Management Agency will buy loans from the guaranteed banks at a discount of 30 per cent, the Minister for Finance has said today.

Dáil ruckus continues throughout.

Lenihan   It is unfortunate that there has been a breakdown of trust in the entire banking system, but the public knows we need the banks.

Opposition TD   You're socialising the banks' losses!

Lenihan   It is not true that we have just 'socialised the losses' – we have socialised future *gains* as well.

Noonan   This is an appalling situation.

Chorus   Fine Gael's Michael Noonan.

Noonan   Why mortgage our children and our grandchildren for the next 15 to 20 years by pouring money into the Anglo black hole?

Lenihan   Nearly every government in Europe, as well as the USA, is burdening the next generation with their borrowings.

Noonan   Were lying an Olympic sport, we could put out a team of bankers who would win gold for Ireland.

Lenihan   The steps we are taking today will provide confidence to the people from whom we must borrow.

November, 2009

Chorus   And then, there's another budget looming.

The **Senior Official** *delivers a brief to* **Lenihan**.

Senior Official   Minister – tax revenues are down again.

Lenihan *delivers it to* **Cowen**.

Lenihan   We need to save 1.3 billion euro on the public sector pay bill *alone* . . . We have to cut wages.

Cowen   We'll negotiate it with the unions. Partnership will get us through this.

Lenihan   Partnership is what got us into this!

Cowen Trust me. I'll talk to them.

The **Senior Official** *hands* **Lenihan** *some papers.*

Senior Official Your briefs for Brussels, Minister.

December 2, 2009

The Cabinet gathers.

Chorus The weekly Cabinet meeting – the Minister for Finance is in Brussels.

Cowen The unions have agreed to a substantial cut in public sector pay for 2010 . . .

The **Ministers** *are impressed.*

Cowen which will be compensated with a 'time-off-in-lieu' arrangement which will run over the subsequent years. (*moving on quickly*) Now, the next item –

Minister 'Time off in lieu?'

Cowen There'll be no net loss to the public service in productivity –

Minister How *much* time?

Cowen Twelve days.

Minister Twelve days holidays?!

Cowen They're not holidays!

Minister You want to prepare the public for another austerity budget by giving civil servants twelve days' holidays?

Cowen We'll pick this up again tomorrow.

Lenihan *phones* **Cowen**.

Lenihan You can't do it, Brian.

Cowen It's a perfectly valid proposal.

Lenihan 'Time off in lieu'? We can't do that – we have to just cut their pay.

Cowen I've staked my authority on it.

Lenihan The sums won't add up.

Cowen They *do* add –

Lenihan And it's a public relations disaster. It will undermine our whole agenda. You're going to have to back out.

Cowen I can't back out.

Lenihan I can't deliver a budget on these figures. The markets are watching.

Cowen Who elected the markets? Fuck the markets!

Lenihan We're building *confidence* – we're confronting this – that's the narrative.

December 8, 2009

Chorus The Dáil.

Dáil ruckus continues throughout.

Cowen To the disappointment of many people, it was not possible to conclude an agreement with the unions.

Chorus The Labour leader, Eamon Gilmore.

Eamon Gilmore The Taoiseach's Minister for Finance is so anxious to get his hands on the Taoiseach's job, he was prepared to sink this agreement.

Cowen I completely reject that!

Eamon Gilmore He clearly does not subscribe to the Taoiseach's view that political loyalty is a virtue.

Cowen The Government was entirely at one with regard to this.

December 9, 2009

Angelus chime

Newsreader In his third budget in his first eighteen months in office, the Minister for Finance is expected to announce a four billion euro cuts package – including one point three billion euro in cuts to public sector pay.

Ruckus.

Lenihan This is the *last* big push of the crisis. Only decisive action will restore confidence . . . We need to rediscover our optimism and our self-belief. We have turned the corner. The worst is over.

Jeering.

Lenihan *returns to his office, and sags.*

His **Senior Official** *enters with a brief.*

Senior Official (*concerned*) Minister?

Lenihan Just not sleeping very well at the moment.

She leaves the brief and exits. **Lenihan** *sits for a moment. He picks up a book and tries to read, but can't concentrate. He takes out an envelope. He starts to slide out the paper inside and then slides it back in again, undecided. Then resolved, he carries it slowly over to* **Cowen**.

Lenihan *hands Cowen the envelope.* **Cowen** *takes it, slides out the paper inside, scans it.*

Beat.

Cowen   How long have you known?

Lenihan   Just a couple of days.

Cowen   How are the– How are the family?

Lenihan *can't answer.*

Cowen   How are you . . . feeling?

Lenihan   I start chemotherapy in January.

Cowen *is upset.*

Cowen   What– What do you want to do?

Lenihan   I'm willing to offer my resignation, of course. (*pause*) I may have to.

Cowen   Do you have to *now?*

Lenihan   No.

Cowen   Good. (*pause*) You know what the media will say. That you're only 'clinging on to power'.

Lenihan   That's what they said about my father.

December 26, 2009

The TV3 News sting plays.

Newsreader   Good evening. TV3 News has learned that the Finance Minister Brian Lenihan has been diagnosed with cancer –

A moment of surprise/pain on **Lenihan**'*s face, but he composes himself for –*

January 4, 2010

A press conference.

A chorus of reporters: 'Minister!' etc.

Lenihan   I am determined to implement the plan for economic recovery. I will supervise the work of my department. I will prepare for and attend Government meetings. I will make myself accountable to Dáil Éireann. I will continue to represent the constituency of Dublin West . . . I will not be accepting invitations for speaking engagements. (*pause*) I do not intend to issue any further statements about this matter.

Reporter   Minister – you said the growth was at the entrance to your pancreas– (*hesitant*) Pancreatic cancer is typically– Its prognosis is– Is it –

Lenihan   It's a growth and it's a growth I intend to defeat or it'll defeat me.

He leaves as they call further questions after him.

An **Official** *approaches him with a letter.*

Official   Minister – an invitation.

Lenihan   I said I'm not accepting any invitations.

Official   It's the Michael Collins commemoration. At Béal na mBláth.

Lenihan   Why would I want to go –

Official   They want you to give the oration.

Lenihan   *What*? Give me that.

He reads it.

Lenihan   Has anyone from Fianna Fáil *ever* been at Béal na mBláth?

Official   Not since you shot him.

August 22, 2010

Chorus   Béal na mBláth, County Cork.

Lenihan   On the walls in the Department of Finance, there are pictures of all the previous Ministers. Michael Collins regularly catches my eye . . . I have taken a particular interest in his work as Minister for Finance, between 1919 and 1922. Here was a man at constant risk of arrest . . . and death . . . yet he still had the time and the ability to build the foundations of a system of financial control . . . He raised the loan to finance the work of the revolutionary government – that was a truly remarkable feat.

Collins was a pragmatist. He believed he could over time bring Ireland *total* independence. He was a driven, ambitious man. He was born to be a leader.

In times of economic difficulty, the greater good may require governments to take unpopular decisions. But that is what leadership in a democracy is about.

People come up to him to shake his hand.

August 25, 2010

Chorus   Meanwhile, NAMA has been taking the loans off the banks – and discovering that they are worth even less than had been thought – meaning the State – the public – will have to pay more to cover the banks' losses.

Projected: **Bond yield 5.436**

The **Senior Official** *collects some papers and presents them to Patrick Honohan, the new Governor of the Central Bank.*

Senior Official   Governor Honohan –

Honohan (*worried*)   But these are worse than we were expecting– When the markets learn about this –

He starts making some calculations.

Angelus chime.

Newsreader   The ratings agency Standard & Poor's has today downgraded Ireland's sovereign credit rating, citing the rising cost of bailing out the banks.

Bond yield 5.698

Senior Official Is the downgrade going to scare the markets?

Honohan *glances at the bond yield.*

Honohan The bond yields are rising – it *is* scaring the markets.

Senior Official Should you say something?

Honohan If the governor of the Central Bank goes on the radio and says 'There's no problem', people think there *is* a problem . . . It's very risky . . . It's all very fragile . . . My saying something could make it worse . . . But Trichet! If *he* said something reassuring – to show the ECB is backing us – that would calm things.

September 2, 2010

A chorus of international reporters: 'Monsieur Trichet!'

Chorus Jean-Claude Trichet, the president of the European Central Bank.

European Reporter Monsieur Trichet – can the ECB help share the burden of bailing out Anglo Irish Bank?

Trichet This is a bank which is *owned* by the Irish government. So it is the responsibility of the Irish government to take the appropriate decisions . . . I have confidence that they will manage this difficult issue as well as they did in the past.

Honohan *overhears.*

The **Senior Official** *enters with a memo.*

Honohan (*watching the yield*) That's going to make it *worse* – the markets don't think the State can afford to carry Anglo's losses!

That's why the bond yield is rising – the greater the likelihood of Ireland not paying back its debt, the higher the interest they charge to lend Ireland money.

Senior Official It doesn't seem that high –

Honohan It can become a self-fulfilling prophecy. The more they charge to lend us money, the greater the debt burden. The greater the debt burden, the greater the likelihood that we won't be able to pay it back. And so the more they charge us to lend us money . . . It can spiral out of control.

Senior Official When does that happen?

Honohan There's no fixed point. But once it goes over seven per cent, the markets think it's unsustainable. Greek bond yields hit seven per cent in early April. Within a month, they were forced into a bailout.

The **Senior Official** *produces the memo.*

Senior Official We have the new projections for the deficit.

Honohan *takes it and studies it. His face falls.*

Honohan I need to talk to the Minister.

Bond yield 5.860

Honohan *enters with papers for* **Lenihan**.

Honohan (*to* **Lenihan**) We could be in trouble.

Lenihan The bank losses?

Honohan It's not just the banks . . . It's the public finances too – the projections for the deficit have got worse.

Lenihan But we're making the cuts. We're out of recession.

Honohan Our projections were . . . too optimistic.

Honohan *shows him his figures.*

Lenihan (*stumbling*) But that's not– We have it– Our figures –

Honohan Your figures are out of date.

Lenihan *Your* figures are *wrong*!

Honohan You need to go further with the budget correction. This could get worse. Very quickly.

Early September 2010

Bond yield 5.871

Lenihan *approaches* **Cowen**.

Lenihan It's not working . . . The figures are worse than we thought. We're going to have to cut deeper.

Lenihan *hands* **Cowen** *a memo.* **Cowen** *scans it.*

Cowen We *can't* cut deeper.

Lenihan A comprehensive programme of tax changes and cuts . . . A four-year plan.

Cowen You want to cut the minimum wage!

Lenihan We have to restore competitiveness.

Cowen Kicking the fellow below me – that's not the Fianna Fáil way.

Lenihan We have to convince the markets.

Cowen Fuck the markets! We'll get through it – a bit of gumption – the meitheal spirit –

Lenihan This is bigger than your 'meitheal'.

Cowen With these cuts – we'll lose the people.

Lenihan So bring *the plan* to the people. Go to the country – seek a mandate.

Cowen We *have* a mandate . . . We'll muddle through.

Lenihan *leaves him.* **Cowen** *reads the memo.*

He starts to sing: The Lakes of Pontchartrain.

Cowen It was one fine March morning, I bid New Orleans Adieu
And I took the road to Jackson Town, my fortune to renew
I cursed all foreign money, no credit could I gain
Which filled my heart with a longing for the Lakes of Ponchartrain
Well I said, 'my pretty Creole girl, my money here's no good
If it weren't for the alligators I'd sleep out in the wood'
She said, 'You're welcome here kind stranger, though my house it's very plain
But we never turn a stranger out on the banks of Pontchartrain'.

September 14, 2010

Bond yield 5.916

Morning Ireland sting.

Cathal Mac Coille Good morning, and welcome to Morning Ireland, coming to you today from the Fianna Fáil 'think in' in Galway.

Senior Official (*running in*) Where's the Taoiseach?

Cathal Mac Coille Later on the programme, we'll be talking to the Taoiseach, Brian Cowen.

Official Weren't you calling him?

Senior Official No – you were.

They look at each other in horror.

Official Oh fuck.

Senior Official I'll get him. You make him a cup of tea.

They rush off.

Cowen *enters, balancing a teacup on saucer, and joins* **Cathal Mac Coille**.

Cathal Mac Coille Taoiseach Brian Cowen, thank you for joining us before your breakfast.

Cowen (*mumbles*) Thank you Cathal.

Cathal Mac Coille Is this budget going to be worse than people have feared?

Cowen (*very slow, hoarse*) Well what people need to know is for the next year we're in discussions at the moment about that . . . Our budget is for the next year . . . We have to align the estimates campaign with the industrial relations agenda . . . Every department will be setting out based on the amount it will be able to have.

Puzzled look from **Mac Coille**.

Sudden panic amongst the officials.

Cowen *is ushered off.*

A chorus of reporters: 'Minister!'

Reporter 1   Was the Taoiseach drunk, Minister?

Reporter 2   How does this look internationally, Minister?

The **Ministers** *step forward reluctantly.*

Chorus   Minister for Foreign Affairs, Micheál Martin.

Micheal Martin   Of course, the Taoiseach was very hoarse during the interview.

Chorus   Minister for Tourism, Mary Hanafin.

Mary Hanafin   He sounded hoarse and congested.

Chorus   Minister for Justice, Dermot Ahern.

Dermot Ahern   It's well known that he has problems with nasal congestion.

Chorus   Minister for Transport, Noel Dempsey.

Noel Dempsey   I'm astounded that we're now doing interviews about the tone of his voice rather than the content.

Mary Hanafin   He was spot on in the content.

Noel Dempsey   The content was very good.

Micheal Martin   From a content perspective –

Mary Hanafin   It's not about the *way* he tells them – it's what he's *saying*.

September 15, 2010

Bond yield 5.947

Lenihan *is reading a newspaper as his* **Senior Official** *enters.*

Lenihan   Listen to this . . .

'The timing of this interview couldn't be worse . . . Prolonged banking problems are fuelling concerns about Cowen's government's ability to weather the storm.' The Wall Street Journal!

Senior Official   And the New York Times . . . the Washington Post . . . Reuters . . . Fox News . . . the Guardian . . . the BBC . . . He's gone viral . . . Twenty six countries. Over 400 publications.

Bond yield 6.099

Lenihan   We're in the middle of the challenge of this nation's life . . . What the fuck is he doing?

September 22, 2010

Bond yield 6.319

John McGuinness *enters.*

Angelus chime.

Newsreader As the fallout from the Taoiseach's Galway interview continues, American chat show host Jay Leno last night called the Taoiseach a 'drunken moron'.

John Mcguinness We can't take any more, Brian.

Chorus The Fianna Fáil backbencher, John McGuinness.

John Mcguinness We've got to get rid of him.

Lenihan He's the Taoiseach!

John Mcguinness He's a taoiseach on probation.

Lenihan The country needs a steady hand now, John.

John Mcguinness You think Cowen's hand is steady?

Lenihan I'm dealing with a banking crisis. And a public finances crisis – a massive deficit.

John Mcguinness And all he's doing is hampering you . . . The party is crying out for new leadership. I'm hearing it all the time.

Beat.

Lenihan Have you got the numbers?

John Mcguinness I can get them.

September 29, 2010

Meanwhile, **Honohan** *has been pouring over figures and brings them to* **Lenihan** *and his* **Senior Official**.

Lenihan Governor.

Honohan We have the final bill for Anglo and Nationwide. They could need a total of 35 billion.

Lenihan Peter Bacon's estimate was 34 billion euro in losses for all *six* banks. And now just two of those banks could cost us 35 billion . . . How much are the others going to cost us?

Honohan We could be looking at more than fifty billion . . . We may not be able to do this on our own.

Bond yield 6.912

Chorus The Dáil. Fine Gael's Michael Noonan, recently appointed finance spokesman.

Dáil ruckus continues throughout.

Noonan   We have for two years proposed that holders of debt should share the pain of the Anglo rescue.

Lenihan   We have to get those overseas holders of debt to fund the Irish state. You can't go to your bank manager and say, 'I want to default,' and at the same time, 'I want more loans.' ... Any Anglo failure would bring down the sovereign.

Noonan   This happened on the Minister's watch and he is responsible for the disaster.

Lenihan   You know well that the reckless lending did not happen on *my* watch.

Noonan   That is true. The Minister was not responsible for the reckless lending – *that* was the *Taoiseach*'s responsibility ...

Cowen   I take my share of responsibility ... But I'm proud of the fact that in good times, when all of the data suggested continuing growth for the economy, we did what we set out to do: to help people at the bottom ...

Opposition TD (*heckling*)   At the bottom of the Galway Tent!

October, 2010

Lenihan's team assembles.

Lenihan   Where are we at? (*to* **Honohan**) Governor?

Honohan   The markets have completely lost confidence in our banks. The banks are losing half a billion a day in funding.

Lenihan   The ECB?

Honohan   The ECB is filling the gap with emergency loans – but that can't continue indefinitely.

Lenihan   And the sovereign?

Official   We've withdrawn from the debt markets – till next year. The State is fully funded – we don't need to borrow till then.

Senior Official   Withdrawing looks weak.

Official   It *is* weak. We had no choice. The interest rate's too high.

Lenihan   Withdrawal from the markets gives us breathing space. We need to finish the four-year plan. It has to be impressive. If we can get the European Commission to endorse it ... *and* get the ECB to make a statement of support for our banks ... that will reassure the markets. We just need a bit of luck.

October 8, 2010

Chorus   In early October, the Minister goes to Washington, for the annual meetings of the World Bank and International Monetary Fund – and takes the opportunity to get some personal advice ...

The **Doctor** *enters, carrying medical documents.*

Doctor   Mr Lenihan?

Lenihan   Doctor.

The **Doctor** *hands him the documents.*

Doctor   There's nothing we can do.

Lenihan   The operation –

Doctor   It would be . . . very difficult.

Lenihan   You mean, you don't want a corpse on your operating table.

Doctor   No.

Lenihan   How long –

Doctor   Not long.

October 18, 2010

Angelus chime.

Newsreader   At a summit in Deauville, France, Angela Merkel and Nicolas Sarkozy have agreed that, where eurozone countries are not able to pay their debts, investors who have lent money to those countries will have to share in the losses, instead of the entire burden being assumed by European taxpayers.

Lenihan *and* **Trichet**, *in separate offices, are listening with their officials.*

Trichet   *Mon dieu!*

Lenihan   Oh good Christ.

Trichet   What are they doing?

Lenihan   This will panic the markets.

Trichet   They are going to destroy the euro! The markets will stop lending to vulnerable sovereigns.

Senior Official   But this is just what we need – a means to make the markets take their losses.

Lenihan   We don't want the markets to take losses – we want the markets to keep lending to us! This will send the bond yields up – it will reinforce the vicious circle.

October 26, 2010

Bond yield 6.913

Dáil ruckus.

Chorus   The Dáil.

Lenihan There is a danger that the markets will refuse to lend to us when we need to return to them next year . . . If that happens, we will have to cut 20 billion from the budget *immediately*. So we have to accept cuts in public spending and higher taxes now – totalling 15 billion euro over the next four years.

Fury from TDs.

Opposition TD This isn't just slash and burn – it's scorched earth.

The anger turns to alarm as they watch the bond yield rise.

Bond yield 7.000

Bond yield 7.374

Bond yield 7.536

November 4, 2010

Honohan *arrives in Lenihan's office.*

Lenihan Governor.

Honohan Deauville has panicked the markets . . . If the markets won't lend to us, we'll need another source of funding . . . We need to talk to Europe.

Lenihan If it gets out that we're even talking about assistance –

Honohan Just technical discussions. To see what they're thinking. We could do it in Brussels.

Lenihan Alright. Set something up. I'll try and steal a march on things here – we'll frontload the cuts. I'll announce a *six* billion correction for next year.

November 5, 2010

Bond yield 7.736

A chorus of reporters: 'Minister!'

Reporter (*in* **Lenihan***'s direction*) Minister, you have an announcement to make?

Minister Brendan Smith *steps in to answer.*

Brendan Smith (*self important*) Yes –

Chorus The Minister for Agriculture – Brendan Smith.

Brendan Smith I'm announcing a scheme today under which 53 tonnes of fresh cheddar will be distributed around the country, with European Union funding. (*modest*) It's a small measure, but it is helpful to those in need.

Lenihan *despairs.*

Bond yield 7.906

NOVEMBER 8, 2010

Bond yield 7.989

The **Senior Official** *leads* **Olli Rehn** *in to* **Lenihan**.

Senior Official   Minister – the European Commissioner, Mr Olli Rehn is here –

Olli Rehn   Your four-year plan is really excellent. Very austere.

Lenihan   Do you think it will be sufficient to restore confidence – to avoid an assistance programme?

Olli Rehn   A 'bailout'? It could be, Brian. (*an afterthought*) Oh – one little thing – have you thought of introducing water charges?

Lenihan *falls into eager conversation with* **Rehn** *as he leaves.*

A chorus of reporters: 'Minister!'

Reporter   Minister – can you guarantee that Ireland will not have to go to the European Union for a bailout?'

Lenihan   Absolutely. We intend to return to the markets next year and we intend to fund ourselves, that's our plan.

We have made it a cardinal plank of our policy that we intend to pay our debts as a state. We will pay our way.

Act III: Contagion
November 2010

November 11-12, 2010

Bond yield 8.918

Chorus Meanwhile, the G20 is meeting in Seoul, Korea. Olli Rehn goes straight there from Dublin and joins a meeting to discuss the Irish debt crisis with Jean-Claude Trichet and the finance ministers of the G7 – amongst them Timothy Geithner.

Trichet When the US let Lehman Brothers collapse, in September 2008, it caused contagion in global financial markets. But now, the euro is at the epicentre of the crisis . . . The markets are afraid that Ireland will not be able to repay its debt . . . So they are looking at the other peripheral countries and asking if they, too, will have similar problems . . . Ireland's bond yield is causing contagion in the eurozone . . . It is a threat to the stability of the euro.

Olli Rehn But the Irish are doing well. They seem to have an appetite for austerity.

Germany They keep underestimating the size of their bank losses. How can we trust what they say?

Trichet The markets no longer trust the Irish banks. They are refusing to lend to them. The ECB has had to lend one fifth of our entire stock of reserves to Ireland. This is not sustainable. We can do no more.

Bond yield 8.950

Italy If Ireland goes under, Portugal could be next. If Portugal goes, then . . . Spain . . . ?

Trichet The eurozone cannot afford to bail out Spain.

Germany That would bring down the euro.

Trichet Ireland could be the Lehman Brothers of Europe.

Bond yield 9.005

Geithner There's too much uncertainty.

Italy Of course there's uncertainty –

Germany That is precisely the problem –

Geithner You're *causing* the uncertainty.

This silences them.

Geithner Deauville! You can't tell the markets you're going to make them take losses, and then be surprised when they don't want to lend to you.

You need to row back on the Deauville declaration – reassure the markets. Remove the uncertainty. And you need to ringfence Ireland – stop the contagion.

Bond yield 9.108

Lenihan *takes a call on speaker phone,* **Cowen** *with him.*

Trichet Monsieur Lenihan – your government needs to enter a programme.

Cowen *bristles.*

Lenihan Monsieur Trichet – we are taking the initiative. Our four-year-plan has impressed Commissioner Rehn. We have withdrawn from the sovereign debt markets till next year. We are fully funded. We don't need to enter any programme.

Trichet Your banks are experiencing a corporate run. They are now entirely reliant on ECB emergency loans – which are supposed to be temporary.

Lenihan And they will be temporary. As soon as the markets get a chance to assess our four-year-plan, confidence will return.

Trichet Monsieur Lenihan, your bond yield is over nine per cent. The markets do not believe you can survive without help. We need to start negotiations.

Lenihan My officials will be in Brussels on Sunday for technical discussions.

Trichet They will be *negotiating* a *programme*.

Lenihan They can *discuss* the *possibility* of a programme.

He hangs up.

Cowen Be careful, Brian.

Bond yield 9.255

Chorus Meanwhile, elsewhere in Europe.

European Reporter Is this on the record?

ECB Source No!

European Reporter *(writing)* An 'ECB source'?

ECB Source Just say '*official* sources'.

European Reporter Okay. So –

ECB Source The markets have lost confidence in Ireland's banks. The loss of confidence has spread to the sovereign, and this has created a spiral –

European Reporter A vicious circle.

ECB Source The only way to *end* this spiral is for Ireland to go into a bailout programme.

European Reporter But the Irish finance ministry is saying they're not going into –

ECB Source But they are *already* in negotiations!

European Reporter (*urgently*) They're *in* negotiations? Already? I'd better get this out there! (*phoning as he leaves*) Put me onto the news desk.

Bond yield 9.296

Chorus And in Dublin –

Senior Official We're getting calls from the foreign press.

Lenihan Just direct them to the embassies.

Senior Official Foreign press *here* – they're arriving in Dublin.

Official (*bursting in*) There's a Sky News van outside the Department!

Lenihan For what?

Official They seem to think we're going into a programme.

Lenihan What the –

Official (*bursting in*) I just got a call from a reporter from Bloomberg – she has a source saying we're negotiating a bailout programme.

Lenihan We are *not* negotiating a programme!

Official (*checking his phone*) Reuters is saying we're in negotiations on a bailout programme!

Lenihan We're *not* in negotiations!

Official They say the final decision is likely to be taken at the Eurogroup meeting on Tuesday.

Lenihan Final decisions about Irish affairs will be taken by this sovereign government! But it *doesn't* arise.

BIG BEN CHIME.

Newsreader The BBC has learned that the Republic of Ireland is in preliminary talks with EU officials for a programme of financial support.

Lenihan We are *not* in 'preliminary talks' – or *any* talks. The State is fully funded into the middle of 2011.

That's the line. Make sure the Cabinet all have it. And tell them to be careful.

November 13, 2010. Saturday

Lenihan *joins* **Cowen**.

Lenihan Honohan thinks we need a bailout ... My officials think we need a bailout ... The markets are squeezing us into a bailout ... The media thinks we're *already* negotiating a bailout ...

Cowen Well fuck them!

Lenihan The G7 – they want us in a programme, Brian.

Cowen Olli Rehn was here a week ago saying we were on the right track with our four-year plan!

Lenihan Things have changed!

Cowen *What*'s changed?

Lenihan The markets – it's got worse.

Cowen Nineteen eighty-four I came into the Dáil. Those were bleak years. Fine Gael and Labour making a fucking mess of the economy. Kids leaving the country in their thousands. The IMF like the wolf at the fucking door. And then Haughey got back in. With MacSharry.

Lenihan And my father.

Cowen And they turned it around. They kept the IMF out . . . We're the *republican* party, Brian. We don't get to sign away our sovereignty . . .

Lenihan We signed away our sovereignty a long time ago . . . The *markets* are sovereign now.

Cowen We're funded till next year.

Lenihan It's the contagion. Portuguese bond yields are rising . . . Spanish.

Cowen Portugal and Spain are still in the markets – that puts them under more pressure than us. We can hold our breath while they drown . . .

Lenihan That's not a pain-free strategy. It's high-risk.

Beat.

Lenihan We could look for a precautionary programme – one that's not drawn down unless we need it . . . A contingency fund.

Cowen So it wouldn't be a 'bailout' . . . ?

Lenihan They'll want a quid pro quo.

Beat.

Lenihan Our corporation tax rate.

Cowen Our corporation tax is a line in the fucking sand.

Lenihan Talks start tomorrow, in Brussels.

Cowen 'Talks'?

Lenihan Discussions. Consultations.

Cowen *Not* negotiations.

Lenihan We'd have to agree that at Cabinet.

Cowen   There'll be time for that yet.

Lenihan   I'll be at the Eurogroup on Tuesday. I'll push the 'precautionary fund' idea.

Cowen   This is a game of bluff. If we say we need help, we've no more leverage – we've lost.

Lenihan   Let's see what happens in Brussels tomorrow. I'll talk to Honohan.

Cowen   Talks about talks.

Honohan (*on phone*)   A precautionary fund, Brian? I can see the sense in it – but I'm not sure there's a precedent . . .

Lenihan   Do what you can, Patrick. Good luck.

November 14, 2010. Sunday

Chorus   On November 14th – a Sunday – Patrick Honohan leads the Irish finance delegation to Brussels.

Honohan   Gentlemen, ladies, thank you for hosting these . . . discussions . . . here in Brussels.

Troika Official   I'd like to welcome the Irish delegation to Brussels.

Chorus   While in Dublin –

French news sting.

French Reporter (*to camera*)   Ici a Dublin, le gouvernement irlandais désavoue que le pays va entrer dans un programme 'bailout'.

Chorus   Minister Bat O'Keefe.

Batt O'Keefe (*to reporter*)   I'm absolutely unaware of any moves from Europe. It's been a very hard-won sovereignty for this country, and this Government is not going to give over this sovereignty to anyone else.

Back in Brussels:

Honohan   What we hope to explore is the possibility of a precautionary financing arrangement – a contingency fund.

Troika Official   I am afraid there is no procedure for a so-called precautionary arrangement, or contingency fund . . . We look forward to discussing the details of a programme of assistance.

Spanish news sting.

Spanish Reporter (*to camera*)   Aquí en Dublín, el gobierno irlandés sigue a negar que el país va entrar en un programa 'bailout'.

Chorus   Minister Dermot Ahern.

Dermot Ahern (*to reporter*)   It is fiction. There is nothing going on at the direction of Government in relation to this.

November 15, 2010, Monday

Bond yield 8.089

Chorus   Monday. Dermot Ahern phones the Minister.

Dermot Ahern   Brian, it's Dermot. Myself and Noel are doing a function later. There'll be press there. What the fuck are all these rumours about a bailout?

Lenihan   Just refer any questions to the Minister for Finance.

Dermot Ahern   But they'll need more than that –

Lenihan   Did you get the brief?

Dermot Ahern   *Yes* I got the brief, but –

Lenihan   Just don't deviate from the line.

Dermot Ahern   What about the negotiations?

Lenihan   There are *no* negotiations.

Reporter   Minister, is the government in negotiations with the IMF and EU for a bailout?

Dermot Ahern   Well I'm not aware of it, nor is Noel.

Beside him, Noel Dempsey shakes his head furiously.

November 16, 2010 Tuesday

Bond yield 8.368

Chorus   Tuesday evening. The Eurogroup meeting, in Brussels. Jean-Claude Trichet:

Trichet   The first item on the agenda is the current situation in Ireland.

Expectant pause.

Germany   It would be helpful if Ireland was present.

Finland   Have they concluded the negotiations?

Trichet   They have not officially started the negotiations.

France   So what are they doing in these– meetings?

Trichet   I think they are calling it 'pre-negotiations'.

Germany   What are 'pre-negotiations'?

Trichet   It is a new stage. The Irish invented it.

Lenihan *bursts in.*

Lenihan I'm very sorry. Fog. Stuck on the runway.

France Maybe you need a new government jet.

Finland (*objecting*) They still have the government jet?

Trichet Our objective this evening is to confirm the Irish entry into a joint EU-IMF assistance programme.

Lenihan I'm afraid I can't –

Trichet Your hesitation is jeopardising your EU partners on the periphery of the eurozone. The rising Irish bond yield is a threat to the stability of the euro.

France The contagion could spread to Spain –

Finland We cannot afford to bail out Spain.

Germany Germany has already bailed out Ireland once – with the Depfa bank.

Lenihan That's not quite accurate –

France So it should be clear that we need to lock this down.

Lenihan We won't be 'locking' anything –

Finland The most important thing is the austerity.

Lenihan We have led the way on austerity –

France I think we're all agreed you need to cut quicker.

Finland And deeper. You need a more aggressive deficit reduction plan – you should cut eight billion euro in the first year, not six.

Lenihan That would destroy our economy – there's no point in –

Trichet You must have fiscal appetite – you need to move forward your budget.

Lenihan That was a disaster the last time. I'm not –

Finland We may also need collateral for the loans.

Lenihan What kind of collateral?

Finland Your Electricity Supply Board, for instance.

Lenihan You want me to hand over our Electricity Supply Board?

Finland Only if you do not make good on your loans.

Germany There may be an alternative concession.

France A Europe in which solidarity is being shown through assistance programmes should also show solidarity through harmonised taxation.

Germany There is a feeling among many Germans that an assistance programme is not compatible with Ireland keeping your corporation tax at the lowest in the EU.

Lenihan   Changes to our taxation regime are a matter of national sovereignty –

Finland   The functioning of the currency union is at stake.

Lenihan   We are fully funded till next summer. We don't need to go into a programme.

Trichet   We cannot afford to wait until next summer. The risk to the eurozone is too great.

Germany   You need to call a press conference now.

Lenihan   I have to report back to my government.

Germany   You need to announce that you wish to start negotiations on a programme.

Trichet   You have to do this tonight!

Lenihan   I do *not* have plenipotentiary powers.

Germany   Time is running out.

France   We need to conclude the negotiations.

Lenihan   The *discussions* can continue in Dublin. On Thursday.

He staggers out.

November 17, 2010. Wednesday

Bond yield 8.388

Chorus   Wednesday.

Lenihan   They want collateral for any loans . . . An *eight* billion correction . . . The corporation tax.

Cowen   You didn't concede anything?

Lenihan   Only to continue the talks tomorrow – in Dublin.

Cowen   Not negotiations?!

Lenihan   Discussions.

Chorus   The Dáil.

Ruckus.

Cowen   There has been no question of the Government being in a negotiation for a bailout. Very simply we are working with colleagues in respect of issues that are arising in the euro area and are affecting Ireland.

Opposition TD (*heckling*)   So they can bail us out.

Cowen (*angry*)   We have had enough of your lip.

Bond yield 8.450

Honohan *paces. Checks his phone. Paces.*

Chorus   Wednesday night. The Governor of the Central Bank is in Frankfurt for a meeting of the ECB governing council the next morning, when he gets word that the Financial Times is to run a story about Ireland in the following morning's newspaper . . .

Honohan (*on phone*)   Saying what?

Senior Official (*on phone*)   Saying deposits are flooding out of our banks.

Honohan (*alarmed*)   That could cause a run. What's the liquidity situation?

Senior Official   Em –

(*checks figures*) They lost a billion today in –

Honohan   A billion!

Senior Official   in *retail* deposits.

Honohan   *Retail*? But that *is* a run . . . That's ordinary people taking their money out – that's unprecedented . . . (*working it out*) It's all the denials! It looks like nobody's in charge . . . Leave it with me. I'll call Trichet. (*to* **Trichet**) Jean-Claude, there is a run on – we need more liquidity support for the Irish banks.

Trichet (*on phone*)   Patrick, we cannot authorise *more* liquidity until the Irish agree to start negotiations on a programme.

Honohan (*to* **Lenihan**, *on phone*)   Brian.

Lenihan (*on phone, tetchy*)   What is it?

Honohan   Trichet wants you to make a formal request for negotiations for a programme –

Lenihan (*angry*)   Why are they trying to rush me?

Honohan   What are you waiting for?

Lenihan   It's too soon to show our hand – we'd lose all leverage.

Honohan   This isn't poker, Brian.

Lenihan   Patrick – it's *always* poker.

Honohan   The public needs reassurance. You need to announce this.

Lenihan   That is a Government decision.

Honohan   You need to call a cabinet meeting.

Lenihan   For Christ's sake Patrick! That's the Taoiseach's prerogative.

Lenihan *hangs up angrily.*

Honohan   They're not ready, Jean-Claude.

Trichet I 'ave given enormous sums of liquidity to Ireland! A fifth of our entire stock of reserves. This is not a sustainable process. I cannot continue to put the money of Europe's citizens at risk!

Honohan They need to work through the political process – that will take a few days, a week. I need to stop this run *now*. I need to reassure people their money is safe.

Trichet That is what a programme will provide – reassurance.

Honohan If I go on the radio and say the European Central Bank will 'stand behind' Irish depositors – will you contradict me?

Trichet I cannot confirm something that is not confirmed.

Honohan I'm not asking you to *confirm*! I'm just asking you *not* to contradict!

Chorus Meanwhile, in Dublin . . .

Ashoka Mody *and* **Ajai Chopra** *approach the hotel* **Receptionist**.

Receptionist Good evening gentlemen, you're very welcome to the Merrion Hotel. May I have your names?

Ashoka Mody Ashoka Mody.

Ajai Chopra Ajai Chopra.

The **Receptionist** *searches on the computer.*

Receptionist Could the reservation be under the company name?

Ashoka Mody IMF.

Receptionist I – M – ?

Ashoka Mody I – M – F.

Receptionist Yes, here they are. Sorry about that.

She types.

Receptionist How long will you be staying, gentlemen?

They look at each other.

November 18, 2010. Thursday

Bond yield 8.563

Chorus The following morning.

Honohan *makes a new call.*

RTÉ Switch RTÉ, which department?

Honohan Morning Ireland, please.

Producer (*tired*) Morning Ireland.

Honohan   Yes. This is Patrick Honohan . . . I'm the governor of the –

Producer   Governor!

Action stations in the studio.

Morning Ireland sting.

Rachel English   We're joined now from Frankfurt by the Governor of the Central Bank . . .

Official (*urgently*)   Minister –

Lenihan   What?

Official   The Governor's on Morning Ireland!

Lenihan   Why didn't you tell me he was going on?

Official   We didn't know!

They listen in.

Rachel English   Governor – The Troika of the IMF, the ECB and the European Commission have arrived in Dublin – they've already been seen on the streets around Government Buildings. There's a palpable sense amongst people that they're not being given the full picture . . . that they're being treated with contempt. So what are the IMF and the ECB here for today?

Lenihan   Hold the line, Patrick.

Honohan   I think the purpose of this whole exercise is to provide reassurance –

Rachel English   Are we talking about a bailout?

Honohan   We don't talk about bailouts.

Lenihan (*to himself*)   Ok.

Honohan   The IMF talks about loans – not bailouts. Loans get repaid.

Lenihan   Hold the line . . .

Rachel English   And you can confirm that they will be giving us a loan?

Honohan   Well *if* it's agreed. If it's agreed, of course, yes.

Rachel English   And when you say if it's agreed, I mean why else would they be here?

Honohan   Oh exactly, I mean the expectation is that negotiations – or discussions – will be effective, and that a loan will be made available.

Rachel English   How big is this loan likely to be?

Honohan   Oh it'll be a large loan. Because the purpose of it is to show that Ireland has sufficient firepower to deal with any concerns of the market. So we're talking about a very substantial loan, for sure.

Rachel English Are we talking tens of billions – 60, 70 billion maybe?

Honohan Tens of billions – yes . . .

Lenihan Jesus, Patrick!

Rachel English So is it your understanding that we will be receiving a multibillion euro loan from the IMF and from the EU?

Honohan (*cautious*) It's not my *call*. It's the government's decision at the end. It's my . . . (*searching for the word*) expectation . . .

Lenihan Christ!

Honohan that this is definitely likely to happen.

Lenihan Patrick – hell is at the gates!

Rachel English Governor Patrick Honohan, thank you.

Lenihan He's shown our hand!

Official He didn't quite –

Lenihan He said we were 'definitely' entering a programme.

Official He said 'definitely *likely*'.

Lenihan Everybody knows what he *meant*. He's played our only cards.

Official (*to* **Senior Official**) Will he fire him?

Senior Official (*dismissive*) He can't fire him! What would the markets think?

Chorus The Dáil.

Lenihan (*to* **Dáil**) I *welcome* this morning's comments by the Governor of the Central Bank.

Dáil ruckus continues throughout.

Lenihan Were these *technical* discussions to result in the availability of a substantial *contingency* capital fund to back Ireland, that would be desirable.

Chorus Michael Noonan.

Noonan If it is poker the Minister is playing, it is liar's poker.

The Minister has no cards left. His colleagues over the weekend with their incredible denials embarrassed the nation.

Fianna Fáil and Fine Gael both spring from the old Sinn Féin. Sinn Féin means 'ourselves *alone*': this is the idea that as a nation we would run our own affairs. This is what the patriot dead fought and died for, and what they achieved was a *sovereign* Irish State.

Now an inept Government, through its arrogance and avarice, has given it away. The Irish Times editorial today asks whether this is what the men of 1916 died for – 'a bailout from the German chancellor with a few shillings of sympathy from the British chancellor on the side'.

That a Fianna Fáil-led Government should be the one to surrender our sovereignty has its own irony. The Minister should be ashamed and his colleagues should share the shame.

November 19, 2010. Friday

Chorus Friday.

Trichet (*to aide*)   Why is he still talking about 'contingency' funds? Mon dieu . . . This has to end. Take a letter. (*dictating*) Dear *Monsieur* Lenihan . . .

The **Senior Official** *hands* **Lenihan** *a letter from* **Trichet**. *As* **Lenihan** *reads-*

Trichet   Only if we receive in writing a commitment from the Irish government that it shall send a request for financial support to the Eurogroup can we authorise further provisions of emergency liquidity to Irish institutions.

Lenihan (*to* **Senior Official**)   We haven't got it nailed down!

Trichet   I am sure that you are aware that a swift response is needed before markets open on Monday.

Lenihan   We need another week.

Senior Official   We don't have another week.

Lenihan   But the corporation tax rate – it's still on the table!

November 20, 2010. Saturday

Angelus chime.

Chorus   Saturday.

Newsreader   The French and German governments have retreated from earlier statements that the Irish corporation tax rate was under threat.

Lenihan *phones* **Cowen**.

Lenihan   They've taken the tax rate off the table.

Cowen   So we'll start negotiations, then.

Lenihan   It's just terms and conditions now.

Cowen   Are your officials ready?

Lenihan   It's like we're dealing with the invader.

Cowen   I'll call a cabinet meeting for tomorrow. Sign off on it.

Lenihan   I'll write to Trichet . . . I hardly feel like the Minister any more.

Desolate pause.

Lenihan Where are you, anyway?

Cowen Arranmore – the Donegal by-election.

A chorus of reporters: 'Taoiseach!'

Reporter Taoiseach – do you think the best place for you to be while the IMF are in Dublin is canvassing on an island off Donegal?

Cowen There are dire issues here regarding salmon-fishing, and it is my job to meet the people and have a good discussion with them about this.

Act IV: Bailout
November to December 2010

November 22, 2010. Monday

Bond yield 8.571

Chorus Monday. In the Department of Finance.

Honohan The Troika are proposing a total package of 85 billion euro. Fifty of that will be to fund the deficit over the next three years, while we're out of the markets, and 35 will be to recapitalise the banks.

Lenihan The bank losses were only supposed to cost 34 billion in total. We've already spent – what? – 46 billion. And they think we need to spend *another* 35 billion?

Honohan That's what they're saying. I think they're wrong – we won't need all of the 35. But they're insisting we write it in to the deal.

Lenihan What if we *do* need it?

Honohan Then the deal won't work. The 35 billion would add too much to our debt. We won't regain market confidence. We'll end up needing another bailout.

Senior Official (*showing in* **Mody**) Minister – Mr Mody of the IMF would like a word.

Ashoka Mody The Europeans want to stuff your banks with capital.

Lenihan We know.

Ashoka Mody It would make the debt burden unsustainable. Again. You'd just be heading for another bailout.

Honohan We know.

Lenihan What choice do we have?

Ashoka Mody 'The fault, dear Brutus, is not in our stars, but in ourselves . . .' (*pause*) The cost of the bank losses is so high because you have taken the entire burden upon the State . . . You need to 'share' it . . . You need to force those who lent recklessly to the banks to take their losses . . . Burn them.

Lenihan We have said we'll pay our debts as a State.

Ashoka Mody You *can't* pay your debts! You have to reduce them.

Lenihan But we've been told all along that was out of the question . . . That it would cause contagion.

Ashoka Mody There could be havoc.

Lenihan (*blanching*) Havoc?

Ashoka Mody But at least it will not be *your* havoc . . . Before, the State was borrowing from the same markets as your banks. So *you* would have been the first victims of contagion. But now, because of the bailout, you are out of the markets for three years. Contagion is somebody else's problem.

Lenihan How much could we save?

Pause.

Ashoka Mody On a first glance at the figures, you could save as much as thirty-six billion euro.

Lenihan *is stunned.* **Honohan** *is quietly skeptical.*

Ashoka Mody Because you are entering a bailout for three years, you will not need the markets' confidence. That means you can afford to burn some of these bank debt holders without worrying that there will be consequences for the sovereign. That means that the actual bailout does not need to be so big . . . And that, in turn, will make your debt burden sustainable – so you will find it easier to regain the markets' confidence . . . It could be a virtuous circle.

Lenihan This could be our salvation!

Angelus chime

Newsreader Following the official start of negotiations on a programme of external assistance, the Green Party has said it will be pulling out of government . . . but not yet.

November 23, 2010. Tuesday

Bond yield 8.583

Chorus Tuesday.

Senior Official Governor?

Honohan I've been looking at the figures. We won't save thirty-six billion.

Senior Official Why not?

Honohan The 36 includes covered debt – debt that is secured on assets. There's no value in burning it – the creditor will just seize the asset. And it includes the subordinated debt – but we've already factored in savings on that.

Senior Official So what *is* the saving?

Honohan It's too early to say – but we could be starting from a figure of maybe twenty billion . . .

November 24, 2010. Wednesday

Bond yield 9.071

Senior Official Wednesday.

Mody *addresses* **Lenihan**, *or phones him.*

Ashoka Mody   We have spoken to IMF headquarters. The director, Dominique Strauss-Kahn, is in favour of forcing losses on the debt holders. He will do what he can to push it.

Senior Official (*to* **Honohan**)   What did you mean, '*starting* from' twenty billion?

Honohan   Twenty billion is the total value of the burnable, unguaranteed bonds. But you can't just write it all off. You have to pay back something on it.

Senior Official   So how much could we *save*?

Honohan   Maybe 60 per cent . . .?

Senior Official   Twelve billion.

Honohan   At a maximum . . . Eight to twelve, maybe.

Ashoka Mody (*to* **Lenihan**)   Dominique Strauss-Kahn is going to organise a conference call with the key decision makers. On Friday.

Lenihan   Trichet won't like it. Nor Geithner.

Ashoka Mody   Strauss-Kahn thinks he can persuade them.

November 25, 2010. Thursday

Bond yield 9.184

Chorus   Thursday.

Angelus chime

Newsreader   In the Donegal South–West by-election, the Fianna Fáil vote has collapsed, allowing the Sinn Féin candidate, Pearse Doherty, to top the poll.

Ashoka Mody (*to* **Lenihan**)   DSK has been talking to Geithner. He thinks he can bring him round.

November 26, 2010. Friday

Bond yield 9.326

Chorus   Friday.

Cowen *joins them.*

Cowen   When will we know?

Senior Official   The conference call is later today.

Cowen   What's the final saving?

Honohan   We think it could be eight to twelve billion.

Cowen   *Think*?

Honohan   There is a degree of complexity that hasn't been fully factored in. Legal issues, for example . . . It's not a miracle cure.

Cowen Is it worth the risk?

Lenihan It's the *narrative* . . .

They look to him.

Lenihan 'Sharing the burden.' Not just foisting it on the citizens . . . We'd finally be punishing the reckless lending . . . (*pause*) The IMF are pushing it. Strauss-Kahn is behind it. Geithner. They'll bring Trichet in. We'll get it over the line. We need this. The country needs it.

Bond yield 9.392

Chorus The conference call. The finance ministers of the G7 . . . The managing director of the IMF, Dominique Strauss-Kahn . . . the President of the European Central Bank, Jean-Claude Trichet . . . and the American treasury secretary, Timothy Geithner.

Strauss-Kahn There is a proposal to force losses on holders of senior debt in some of Ireland's banks as part of the 85 billion programme being negotiated with the EU and IMF.

Trichet *Mais-*

Germany Investors should bear responsibility for their losses.

Strauss-Kahn Our team in Dublin feels the programme currently being negotiated is not sustainable. It will add too much to Ireland's debt burden. It should be relatively straightforward to force losses on some of these debt holders.

Trichet But –

Germany Good. It will lay down a marker.

Trichet But Europe at this moment needs credibility.

Strauss-Kahn Market credibility comes from a sustainable debt burden.

Trichet Credibility comes from paying our debts.

Geithner What's the saving to Ireland?

Strauss-Kahn Eh –

Trichet They think it could be eight to twelve billion.

Geithner Eight to twelve? Billion? (*pause*) We spent seven hundred billion dollars on our bank rescue plan. You've put together a trillion dollar rescue fund for Europe. You've spent a hundred and ten billion euro on Greece. You're going to spend 85 billion on Ireland. And you're going to risk global contagion, again, for a saving to Ireland of *twelve* billion?

Strauss-Kahn We think the risk of 'global contagion' is overstated –

Geithner You think the risk is *overstated*? Money is running from Europe as we speak! Look at the bond yields! Ireland – Portugal – Italy – Spain – contagion is happening!

Germany But the public cannot keep paying these private debts!

Geithner You know – you sound a bit like Herbert Hoover in the 1930s.

Germany What has Herbert Hoover got to do with –

Geithner He let the banks collapse. Their investors lost money. He didn't bail them out. And what happened?

> Everybody panicked. There was global contagion. The Great Depression. It lasted a decade.
>
> You know what banks used to do to stop runs? They used stack money in their windows . . .

Mexico in 94 . . . Indonesia in 97 . . . South Korea . . . Thailand . . . We learned to stack enough money in the fucking window. To stop the contagion. Before it infected the world . . . Money is running from Europe as we speak. And if you let Ireland burn holders of debt in its banks, that run is going to accelerate. Nobody will lend a dollar – a euro – to Europe if they think that, as soon as you need money, you're going to welch on your debts.

Germany But the moral hazard – the public cannot keep paying for speculators' losses.

Geithner The moral hazard will pale beside the cost of a panic on Europe's debt markets . . . Ireland needs to take the bailout money and stack it in the fucking window – and not be threatening to take money off market lenders . . . Confidence is a fragile thing. When it evaporates, it evaporates quickly. And it's hard to get back once it's lost.

Trichet *Bien sur.*

Geithner You need to close this down. There's too much uncertainty.

Strauss-Kahn The negotiations are due to run another week.

Geithner Another *week* of speculation? Of erratic Irish pronouncements? This is a clusterfuck. Close it off.

Back in Dublin:

Ashoka Mody The US contributes a fifth of the budget of the IMF. That's it.

Lenihan You said . . . we could save thirty-six billion . . .

Ashoka Mody That was a starting estimate. But it doesn't matter. You can't save anything now.

Lenihan But Strauss-Kahn –

Ashoka Mody We should have known.

Lenihan Geithner was –

Ashoka Mody It's the 'Geithner doctrine': you don't forces lenders to take losses in a crisis. We thought maybe the circumstances here were different – that the Irish case could be an exception. But it turns out there are no exceptions to the Geithner doctrine . . . And Trichet was implacable anyway . . . We got it wrong.

Mody *leaves.*

November 27, 2010. Saturday

Chorus Saturday night, Government buildings. The Cabinet meeting.

Minister 1 You call this the result of a *negotiation*?

Minister 2 This is humiliating.

Minister 3 It sounds more like a surrender.

Lenihan This is the outcome of a difficult negotiation conducted in good faith by our top officials –

Minister 1 In good faith!

Lenihan Yes –

Minister 1 You *lied* to us!

Lenihan Nobody lied to you. There were no negotiations –

Minister 2 There was a delegation of Irish officials in Brussels –

Lenihan For discussions –

Minister 1 Shouldn't those discussions have started at *Cabinet*?

Lenihan Things were changing very fast . . .

Cowen We are where we are.

Minister 3 There must be an alternative to this bailout –

Lenihan There's no alternative.

Minister 3 There's *always* an alternative. What if we –

Lenihan The country can't pay its way. We're relying on our lenders to keep the schools and hospitals open. Market lenders have abandoned us. This is our only option.

Minister 3 What if we cut the deficit –

Lenihan We *are* cutting the deficit –

Minister 3 Cut it in one year. So we wouldn't be dependent on the markets.

Cowen Go from 50 to 30 billion? In *one* year?

Minister 3 If that's the price of independence.

Cowen We can't do that. It would destroy the country.

Lenihan It would be like closing every school and hospital in the country!

Minister 2 Well what if we burned the –

Cowen People get lost on 'what if' scenarios. Let's not add to uncertainty. We have to try and keep things simple. We need to fund the state and fix the banks. We cannot have a European Lehman's here. Let's keep it simple.

Minister 3 We're not too many steps away from a serious breakdown of social cohesion.

Cowen I know there are all sorts of problems. But this is where we have to go. There are no options here. Are we agreed?

Minister 1 This deal is going to destroy the party.

Cowen Yes. That might be the price of it. (*pause*) Are we agreed?

He looks around the room.

November 28, 2010

Lenihan *is left, standing, alone. He pulls his jacket tighter about him, against the cold. He takes out his phone.*

John McGuinness Brian.

Chorus John McGuinness, Fianna Fáil backbencher.

Lenihan It's over, John.

John Mcguinness Where are you?

Lenihan The airport. Baldonnell. En route to Brussels. (*pause*) We can't run our own affairs, John. No other Irish finance minister has ever had to admit that.

John Mcguinness If we go into an election after this, with Cowen as leader, we'll be wiped out.

Lenihan I can't move against the Taoiseach now.

John Mcguinness *You* won't have to make the move. (*pause*) 'He who wields the knife never wears the crown' . . . (*pause*) I'll wield the knife.

Lenihan I'm dying, John. I won't have long.

John Mcguinness You might have long enough.

Lenihan You want me to be El Cid.

John Mcguinness El Cid?

Lenihan El Cid – the Spanish medieval –

John Mcguinness What?

Lenihan He was a military leader in 11th century Spain . . . When he died they propped him back up on his horse, in his armour, and sent the horse back into battle.

November 28, 2010

Lenihan, **Trichet** *and* **Rehn** *greet each other.* **Rehn** *carries copies of the Memorandum of Understanding and places them on the table. He signs them. He gestures to* **Lenihan**. **Lenihan** *defers to* **Trichet**.

Lenihan   Monsieur Trichet –

Trichet   But Monsieur Lenihan – the ECB has merely an advisory role in these matters.

Lenihan *signs both copies.* **Rehn** *shakes his hand.* **Trichet** *watches.*

Angelus chime.

Newsreader   The Government has announced that the country is to enter an eighty-five billion euro 'assistance programme' jointly administered by the 'Troika' of the IMF, the European Commission and the European Central Bank.

December 1 2010

Chorus   The Dáil.

Dáil ruckus continues throughout.

Lenihan   We have every reason to be confident about the future of this country.

Cries of 'Shame!' etc.

Chorus   Michael Noonan.

Noonan   This deal is a very bad deal . . . And in one respect, this deal is a downright obscenity . . . By refusing to force losses on the holders of Irish bank debt, those losses have been transferred to the Irish people – in many respects to the poorest of the Irish people.

Lenihan   If you think we could renege on senior debt holders against the wishes of the ECB, you are living in fantasy land.

Noonan   The deal needs to be re-negotiated. In the election, we will look for a mandate to do so.

Act V: A Democratic Revolution
January to April 2011

January, 2011

Chorus In January 2011, with the prospect of an election looming, the Minister for Finance is under pressure to finalise the Finance Bill that will give effect to the terms he has agreed with the Troika of the IMF, the European Commission and the ECB.

Lenihan Where are we at with the Finance Bill?

Senior Official The latest draft is with the AG's office.

Official There's some blowback from backbenchers on the Universal Social Charge.

Lenihan Tell them it's just a tidying-up exercise – gathering all the existing levies together.

Official But it's not just a –

Lenihan Just *deal* with it.

Senior Official The Troika are looking for a schedule for the first ten billion recapitalisation.

Lenihan (*dismissing them*) Tell them you'll get back to them later in the week.

Senior Official (*to* **Official**) 'Get back to them'? But they've moved into my fucking office.

January 9, 2011

Angelus chime.

Newsreader According to new revelations today, shortly before the bank guarantee of 2008, the Taoiseach Brian Cowen played golf with Anglo Irish Bank chairman, Sean Fitzpatrick.

Dáil ruckus.

Cowen That game took place and I did not discuss Anglo Irish Bank matters with him. And that is the truth.

Outrage.

Chorus John McGuinness.

John Mcguinness He's finished, Brian. You have to move.

Lenihan I can't jeopardise the Finance Bill, John.

John Mcguinness If the government collapses you won't *have* a finance bill.

Lenihan If I challenged the Taoiseach now . . . it could provoke a crisis.

John Mcguinness This *is* a crisis!

Lenihan   Just let me get this bill through.

January 13, 2011

Cowen   What are you hearing on the backbenches?

Backbencher   We're with you, Boss.

Cowen   Maybe it is time to go.

Backbencher   And leave it to that fucker?

Cowen   Half my cabinet's offered their resignations.

Backbencher   Fucking quitters! We should have a confidence motion. Rally the troops. Force out the fuckin rebels.

John Mcguinness (*to* **Lenihan**)   He's holding a confidence motion. You have to move.

Lenihan   The time's not right. For the country.

John Mcguinness   This is politics! You don't get to choose the time!

January 18, 2011

Chorus   On the day of the Fianna Fáil motion of confidence in the Taoiseach, the Minister for Finance goes on the News at One to discuss the economy.

John Mcguinness (*listening*)   Be careful, Brian.

NEWS AT ONE SIGNATURE TUNE.

Presenter   Minister – we've been told that you're *not* expected to support Brian Cowen in the confidence motion this afternoon.

Lenihan (*blustering*)   The financial survival of this country– I'm down in the engine room, getting muck on my hands– It's very important that I work in that engine room and finish the agenda of the government.

Presenter   So what are you going to do in the vote this afternoon?

Pause.

Lenihan   The Taoiseach– The Taoiseach has been totally supportive to me on the financial programme that I have brought to the Cabinet. He has supported me to the hilt. So I'm supporting the Taoiseach.

McGuinness *is dismayed.*

Presenter   Did you give people to understand that you would be supportive of a motion of no confidence?

Lenihan   No– (*falters*) I made it clear to those who approached me that the financial work facing the country made it impossible for me to disrupt the good working relationship that any finance minister should have with the Taoiseach . . . I didn't have the luxury of indulging my ambitions on this particular matter. As far as I'm concerned, the country comes first.

Presenter   Minister, thank you. Now I think we have John McGuinness, Fianna Fáil TD for Carlow/Kilkenny on the line. John McGuinness – Brian Lenihan *didn't* encourage a heave against the Taoiseach?

John Mcguinness   That is not what he has been saying to the backbenchers over the last number of months. He *did* encourage dissent, he did encourage us to look at the numbers, and he did express an interest in the leadership.

January 19, 2011

Backbencher   That's the end of Lenihan's challenge. Now you need to reshuffle.

Cowen   I can't move Lenihan. The markets –

Backbencher   Micheal Martin's already quit. How many of the others have said they want to retire at the election?

Cowen   Harney. Ahern and Dempsey. O'Keefe. Killeen.

Backbencher   Let's get rid of them now.

Cowen   But they're expecting to serve out their term –

Backbencher   Fuck them! A hundred-and-twenty-grand pension will ease their retirement. That makes space for *six* promotions – that'll put a new face on the cabinet. Cheer up the backbenches. Let's get calling.

He dials and hands the phone to **Cowen**.

Backbencher   Barry Andrews.

Cowen *takes the phone.*

Cowen   Barry? Did I disturb you? (*to* **Backbencher**) What time is it?

Backbencher   Just past midnight.

Cowen (*to* **Barry**)   Sorry Barry. Listen. I want to you be my new Minister for Health.

January 20, 2011

Angelus chime.

Newsreader   RTÉ News has learned that the junior coalition partner, the Green Party, has objected to the Taoiseach's attempt to appoint new ministers in the run up to the election. With half the cabinet already having resigned, it is not clear this morning who is to replace them.

Backbencher   The Dáil is going fucking mental. You have to get down there.

Cowen   But I don't have a fucking cabinet!

Backbencher You'll just have to share the empty portfolios out amongst the remaining ministers!

Dáil ruckus.

Cowen I am reassigning the portfolios of those who have resigned as follows.

The ministers line up beside him and dutifully shake hands with each other, confusedly.

Cowen The Tánaiste, Mary Coughlan, becomes the Minister for Education and Health . . . Pat Carey becomes the Minister for Community, Equality, Gaeltacht Affairs . . . and Transport . . . Mary Hanafin becomes the Minister for Tourism, Sport, Culture . . . and Enterprise. Éamon Ó Cuív is the new minister for Social Welfare . . . and Defence. And Brendan Smith is the new Minister for Agriculture . . . and Justice.

Uproar.

January 22, 2011

Angelus chime.

Newsreader Brian Cowen has announced his resignation as leader of Fianna Fáil. He will remain as Taoiseach till the general election in March.

Lenihan The government won't survive till March. We need to get the Finance Bill through.

Senior Official It's not ready.

Lenihan We need to get the opposition on board. I need to talk to Fine Gael and Labour.

Senior Official I'll put out some feelers.

Lenihan Oh – will you help me with the speech?

Senior Official What speech?

Lenihan For the leadership.

January 24, 2011

Senior Official Minister – Deputy Michael Noonan is here.

Noonan The country needs an election. Quickly.

Lenihan Michael – the country needs the Finance Bill to go through first.

Noonan The *new* government will put through their *own* finance bill.

Lenihan In which case you'll just have to make the same cuts as us – and take the blame for it.

Noonan We can't support your finance bill.

Lenihan   You don't need to. We still have the numbers. The Greens have left government but they're prepared to support the Finance Bill from the backbenches . . . But you've put down a 'no confidence' motion. That's scheduled to happen *before* the Finance Bill. The Greens have said they can't vote confidence in the government any more. So if the confidence motion goes ahead, the government will fall – we'll move straight into an election, without a finance bill. That will damage market confidence. And *you*'ll have to pick up the pieces after the election.

Noonan   What are you suggesting?

Lenihan   Withdraw your 'no confidence' motion. You can oppose the Finance Bill – safe in the knowledge it will pass. We'll get it done by the weekend, dissolve the Dáil and move straight to the election.

January 26, 2011

Angelus chime

Newsreader   The race to succeed Brian Cowen as leader of Fianna Fáil has been won by Micheál Martin, with Éamon Ó Cuív in second place and Brian Lenihan third.

February 1, 2011

Angelus chime

Newsreader   Following the passing of the Finance Bill, the Dáil has been dissolved and the general election campaign is underway.

March 29, 2011

Chorus   In the General Election, Fianna Fáil is reduced from 77 to 19 seats. Brian Lenihan is the sole Fianna Fáil TD elected in Dublin. Fine Gael and Labour form a coalition government and Michael Noonan becomes Finance Minister. A few weeks later, the new Minister brings a proposal to Cabinet.

Noonan   Taoiseach, ministers . . . We are the sovereign government of the Irish Republic. We said during the campaign that we would seek to force holders of senior debt in our banks to 'share' in the losses of those banks . . . losses that could be over 60 billion euro . . . losses that the Irish people have shouldered. (*pause*) There is 3.7 billion euro of unguaranteed, unsecured senior debt in Anglo Irish Bank and Irish Nationwide. These are failed banks. I am proposing that we move to close these banks and that the holders of this debt should take their share of the losses.

The meeting breaks up in mutual congratulations.

This segues into a meeting of officials.

Senior Official   The Cabinet has agreed the new banking strategy. The Minister is going to announce it in the Dáil on Thursday. (*to one* **Official A**) Talk to the Troika – we'll need to keep them in the loop. (*to* **Official B**) Start work on his statement.

Official B   He's going to announce the burning?

Senior Official   Not the details – just the intention. We'll need new legislation to put it into action.

Official A (*finishing phone call*)   The IMF is supportive.

Senior Official   The Commission?

Official A   I'm on it.

March 30, 2011

Official B   I have a draft of the statement . . .

Senior Official   What have you got on the burning?

Official B (*reading*)   'The Government will legislate if necessary to allow for burden sharing with senior bondholders in Anglo Irish Bank and Irish Nationwide.'

Senior Official   That's fine. No– Wait –

She thinks.

Senior Official (*dictating*)   'Having *consulted* with the external partners . . . the Government will legislate if necessary . . .'

Official B   Got it.

Official A (*from another phone call*)   It looks like the European Commission is on board also.

Senior Official   Get the statement over to the ECB.

Official A   They won't like it.

Senior Official   We've been talking to them. Things have moved on. I think they'll back it this time. We need their endorsement – a statement of confidence for the markets.

March 31, 2011

12.30PM

Official A (*reading a news story*)   The head of the Bundesbank has come out in favour of burning! Ireland should 'make creditors participate in losses', he said.

Senior Official   That could be a game changer. Any word from the ECB?

Official B   Not yet!

Official A   What time's the Minister's speech?

Senior Official   Four thirty.

1.30PM

Noonan   Where's my speech?

Official B (*handing it to him*)   Minister.

He scans it, approves, hands it back.

Noonan   The ECB?

Senior Official   Any moment now, I'd expect.

Noonan leaves.

They wait.

3.57PM

Official A   The ECB! An email. (*reads*) 'The Governing Council meeting was very clear: you need to go back to the old version of the statement and strike out the whole paragraph on 'burden sharing' with bond holders.'

Stunned silence.

Official A   They can't do that.

Senior Official   They're doing it.

Official A   Again.

Official B   Call their bluff. They can't do anything about it.

Official A   They could call in their loans.

Official B   That would collapse Anglo – it would set the euro crisis off again.

Senior Official   We need their backing for the new banking strategy. To reassure the markets. Otherwise this is all pointless.

Noonan   Do the sums again.

Senior Official   Minister – you're due in the Dáil.

Noonan   Where's my speech?

Official B   Here.

Noonan   Which version?

Official B (*confused*)   There are two versions?

Noonan   We need a version *with* the 'burning' paragraphs . . . And a version *without* them.

Official B   I'll get it.

Noonan   Follow me with it. I'll try Trichet again on the way.

4.20PM

Noonan *walks and phones.*

Senior Official   You've ten minutes to get to the Dáil, Minister.

Trichet (*to* **Noonan***, on phone*)   Non, non, non! Monsieur Noonan – if you force losses on the debt holders, a bom*b* will go off.

Noonan   This will not affect the ECB, Jean-Claude –

Trichet The bom*b* will not go off in *Frankfurt* – it will go off in *Dublin*. You have been rebuilding confidence – this will destroy it.

Noonan But Anglo is a dead bank. The markets are expecting to take losses on it. This will not have contagion effects–

Trichet Monsieur Noonan – failure to repay the debts of Anglo Irish Bank will be a default. The rules of the ECB state that we cannot give emergency loans to a bank that defaults.

Noonan I have the authority of the Irish government to do this. We have taken a government decision –

Trichet Anglo Irish Bank currently has 41 billion euro of emergency loans from the ECB. If Anglo defaults, the government will become liable for that.

4.30PM

Noonan (*to* **Officials**) Who's doing the sums?

Official B The *total* value of the debts we can burn is 3.7 billion . . . We'd probably save about half that. Say 1.8 billion . . . But if interest rates rise on the other banks, that would eat into the savings . . .

Noonan How much of a saving are we left with?

Official B It's all about confidence – it depends on how the market reacts –

Noonan Give me a figure.

Official B A few hundred million euro . . . ?

Noonan *reacts with dismay.*

Official B It's not nothing.

Official *gives him the two speeches.*

Noonan *thinks and then tears up one of the speeches.*

4.40PM

Chorus The Dáil.

Noonan (*composing himself*) I regret delaying the House momentarily . . .

Minister A (*excited*) This is what we promised!

Minister B Worth waiting for!

Noonan The new Government has received a very strong mandate for change, renewal and doing things differently. It is a mandate to act, and we will act.

For the benefit of our people . . . and of the market . . . I want to be clear that we are committed to the EU-IMF programme . . . The fact is that the European Central Bank is keeping banking going in this country . . . No Opposition member would thank us if he went to his local bank machine tomorrow morning and it did not work and no money was available.

He shuffles through his pages, momentarily confused – they are mixed up.

Minister B (*outraged*)   What about the Anglo bondholders?

Minister A   We made a cabinet decision!

Noonan   From here, let us move forward with purpose.

Desultory applause and, over it, mutterings from TDs:

A chorus of reporters: 'Minister!'

Reporter   Minister, you promised to burn bondholders, to share the burden of rescuing the banks –

Noonan (*flustered*)   We're not going to go there until we go *with* our European colleagues – we may seek to reopen these discussions in the future.

Clamour of further questions – 'But Minister', 'One more question, Minister' – as **Noonan** *leaves.*

April 6, 2011

Senior Official   The Dáil. It's empty, almost.

Lenihan (*slowly*)   This Government's narrative suggests that theirs is a radical 'new' policy, different to the 'mistakes' of our policy. In fact, it is the same policy as ours. And is the correct one.

He sits down, slowly. She goes to him.

Senior Official (*concerned*)   Brian –

Lenihan   I'd like to get this all down on paper.

Senior Official   All?

Lenihan   The last few years. The crisis.

Senior Official   I could bring a tape recorder. We could make some recordings . . . Get them transcribed . . . A memoir . . . What do you want to say?

Pause.

Lenihan   I kept the ship afloat.

Epilogue

*The **Chorus** retrieves the book Stress Test.*

Chorus Brian Lenihan does not get to leave a memoir. Others do, though. Jean-Claude Trichet:

Trichet Europe is in the vanguard of nations working peacefully together. We have proved that our single currency is stable and credible. We have replaced confrontation and conflict with cooperation and consensus.

Chorus And Timothy Geithner:

She opens the book.

Chorus 'In any financial rescue, many of the toughest decisions involve how to set conditions – what kind of medicine will help, what's the right dose, what might kill the patient . . .'

She looks up.

Chorus Actually, I prefer this line: 'What's the best way to defuse a bomb?'

Beat.

Chorus 'The way you don't die . . . In other words, the way that works.'

She closes the book.

Senior Official The 'Geithner doctrine'.

Blackout.

Selected Bibliography

See also bibliography for Guaranteed!.

Arnold, Bruce, and Jason O'Toole. *The End of the Party: How Fianna Fáil Lost Its Grip on Power*. Gill Books, 2011.

BBC Radio 4. *Bailout Boys Go to Dublin*. Radio documentary. Presented by Dan O'Brien. First broadcast April 24, 2011.

Cardiff, Kevin. *Recap: Inside Ireland's Financial Crisis*. The Liffey Press, 2016.

Donovan, Donal, and Antoin E. Murphy. *The Fall of the Celtic Tiger: Ireland and the Euro Debt Crisis*. Oxford University Press, 2013.

Fallon, Johnny. *Brian Cowen: In His Own Words*. Mercier Press, 2009.

Geithner, Timothy. *Stress Test: Reflections on Financial Crises*. Crown Business, 2014.

Joint Committee of Inquiry into the Banking Crisis. *Report of the Joint Committee of Inquiry into the Banking Crisis*. Dublin: Houses of the Oireachtas, 2016. https://inquiries.oireachtas.ie/banking/

Leahy, Pat. *The Price of Power: Inside Ireland's Crisis Coalition*. Penguin Ireland, 2013.

Minihan, Mary. *A Deal with the Devil: The Green Party in Government*. Maverick House, 2010.

Murphy, Brian, Mary O'Rourke, and Noel Whelan, eds. *Brian Lenihan: In Calm and Crisis*. Merrion Press, 2011.

Trichet, Jean-Claude. "My 25-Year Journey with the Euro." *Nikkei Asian Review*, September 1, 2014. https://asia.nikkei.com/nar/articles/jean-claude-trichet-1-my-25-year-journey-with-the-euro. First in a series of biographical columns.

Ali White as the Narrator and Peter Daly as Michael Noonan in *Bailed Out!*. ©Photo by Pat Redmond